Combining Economic and Political Development

International Development Policy

Editor-in-Chief

Gilles Carbonnier (*Professor of Development Economics, The Graduate Institute, Geneva*)

Guest Editor

Giacomo Luciani (*Adjunct Professor of International Affairs, Graduate Institute, Geneva and Scientific Advisor of the Master in International Energy at the Paris School of International Affairs, Sciences Po*)

VOLUME 7

The titles published in this series are listed at *brill.com/idp*

Visit *International Development Policy* and associated documents online
http://devpol.org and *http://debate.devpol.org*

Combining Economic and Political Development

The Experience of MENA

Edited by

Giacomo Luciani

BRILL
NIJHOFF

LEIDEN | BOSTON

Cover illustration: A general view of anti-Mursi protesters gathering at Tahrir Square in Cairo November 27, 2012. Opponents of President Mohamed Mursi clashed with Egyptian police on Tuesday as thousands of protesters stepped up pressure on the Islamist to scrap a decree they say threatens the nation with a new era of autocracy. Photographer © Mohamed Abd El Ghany / Reuter

Library of Congress Cataloging-in-Publication Data

Names: Luciani, Giacomo, 1948- editor.
Title: Combining economic and political development : the experience of MENA / edited by Giacomo Luciani.
Description: Boston : Brill, [2017] | Series: International development policy ; 7 | Includes bibliographical references and index.
Identifiers: LCCN 2016053244 (print) | LCCN 2017002038 (ebook) | ISBN 9789004336445 (pbk. : alk. paper) | ISBN 9789004336452 (E-book)
Subjects: LCSH: Middle East--Economic policy. | Africa, North--Economic policy. | Arab Spring, 2011-
Classification: LCC HC415.15 .C66 2017 (print) | LCC HC415.15 (ebook) | DDC 338.956--dc23
LC record available at https://lccn.loc.gov/2016053244

Typeface for the Latin, Greek, and Cyrillic scripts: "Brill". See and download: brill.com/brill-typeface.

ISSN 1663-9383
ISBN 978-90-04-33644-5 (paperback)
ISBN 978-90-04-33645-2 (e-book)

This book is printed on acid-free paper and produced in a sustainable manner.

Contents

Foreword

It is my pleasure to introduce this new thematic volume of *International Development Policy* (IDP). The journal's seventh annual issue focuses exclusively, and for the first time, on the Middle East and North Africa (MENA), a region beset by armed conflict, social and economic turmoil and set against the backdrop of lower oil prices and political uncertainty.

The volume explores the economic implications of democratic transition efforts in the region since the start of the so-called Arab Spring in December 2010. It analyses the challenges facing governments in addressing the underlying economic problems that have led to widening national and regional inequality and contributed to the initial unrest, while questioning the complex relationships with Europe, the USA and the rest of the world. Importantly, the volume highlights the value of short-term policy measures that may offer the potential for quick and visible economic wins to help consolidate democratic processes and strengthen institutional governance at critical junctures.

The volume consists of eleven chapters including an introduction by the guest editor, prof. Giacomo Luciani. As he underscores, this collection of articles pursues specific objectives while complementing the existing literature on economic and political developments in the MENA region. While acknowledging policy priorities aimed at producing positive results in the long run, such as public sector reform and economic diversification, there is a sense of urgency when it comes to offering new opportunities to respond to the challenge of rising labour market demand, with a projected North African workforce expected to grow by more than 80 million between 2010 and 2050.[1] The authors further insist on the imperative of seeking out and implementing innovative policies 'that will allow for rapid improvement in the living conditions of a majority of people and sustain consensus around the consolidation of democracy'. These include measures such as the abolition of fuel subsidies combined with a targeted system of unconditional cash transfers, and policies that favour currency devaluation and reform of the banking sector to support small-scale enterprises.

I commend Giacomo Luciani for pulling together a timely and thought-provoking volume that brings together authors displaying a wide breadth of expertise not only with regard to the highly complex challenges and problems facing the region, but also with regard to potential economic policy measures in support of inclusive development and democratisation. The volume thus

1 AfDB, OECD, UNDP (2015), African Economic Outlook, pp. xii–xiii.

contributes to filling gaps in our understanding of how economic and political development processes may support democratic transition in spite of adverse political-economy dynamics. It also illustrates the broader intent that lies at the heart of our journal which seeks to serve as a bridge between academic research and policy making.

I extend special thanks to the Kuwait Foundation for the Advancement of Sciences (KFAS) and the Kuwait Program at Sciences Po, as the sponsors of the conference that provided financial support and material for this publication. I also underline my appreciation to Ghassan Salamé, the founding Dean of the Paris School of International Affairs at Sciences Po (PSIA), as well as to two anonymous peer reviewers for their insightful remarks and suggestions.

While I hope this collection will have particular appeal to new readers in the MENA region, I am confident that the volume will raise interest among our regular readership of scholars and practioners elsewhere thanks to the relevance and diversity of contributions on a region whose future bears central importance to us all.

Gilles Carbonnier, Editor-in-Chief

Preface

International Development Policy is a critical source of analysis of development policy and international cooperation trends and is aimed at scholars, policymakers, development professionals, and journalists. It offers a diverse range of academic views from both industrialised countries and emerging economies.

International Development Policy is edited by the Graduate Institute of International and Development Studies, an institution of research and higher education dedicated to advancing world affairs. Located in Geneva at the heart of an international centre of multilateral governance, the Graduate Institute benefits from a rich legacy linked to the founding of the international system and the League of Nations in the 1920s, and the emergence of the developing world in the 1960s.

http://graduateinstitute.ch/publications
http://devpol.org | http://debate.devpol.org

We extend our thanks to the Swiss Agency for Development and Cooperation (SDC) for its financial support.

Schweizerische Eidgenossenschaft
Confédération suisse
Confederazione Svizzera
Confederaziun svizra

List of Illustrations

Figures

Tables

List of Acronyms and Abbreviations

ADM	Archer Daniels Midland (company)
AOAD	Arab Organization for Agricultural Development
BTU	British thermal units
CAR	capital adequacy ratio
CEO	Chief executive officer
CIHEAM	International Centre for Advanced Agronomic Studies
EDBI	Ease of Doing Business Index (World Bank)
EIA	US Energy Information Administration (Washington D.C.)
EIU	The Economist Intelligence Unit
EGP	Egyptian pound (currency)
ENPARD	European Neighbourhood Programme for Agriculture and Rural Development
EU	European Union
FAO	Food and Agriculture Organization
FDI	foreign direct investment
FS	Food Security
GAFTA	Greater Arab Free Trade Area
GFSI	Global Food Safety Initiative
GHI	Global Hunger Index (of the International Food Policy Research Institute (IFPRI),)
G20	Group of 20 leading industrialised and developing nations (Argentina, Australia, Brazil, Canada, China, France, Germany, India, Indonesia, Italy, Japan, Korea, Mexico, Russia, Saudi Arabia, South Africa, Turkey, United Kingdom, United States and European Union).
GCC	Gulf Cooperation Council
GDP	gross domestic product
CIHEAM	International Centre for Advanced Agronomic Studies
IEA	International Energy Agency (OECD, Paris)
IMF	International Monetary Fund
IOM	International Organization for Migration
IPO	Initial Public Offering
ISIL	Islamic State in Iraq and the Levant
JOD	Jordanian dinar (currency)
MEFTA	Middle East Free Trade Area
MENA	Middle East and North Africa
MESC	Allied Middle East Supply Center (Cairo)
NEPCO	National Electric Power Company (Jordan)

NOAA	National Oceanic and Atmospheric Administration
NGLS	natural gas liquids
NPL	non-performing loan
OECD	Organisation for Economic Co-operation and Development
ONE	Office National de l'Electricité (Morocco)
OPEC	Organization of the Petroleum Exporting Countries
RRE	resource rich economy
RST	Rentier State Theory
RTA	Dubai Roads and Transports Authority
SAMA	Saudi Arabian Monetary Agency
SCI	specialised credit institution
SOB	state-owned bank
SOE	state-owned enterprise
SWF	sovereign wealth fund
WTTC	World Tourism and Travel Council
IFAD	International Fund for Agricultural Development
WFP	World Food Programme
UAE	United Arab Emirates
UfM	Union for the Mediterranean
UNDP	United Nations Development Programme
UNHCR	United Nations High Commissioner for Refugees
UNWRA	United Nations Relief and Works Agency for Palestine Refugees in the Near East
US	United States of America
USD	United States dollar (currency)

Notes on Contributors

Alissa Amico
is the Managing Director of GOVERN, which works with public sector and corporate leaders to advance corporate and economic governance in the Middle East and North Africa (MENA) and other emerging markets. Until 2015, Alissa was responsible for overseeing the Organisation for Economic Cooperation and Development's (OECD) work on financial markets and corporate governance in the MENA.

Laura El-Katiri
is an Abu Dhabi-based analyst and consultant. She has a professional and academic background in economics and energy policy in the MENA, with special focus on the Gulf Cooperation Council (GCC) members. Her work includes various aspects of strategic policy making, including regional oil and gas market development, utility sector and demand-side management, energy pricing and subsidy reform, renewable energy, climate change and sustainable economic development.

Philippe Fargues
is a sociologist and demographer. He is the founding Director of the Migration Policy Centre at the Robert Schuman Centre for Advanced Studies, European University Institute, in Florence, Italy. He has held senior positions at the National Institute for Demographic Studies in Paris and the American University in Cairo, and has taught at Harvard and various universities in France, the Middle East and Africa. His research interests include migration, population and politics, demography and development.

Bassam Fattouh
is the Director of the Oxford Institute for Energy Studies and Professor at the School of Oriental and African Studies, University of London. He has published articles on the international oil pricing system, OPEC pricing power, security of Middle Eastern oil supplies, and the dynamics of oil prices. He served as a member of an independent expert group established to provide recommendations to the 12th International Energy Forum (IEF) Ministerial Meeting in Cancun (29–31 March 2010).

Steffen Hertog
is an associate professor of Comparative Politics at the London School of Economics and Political Science. He is a comparative political economist with a particular focus on the Middle East and is the author of *Princes, Brokers and Bureaucrats: Oil and State in Saudi Arabia* (Cornell University Press, 2011)

and—with Diego Gambetta—of *Engineers of Jihad: the Curious Connection between Violent Extremism and Education* (Princeton University Press, 2016).

Giacomo Luciani
leads the Master in International Energy at the Paris School of International Affairs, Sciences Po; and is adjunct professor of interdisciplinary studies at the Graduate Institute, Geneva. From 2010 to 2013 he was Princeton Global Scholar at the Woodrow Wilson School of Public and International Affairs and the Department of Near Eastern Studies.

Samir Makdisi
is Professor Emeritus of Economics and Founding Director of the Institute of Financial Economics at the American University of Beirut. He is a former Minister of National Economy for Lebanon (1992) and Deputy President of AUB (1992–1998), and is co-editor—with Ibrahim Elbadawi—of a forthcoming book, *Democratic Transitions in the Arab World* (Cambridge University Press).

Adeel Malik
teaches political economy of the Middle East at the University of Oxford and holds the Globe Fellowship in the economies of Muslim societies at the Oxford Centre for Islamic Studies. He is also a research fellow in economics at St Peters College, Oxford.

Bassem Snaije
is the Managing Partner of Cosmos Advisors SARL. His career in investment banking and capital markets began in 1983. He has worked in Paris, London and New York, trading global financial markets and advising global institutional and private clients. Snaije regularly lectures in Political Economy at the Paris School of International Affairs, Sciences Po.

Robert Springborg
is Professor (ret) of National Security Affairs at the Naval Postgraduate School, Monterey, USA, and Non-Resident Research Fellow at the Italian Institute of International Affairs, Rome, Italy. He was Kuwait Program Visiting Professor at Sciences Po in 2014.

Eckart Woertz
is Senior Research Fellow at the Barcelona Centre for International Affairs (CIDOB) and scientific advisor to the Kuwait Chair at Sciences Po in Paris. He specialises in the political economy of the Middle East, food security, energy, sovereign wealth funds, and financial markets. Eckart Woertz is the author of *Oil for Food* (Oxford University Press, 2013).

CHAPTER 1

Introduction: In Search of Economic Policies to Stabilise Democratic Transitions

Giacomo Luciani

Abstract

Democratic transitions in the Middle East and North Africa have mostly failed to consolidate and have been hindered by the difficult economic heritage of previous authoritarian governments. Yet newly established democratic governments must deliver on the expectations of their people, especially the poorer strata, otherwise disillusionment may open the door to restoration of authoritarian rule. The introductory chapter reviews existing literature on the topic and presents the contributions of the collective volume to this crucially important discussion. Can democracy succeed? Various ideas for economic policies that may help consolidate the democratisation process are proposed, while major obstacles on the way to democratic success are also highlighted.

1 Introduction

With the solitary exception of Tunisia, where a still fragile process of democratic consolidation appears to be making progress in the face of multiple challenges, the Arab Spring has led to either a restoration of authoritarian rule (in Egypt, and in Bahrain and the other members of the Gulf Cooperation Council (GCC)) or civil war (in Iraq, Syria, Libya and Yemen).

This state of affairs is obviously unsettling. For decades the political economy debate about the Middle East and North Africa (MENA) has focused on the causes and negative consequences of authoritarianism, and has preached democratic good governance, promising instantaneous and almost unconditionally improved growth and integration into the globalisation process (Acemoglu et al., 2014; World Bank 2016). Then an opportunity for transition to democracy arises—largely unexpected and certainly unpredicted—and almost universally fails. Unavoidable questions then confront us: is democracy possible? Is it desirable? How can we increase the chances for newly established democratic governments to deliver and consolidate?

The Arab Spring has encouraged a broad debate concerning its causes; less so about how it might develop. Much of the literature has focused on ideology,

 | DOI 10.1163/9789004336452_002

identity and longing for human dignity (Achcar, 2013; Hanieh, 2013; Kamrava, 2014; Selvik and Utvik, 2016). The analysis has mostly been conducted at the level of individual countries; the regional dimension of the phenomenon has generally not been recognised and explained. Economic causes of discontent are frequently mentioned, but are rarely supported by empirical data (notable exceptions are Alvaredo and Piketty, 2014; Azmeh, 2014; Beinin, 2016; Hakimian, 2013a and 2013b; Luciani, 2016; Nugent, 2012; and Verme et al., 2014).

It is of course necessary to form a better understanding of the causes and meaning of the Arab Spring in order to meaningfully discuss its eventual failure. That said, the focus of this collection is not on the causes, but on the dilemmas that governments in power, whether incumbent or issuing from a democratic transition, must face in addressing the unresolved underlying issues that led to the revolt. Important recent contributions that have addressed in a similar manner the issue of post-revolution economic policies include, notably, works of Magdi Amin et al. (2012), Hafez Ghanem (2016a), Schiffbauer et al. (2015), and the World Bank (2014).

What needs to be done to deliver the minimum improvement in living conditions that will convince the people that indeed things are changing for the better? Can a democratic government implement the measures necessary? Or do we still need a degree of authoritarianism before a successful democratic transition is conceivable? What can the democratic world do to support the consolidation of democratic transitions? Or should democratic countries accept that an authoritarian parenthesis is inevitable and keep searching for the oxymoron: a democratising authoritarian government?

For Europe at least, these are not just academic questions. The civil wars, restorations of authoritarian rule, and developmental failures in the Middle East and North Africa have led to an unprecedented wave of refugees and economic migrants that the European Union and other European countries are unable to deal with. Faced with a humanitarian crisis of biblical proportions, Europe is falling apart, turning into not one, but multiple fortresses. It is a political return to the Middle Ages, where localism and defence against encroachment from outside are the leading values.

If democracy is to be saved, it has to be saved everywhere. In a globalised world, it is simply impossible to be indifferent to the fate of neighbouring countries. The European Union (EU) has long had a concept of its 'neighbourhood' and formulated policies—on paper at least—to support the respect of human rights, and good governance and democracy. The fact is that policies adopted so far have accomplished nothing, and have almost exclusively been disasters. In its latest revision the European Neighbourhood Policy appears to have abandoned any ambition to foster democratisation (Schuhmacher, 2016). Is there anything that could be done better? Are we following the right recipes?

We badly need to engage in this debate, and academics have a moral duty to put their minds to it.

2 The Economic Heritage of Authoritarianism

At least since the turn of the millennium, if not earlier, Arab authoritarian governments have come to terms with the 'Washington Consensus', with variable degrees of enthusiasm. They have pursued policies of fiscal stabilisation, which progressively allowed typical features of the past—such as high inflation, capital controls, trade protectionism and multiple exchange rates—to be overcome. Economies were opened and active participation in the globalisation process was sought. International specialisation in goods and services for which the countries could claim comparative advantage was accepted, which resulted in less emphasis on industry and subsistence agriculture, more on export agriculture (Woertz, this volume) and export services such as, principally, tourism.

Generally, these developments were lauded by international financial organisations. It was expected that the Arab economies would be able to attract increased foreign direct investment, which would have led to accelerated growth, improved productivity and competitiveness, and the creation of jobs in line with population growth and the youth bulge (Fargues, this volume). The outcome of these policies was partially, yet not entirely disappointing.

Things have also been problematic from the point of view of democratic transition. Capital-intensive investment in mining and industry displays strong resistance to political disturbances, because the large amount of sunk capital encourages resilience, plus generally projects are remote from densely inhabited centres and are not as vulnerable as sometimes believed. It is therefore generally the case that such investment may be slowed down but not reversed; nor is production interrupted should political instability occur, except in extreme cases where the security of company personnel is directly threatened. In contrast, financial investment and tourism are extremely vulnerable to political instability, and this is the other side of the democratic transition coin. As soon as the incumbent authoritarian regime collapses, foreign investment will stop coming in, domestic and foreign money will tend to flow out, and international rating agencies will revise the country's rating downwards. This immediately creates a negative spiral, which a newly elected democratic government (or, more likely, a provisional government lacking full democratic legitimation and with a very uncertain life expectancy) will find difficult to reverse.

Tourism is also extremely vulnerable to political disturbances and uncertainty. The vast majority of potential tourists are not interested in witnessing a revolution. In the time that popular uprisings will take to provoke the fall of the authoritarian regime, the tourist trade will quickly dry up. Once a democratic transition is underway, tourists will still normally want to be reassured that conditions are stable and security is guaranteed; recovery will be gradual. This means that a newly elected democratic government is likely to be confronted with rapidly deteriorating economic conditions in the tourism sector, depending on the importance of that sector in the national economy. Furthermore, even once the democratic transition is well underway, it is not difficult for opponents or extremists to stage terrorist attacks targeting tourists, which will have the immediate effect of precipitating a new crisis or extending the existing one. The damaging economic impact of terrorism is evident and feared even in Europe or the United States, but much more so in MENA, including in such primary tourist destinations as Egypt, Tunisia or Morocco.[1]

Tourism is also a labour-intensive sector, which supports local agriculture, handicrafts and small-scale commercial activities. A sudden downturn in tourist activity is likely to be immediately felt by a significant share of the population, mostly from relatively low-income or poorer strata.

With respect to fiscal policy, authoritarian regimes have pursued balanced budgets primarily by cutting down on social services (generally by simply not increasing expenditure in line with population growth, and letting quality progressively deteriorate). Such regimes have, however, tended to maintain and in some cases even expand entitlements in the form of subsidised or exceedingly low prices for selected necessities (primarily basic food items) and energy products (oil products, gas and electricity). The latter have mainly a regressive impact on income distribution (as documented by El-Katiri and Fattouh, and Hertog—both in this volume) while the former are more benign (as explained by Woertz and, in the case of Egypt, by Springborg, both in this volume). Nevertheless, it is energy subsidies that have come to absorb an exceedingly important share of government budgets, in part because the price of oil increased rapidly between 2003 and 2008 and remained very high subsequently. Newly empowered democratic governments were therefore immediately confronted with the challenge of announcing unpopular measures while their legitimacy and hold on power was still quite shaky.

Notwithstanding evident weaknesses, the economic growth record of the authoritarian regimes over the 2000–10 decade was not altogether negative

1 In Egypt, international tourism revenue in 2015 totalled USD 6.1 billion, while in 2010 it had stood at USD 12.5 billion. In Tunisia tourist revenue peaked in 2008, was down by roughly one-third by 2013, and further declined in 2015 following terrorist attacks on tourist facilities. See also World Bank (2016).

(Amin et al., 2012; Ghanem, 2016a; Hakimian, 2013a and 2013b; Devarajan and Mottaghi, 2014). Arab countries, and not just the major oil exporters, experienced a decade (or more) of rapid growth up to 2010; growth suffered subsequently because of the negative impact of the Spring, especially on certain sectors. However, this growth did not benefit all equally: although most measurements of income distribution do not show increasing concentration (Hakimian, 2013b), employment opportunities for young people (especially if educated) worsened significantly. Ghanem (2016a) also points to unemployment among educated young entrants to the job market, but also to the worsening or stagnating conditions in marginalised regions (e.g. Upper Egypt) or sectors (e.g. agriculture). Finally, Alvaredo and Piketty (2014) convincingly argue that data sources that are currently available at the national level in Egypt or other MENA countries are insufficient to derive reliable estimates of top income shares, and that income inequality is extremely large at the level of the Middle East region taken as whole. It is the perception of such growing inequality, further fuelled by the growing role of regional media and the constant image of Dubai-style success that they project, that ignited the resentment and revolt against incumbent authoritarian regimes. The widening gap in incomes and wealth at the regional level is the key target of popular revolt: democracy must succeed in bringing about a reversal of this trend.[2]

3 Well-Established Recipes Do Not Support Democratic Transitions

Faced with a declining economy, falling government revenues and excessive expenditure on subsidies, governments issuing from the demise of authoritarian regimes were encouraged to persist in the policies of the Washington Consensus—that is, primarily cutting outlays by reducing subsidies and other expenditure, privatising government-owned enterprises, and improving tax collection.

Such policies promise immediate political costs but deferred advantages—hardly the ideal path for a democratic government in need of consensus and consolidation. True, democratic legitimation is necessary if one is to pursue controversial or unpopular policies, but democracy needs to be well rooted for that. A country undergoing democratic transition needs both a high degree of consensus to establish a national pact that will underpin a new constitution,

2 After the revolt, the Arab Barometer conducted a survey asking Tunisians what was the main reason for their revolt. More than 60 per cent of respondents indicated a 'weak economy' was their main motivation. (Cited in Ghanem, 2016a).

and compromises among a broad spectrum of political forces. This does not bode well for potentially unpopular measures.

Revolt against incumbent authoritarian regimes certainly is motivated largely by a desire for freedom, for respect for human rights, and for dignity; but the poorer strata of the population also expect an improvement in their material conditions—at least some sign that income distribution may be moving in the right direction. Traditional macroeconomic stabilisation policies go in the opposite direction.

In fact, evidence of growing income inequality everywhere in the world, in advanced as well as in emerging countries, points to the conclusion that the globalisation process has supported a greater concentration of income and wealth rather than the opposite. Thus, while reverting to greater isolation from the global economic environment is not an option for any country, and certainly not for a country pursuing democratisation, the rules of globalisation are not helpful (Springborg 2016).

The debate on income inequality has greatly intensified among economists since the turn of the century with reference to all countries, not just to the MENA region (Piketty, 2013; Atkinson, 2015). It has become evident that the process of globalisation has had profound consequences for the distribution of income in industrial and in emerging countries, leading to a greater concentration of income and wealth at the global level. In mature democracies, this trend is viewed as a potential threat to the satisfactory functioning and stability of institutions, but little attention has been paid to the consequences that it might have on democratisation processes. The standard line is that concentration of income and wealth may lead to growing dissatisfaction and eventually revolt: but in the initial stages of democratic transition, the limited opportunities to implement redistributive policies may endanger the process itself.

At the heart of the problem is increased international competition, which has led to deindustrialisation and the weakening of labour movements in all countries where industry and trade unions used to be important players.[3] The liberalisation of international trade and capital movements has brought about a radical change in the labour/capital bargaining balance. While some minority voices advocate a reversal of the globalisation process and a return

3 Beinin (2016) insists on the importance of the role of trade unions and labour activism in Egypt and Tunisia. In the case of the latter country, trade unions also plaid a significant political role in the transition process in the context of the so-called Quartet. Nevertheless, formal employment in both countries remains limited, and in the rest of the region trade unions are hardly a significant force.

to greater national control over the economy to protect a broad range of welfare and rights-related legislation, it is unlikely that the world will go back to protectionism.

The more sophisticated discussion of inequality in a globalised context seeks ways of mitigating the trend towards growing concentrations of income and wealth by considering measures that are compatible with freedom of trade and capital movements. In this context, the role of education and of progressive taxation on income and wealth are frequently cited as the appropriate solutions—although fiscal competition constitutes a grave threat to the ability of individual states, even in the European context, to manage or tighten their taxation systems.

Almost all redistributive policies are administratively complex and require time to implement and even more time to show their effects. This means that they are not adapted to conditions prevailing in countries that are undergoing a democratic transition. We therefore face a potential vicious circle: if strong and accountable institutions are needed for successful participation in the globalisation process, but the latter worsens income and wealth inequality, which constitutes a powerful obstacle to democratic transitions, then countries with weak/unaccountable institutions are condemned to economic marginalisation and to having inferior institutions.

4 The Quest for Alternatives

It is this critical nexus that the chapters in this book explore from different angles. The broad question is: what economic policies and development priorities should be pursued by governments in the early phases of democratic transition processes? As mentioned already, the literature addressing this question so far has been limited.

Both of the major contributions to the literature originate from collective efforts undertaken under the aegis of the Brookings Institution. The first project took place in 2011 and led to the publication of a volume by Magdi Amin et al. (2012). The second took place five years after the eruption of the Spring (as is self-evident from the title *The Arab Spring Five Years Later*) and led to the publication of two volumes, one entirely written by Hafez Ghanem (2016a) and the other edited by the same (2016b).

The first book sets off from premises that are very similar to our own: 'Most successful transitions involve simultaneous political and economic reform, and this is likely to be the case for Arab countries as well' (Amin et al., 2012, 2). The importance of the regional dimension for both understanding the Arab

Spring and defining policies for democratic transitions is also underlined.[4] The book's main message is that 'four main economic transitions are required':

> First, more opportunities for young people need to be created. There are large intergenerational inequities in the distribution of the benefits of economic growth, in favor of a group of public sector employees, elites, and other rent seekers to the disadvantage of the large youth population in the region. (...)
>
> Second, the Arab economies need to modernize their public sectors. There is still a strong demand for a developmental state role in Arab economies and a significant suspicion over the impact of liberal economic reforms that, under the old regimes, served to benefit only a few well-connected private groups. (...)
>
> The third transition is in the private sector. Today, large elements of the private sector are seen as synonymous with corruption. Yet there is no sustainable economic model for the region that does not have the private sector playing a leading role. (...)
>
> The fourth economic transition is in the approach to the rest of the world.
>
> AMIN ET AL., 2012, 6–7, 9

These are all well-identified priorities, but mostly for pursuing in the longer term. Will weak governments engaged in transitioning to democracy have the time to pursue them? Is it not necessary to focus on some more immediate benefits? It is possible that, given that the book was the outcome of brainstorming that took place while the Spring was still unfolding, the urgency of stabilising the transition was not yet acutely felt.

Writing five years later, Ghanem (2016a) seems resigned to the inevitability of a neo-authoritarian parenthesis to put in place policies that, in due course, will facilitate transitioning to democracy. Thus he writes: '...can a country with no democratic tradition and with weak institutions become a well-functioning democracy and improve the lives of its citizens overnight? The answer is obviously no. Democratic transitions take years, even decades to succeed, and there are many twists and turns along the way. Moreover, they can be costly

4 '... there is a commonality to Arab history, language, and culture so it is reasonable to suppose that there is a regional identity that should not be ignored. Such a view is reinforced by the contagion demonstrated during the Arab Spring and the close links of people, ideas, news carried from country to country, and aspirations across the region' (Amin et al., 2012, 5).

and require heavy human and economic sacrifices. Ask any Arab today if he or she feels that the region is better off than before the Arab Spring. What do you think the answer will be?' (Ghanem, 2016a, 2). He continues, telling us about a conversation with a Cairo taxi driver who is happy about President al-Sissi and proud of having overthrown two presidents before him (Mubarak and Morsi): he says that if al-Sissi does not perform, the people will get rid of him as well. Ghanem believes this has established some basic accountability of power; therefore, 'the Arab world appears to be moving toward more open and inclusive governance' (Ghanem, 2016a, 2). Clearly the author believes that the neo-authoritarian regime of al-Sissi may deliver where Mubarak failed: providing for more inclusive growth.

Ghanem's proposed cocktail of policies for achieving more inclusive growth is composed of four priorities: 'institutional reforms to improve implementation of policies and programs; reforms of the business environment, with a special emphasis on developing small and medium-sized enterprises (SMEs); rural development and support to lagging regions; and improving the quality of education'. None of these is objectionable, and clearly these are all priorities that can only be pursued in the longer run, as improvements will be slow to materialise. But none of these is new either: why were previous authoritarian regimes unable to pursue these priorities (they did in the 1950s and early 1960s, but progressively steered away and towards elite integration in regional oil rent circulation)? How can we expect that newly established authoritarian regimes, whose repressive inclination is only too evident, will behave differently to their predecessors?

The essays in this volume continue this debate, in many ways confirming the difficulty of proposing a cocktail of policies that will allow for rapid improvement in the living conditions of a majority of people and sustain consensus around the consolidation of democracy.

In Chapter 2, Samir Makdisi summarises the main conclusions of research on the historical entrenchment of Arab autocracies and of their subsequent unravelling in a few countries. He concludes that notwithstanding the unprecedented wave of popular revolt, 'the region's democratic prospects remain highly uncertain'. His key message concerning policies for the consolidation of democratic transitions is clear:

> At the socio-economic level what would be required is the design and implementation of a broad based and what has come to be referred to as inclusive strategy, one that should create expectations that growth, expanding employment opportunities, and equity will play a major role in the transition to a new economy.
>
> MAKDISI, this volume

In Chapter 3, Adeel Malik revisits the rentier state theory and argues that its scope should be greatly enlarged to encompass numerous other sources of rent besides mineral extraction. He believes that rent formation and circulation is the key explanatory variable of unsatisfactory growth results and the stability of autocratic regimes in the region. He points specifically to the way in which non-tariff barriers, bank lending and freedom of capital movements have been used to favour the formation and enrichment of elites close to the incumbent autocratic regimes. As he writes, 'it is easier to remove regime leaders than to eliminate the rentier structures that feed the associated elite coalitions', thus pointing to the difficulty of moving from one set of economic structures to another that would be more inclusive. This also points to the crucial importance of dismantling existing mechanisms for rent circulation and the very sources of internal rents if the door to more inclusive economic development is to be opened.

El-Katiri and Fattouh (Chapter 4) focus on energy subsidies as a very important form of rent circulation, documenting the extraordinary and crippling burden of these subsidies on the budgets of states that are not major exporters, such as Egypt, Tunisia and Yemen. For oil exporting countries the burden is 'virtual', in the sense that it translates into forfeited earnings rather than actual expenditure; but for all net importers of petroleum products the subsidies entail actual expenditure, which accounts, depending on the year and the average price of crude oil, for a very substantial share of government expenditure (in 2013–14 upward of 30 per cent in the case of Yemen, close to 20 per cent in the case of Egypt). It is clear that the opportunity cost of such outlays—that is to say, the possible alternative ways in which this money could be spent, is extremely significant.

El-Katiri and Fattouh underline that a reform of energy subsidies needs to be well prepared and compensated by some balancing measure in order to be successful. Thus subsidy reform succeeded in both Morocco and Jordan (which, not by chance, are the two 'democratising monarchies' in the region, notwithstanding limitations to their democratic progress), but failed in Yemen. Energy subsidy reform also succeeded in Egypt, but was implemented only after the restoration of authoritarianism and in the context of strong repressive measures. Finally, energy subsidy reform succeeded in Iran, whose case is especially interesting because the increase in energy prices was offset by cash payments to all citizens; 50 per cent of the sums saved were allocated to cover these payments. The burden of energy subsidies in Iran was even higher than in the Arab countries concerned, but compensation with universal cash payments was undoubtedly a success. The programme later ran into difficulties, including due to international sanctions; but the experience demonstrated that a bold, if 'populist', move can send a signal of radical change—although in the case of the Ahmadinejad Administration the political context was certainly not one of democratisation.

In Chapter 5, Steffen Hertog argues strongly in favour of universal cash transfers.[5] He analyses the two main distribution mechanisms in use in the region—public sector employment and subsidies—and concludes that both have perverse effects. He stresses how 'apart from public employment and subsidies, Arab governments offer little by the way of social security policies' and traces the reasons for this to the priorities of authoritarian regimes. This creates a vicious circle whereby new redistribution policies cannot be initiated until the burden of excess employment and subsidies is lifted—yet abandoning the old policies without adequate compensation will be perceived as being profoundly unpopular. More modern social security policies are not created and put in place overnight, so a deterioration of living conditions may be unavoidable and politically unaffordable.

Hertog therefore clearly distinguishes between an agenda for the long run ('In the long run, Arab countries should build up conventional social security mechanisms such as means-tested income support, unemployment assistance, unemployment insurance, and active labour market policies such as retraining and job placement services') and one for the short run: 'direct, unconditional cash grants for all adult citizens'.[6] Hertog offers an articulate defence of the advantages of this solution in the MENA environment. He argues that such a policy would be beneficial for labour markets because it may be tailored to encourage private sector employment (excluding government employees from receiving the grants) and in this way equilibrate at least in part the attraction of public vs private sector jobs. It would also, I wish to add, constitute an incentive to remain in the home country, rather than adding to the relentless

5 The idea is found also in both Amin et al. (2012) and Ghanem (2016a). Amin et al. (2012, 89) write: 'A system that replaces the current energy and food subsidies with direct income transfers to the poor will be fairer and more efficient. However, Arab regimes have so far been unable to make such a change. (...) It remains to be seen whether the new governments resulting from the Arab Spring will be able to build the necessary consensus to bring about such a major policy change'. Ghanem (2016a, 33–34) writes: 'The idea of putting in place a social protection system based on targeted cash transfers has been studied in the Arab world for several years and could be quickly implemented. Experience from around the world indicates that such a system is much less expensive, more efficient, and fairer that price subsidies'.

6 The debate on the widening inequalities with regards to income and wealth taking place in practically all countries, whether attributed to globalisation or other causes, has greatly intensified in recent years. Various proposals for a 'citizens' income' have been put forward, especially in advanced countries. For a recent proposal focusing on the UK, see Painter and Thoung (2015). The approach is discussed also in Atkinson (2015, Chapter 8).

stream of refugees and economic migrants that flows towards Europe—a good reason for European countries to provide financial and administrative support, at least in an initial phase, under the banner of facilitating democratic consolidation and easing immigration pressures.

There may be multiple ways of refining this approach and improve targeting. Restricting cash grants to the poorer strata is difficult because of the uncertainty of available income data and the potential for corruption and cheating; but it might be possible to focus a cash grant scheme on those age groups that encompass young entrants into the labour force[7]—between 14 and 30 or 35. There might be multiple reasons for this approach: citizens in these age groups are the most politically active (and potentially attracted to extremist ideologies); in addition, one key component of the unstable political environment throughout the region is the unprecedented youth bulge, which—as highlighted by Fargues in Chapter 9 (and also by Hakimian, 2013b and Ghanem, 2016a)—characterises the Arab demography of the past and current decade.

Such a youth bulge is, on the one hand, a 'demographic blessing', because it temporarily reduces the ratio of dependents to the active population; but, on the other hand, it also constitutes an impossible challenge for the governments of the region, which are expected to create enough jobs to productively employ all new entrants. Migration has been a frequent response to this state of affairs among young entrants into the workforce that have found no opportunities at home. It is significant that the collapse of authoritarian regimes has led to an increased migration push that, as Fargues documents, has not exclusively been motivated by economic reasons.[8] There is also some evidence that diasporas have fed a culture of revolt, either through 'political remittances' or by offering better opportunities for resistance in regions that experienced the highest migration rates (successful migrants offering potential support to those left behind). Fargues cites the example of positive correlation between regional rates of emigration in Tunisia and voting for Ennahda in the first election after the fall of Ben Ali. Political and economic mobilisation of diasporas offers a potential opportunity for governments aiming at consolidating the democratic transition. At the same time, migration also offers a safety valve for letting off the steam of political discontent (exit rather than voice); and the very high share of expatriates in the major Gulf oil producing countries is an objective

7 Child benefits are a frequently advocated component of redistribution policies: see e.g. Atkinson (2015, Chapter 8). Child poverty obviously deserves to be targeted, but in the regional context it may be feared that child benefits may end up supporting high fertility rates in countries where this is still a problem.

8 Christian and other religious minorities have felt threatened by political developments and have manifested an even stronger desire to migrate.

obstacle to democratisation (Khalaf and Luciani, 2006; Luciani, Chapter 11 in this volume; Mehlum, Moene and Ostenstadt, 2016). This may also have the effect of weakening, at least temporarily, resistance to an authoritarian comeback—with people reverting to focusing on individual efforts at exit rather than collective voice.

Can migration become a tool for the consolidation of democracy rather than being just a phenomenon ignored in the sending countries, and resisted in the receiving ones? Could one think of policies to encourage return migration, in particular with incentives to repatriate know-how and establish new micro and small enterprises—a phenomenon that has played such an important role in the economic success of Turkey in the last three decades? Or could one establish policies to encourage remittances and investment in the country of origin?[9] Could receiving countries tie conditions for access and progress in the direction of democracy together (and not just to protracted civil war: in other words, create an incentive for a positive, not just a negative, outcome of the transition)?[10] Currently, Europe ends up paying the price for various catastrophes on humanitarian grounds, but does precious little to support the consolidation of democratic transitions.

Migration patterns are a sore point in relations with Europe, but also in inter-Arab economic relations, a point stressed by Luciani in Chapter 11. In the immediate aftermath of the first wave of increases in oil prices (1970–1985) some of the major oil exporters opened their doors to workers from other Arab countries quite wide: Iraq formally had a policy of encouraging migrants from the region, Yemenis could travel to Saudi Arabia without a visa, Kuwait hosted a large Palestinian population, a large number of Lebanese and Jordanians moved to the Gulf, and Libya took in a significant number of Egyptians and Tunisians. This pattern was brutally reversed in 1990, following the Iraqi invasion of Kuwait, because Palestine, Jordan and Yemen supported or did not condemn the Iraqi action, thus leading to mass expulsions from the GCC countries. Iraq suffered first from the impact of the war with Iran, and soon thereafter from the defeat that followed the invasion of Kuwait, so that it ceased being an attractive destination. Libya remained an important destination, especially for

9 Receiving European countries could establish facilities to provide credit to migrants wishing to return and set up businesses, or simply invest in their country of origin. Inadequate access to credit is a key obstacle to the development of small enterprises in MENA.

10 As I write these lines, Germany has announced that it is putting Tunisia, Algeria and Morocco on a list of 'safe countries', thus making immigration from these countries more difficult, while keeping the doors open to immigration from Syria and other countries in the throes of civil war (the Guardian, 2016). One can readily understand the logic, but democratic consolidation is thus not made any easier.

Egyptian workers, until the country plunged into civil war. In the end, the role of inter-Arab migration as a potential equaliser of regional incomes deteriorated drastically. According to figures presented by Fargues (Chapter 9), the total number of Arab migrants in 2012 was just above 17 million, of which 8.6 million went to other Arab countries, 5.6 million to Europe and just 3 million to the rest of the world:[11] inter-Arab migration therefore represents only 50 per cent of the total, and—in fact—probably less.

Agriculture is another key area with an influence on the outcome of democratic transitions, but is mostly neglected by newly elected governments and by external actors interested in their success. In Chapter 8, Eckart Woertz highlights how agriculture, while contributing relatively little to total GDP, consumes the bulk of scarce water resources and still employs a large share of the workforce in many countries in MENA (close to 50 per cent in Sudan, South Sudan and Mauritania; 35 per cent in Yemen; 27 per cent in Oman; 23 per cent in Egypt and Morocco…). Insufficient attention has been paid by new democratic governments to living conditions in the countryside: in the context of policies of opening to international trade and investment, previous policies in support of the peasantry have been reversed, leading to continuing migration from rural to urban areas, and to a 'ruralisation of cities'—that is to say, an increase in the number of poor and marginalised inhabitants of the major urban areas. The transition towards capitalist agriculture has not led to significantly increased productivity and lower prices: 'People in many MENA countries including Egypt, Algeria and Morocco, spend more than a third of their disposable income on food'. Hence, food subsidies are difficult to eliminate and 'have great significance with regard to political legitimacy. This could be seen during the Arab Spring when Egyptian protesters strapped loaves of bread to their heads'. Relative to fuel subsidies, 'Food clearly commands a greater emotional appeal and—because of their self-targeting nature—the abolition of subsidies on staple foods would disproportionately hurt the poor'. But containing the cost of food for the urban dweller contrasts with improving the lot of people living off agriculture. The matter is made more difficult by widespread agricultural protectionism in industrial countries: the EU surplus in trade of agricultural products with MENA has been growing, for example.[12]

11 This includes Syrian refugees, which cluster in neighbouring countries. Civil wars and the ensuing wave of refugees swelled the ranks of regional migrants.

12 As discussed in Chapter 11, empirical research has demonstrated that the agreements concluded under the European Neighbourhood Policy have led to an increase in European exports but not of those of the Southern partners; agricultural protectionism is largely to blame.

It is clear that improving the income and living conditions of the rural population in MENA would contribute to relieving migratory pressures, both internally towards urban areas that are overcrowded and incapable of accommodating new arrivals, and internationally—that is to say, towards Europe.

Eventually, however, whether policies to promote the significant potential of agriculture are successful or not, employment in the sector will need to decline both absolutely and as a share of the total. Inevitably, it is growth in industry and export-oriented services that will have to provide the jobs and opportunities required to accommodate the growing number of new entrants into the workforce. But services are vulnerable—we have already commented, in particular, on tourism in this respect. It is unrealistic to envision that the MENA region may simply bypass the industrial phase of development and directly pass from agriculture to services. Industry remains an essential component of any diversified economy, and so-called post-industrial societies are having growing misgivings about having too easily liquidated large parts of their industrial systems in the context of globalisation.

But when it comes to industry, MENA countries suffer from the weakness of their private sectors, in terms of both financial and industrial capabilities. 'While it is now widely accepted that private sector-led growth is necessary if structural unemployment in the region is to be addressed, state-led development remains a pervasive characteristic of the Arab world', writes Alissa Amico in Chapter 6 of this volume. '(...) question marks surround private sector's capacity to act as a locomotive of economic growth in the Arab world', and in practice the only alternative to continuing reliance on state-owned enterprises is privatisation, leading to foreign ownership. But multinational corporations will prioritise the elimination of excess employment, which is problematic in the short run for recently established democratic governments. Furthermore, large-scale sales of state-owned assets to foreign corporations would inevitably run against nationalist feelings and suspicions of corruption.

Improving the governance of state-owned enterprises and restoring them to profitability, so that they can contribute to the accumulation of capital and economic growth, is therefore an additional challenge for newly elected democratic governments. Where authoritarian incumbents failed in most cases, democrats must succeed: not an easy challenge in the face of popular expectations. In fact, employment in state-owned enterprises has rapidly increased in Tunisia, confirming the populist tendency to use economic assets as distributional rather than developmental tools.

A specific category of state-owned enterprises that deserves special attention and is in dire need of urgent reform is banks. State-owned banks dominate the banking sector in MENA and constitute a key pillar of rentierism and authoritarian control. Through control of the banking sector and selective, non-transparent and politically conditioned access to credit, state-owned banks facilitated the formation and survival of a non-performing class of crony capitalists to support the authoritarian regimes. The flip side of this coin has been the exclusion from access to credit of most small-scale and/or politically unconnected entrepreneurs, whose ability to contribute to growth and the creation of jobs has correspondingly been reduced (Diwan, 2016; Ghanem 2016a; Schiffbauer et al., 2015).

Restoring the role of banks and other financial institutions as intermediaries that enable entrepreneurs by facilitating their access to finance is an essential component of democratisation processes. Bassam Snaije argues in Chapter 7 that democratic institutions and governance are contextual with the development of financial markets, with special emphasis on the market for debt securities. He notes how the structure of financial markets in MENA differs significantly from that of Organisation for Economic Co-operation and Development (OECD) countries, inasmuch as it is dominated by bank credit, predominantly with short maturities; while the market for equity and debt securities is much less important. Furthermore, most banks, in particular those in countries outside the GCC, are either state-owned or controlled by families that are close to authoritarian power holders. Snaije believes that banking reform and enhancing the role of equity and debt securities markets should be a priority for democratising governments, in order to allow new participants to access finance, foster growth and promote agreements of trust that are not based on personal acquaintance and proximity to power.

Faced with the difficulty of formulating economic policies that will help consolidate a democratic transition, is the solution a return to 'modern autocracy' in the hope that it may eventually evolve in a genuinely democratic direction? This is where the case of Egypt is crucially important: not only is Egypt the most populous and geographically and politically central Arab country, it is also the one in which the credibility of the potential 'authoritarian route to democracy' is the subject of experiment. After the collapse of the democratically elected Morsi Administration, largely due to its utter inability to govern a collapsing economy and manage a transparent and inclusive democratisation process, the Army is back in power under Marshal al-Sisi: will he deliver the economic miracle that Egypt needs? In Chapter 10, Robert Springborg expresses his profound scepticism in this respect. The conclusion of his detailed analysis of Egypt's economic ills and the current regime's approach to them is stark: '...al-Sisi's Egypt is doubling down on what preceding regimes in that country and those elsewhere in the world have demonstrated to be a failed strategy for economic development'. Indeed, Egypt may eventually become another basket case, like Yemen or the Sudan. Repression will then maintain political stability only temporarily.

In the final chapter in this volume, Giacomo Luciani focuses on the regional environment of the Arab Spring and Arab economies. He argues that the Spring was indeed a regional rather than country-specific phenomenon, and all Arab countries are—in one way or another—involved in a regional civil war, although that war is currently only being actively fought in four of them (Iraq, Libya, Syria and Yemen). The outcome of the regional civil war will eventually determine the political future of all MENA countries. Regional economic integration has been prevented by multiple political conflicts, yet is essential for the success of the very economic policies that might consolidate democratic transitions—assuming that the outcome of the Arab civil war will point in that direction.

5 Conclusion: Does Democratisation Have a Chance?

It is clear from the above discussion and from the remainder of this volume that democratic transitions face a serious problem inasmuch as they can expect to face deteriorating economic conditions while expectations of rapid improvement among a majority of the people, especially the poorer strata, are high. Our research has pointed to some initiatives that may be undertaken relatively quickly and give a strong signal in the direction of greater inclusion. It remains difficult to move rapidly and obtain visible results quickly, but newly installed democratic governments should be bold.[13]

The abolition of fuel subsidies that only benefit the middle classes and the rich is a case in point: fiscal space gained with this measure might be used, as suggested by Hertog, for a programme of unconditional cash transfers to either all citizens or some easily verified categories; in any case avoiding complex bureaucracy that would invite corruption. This would benefit citizens that presently derive minimal or no advantage from fuel subsidies.

The merits of a large enough devaluation should be carefully considered. The drawbacks of an overvalued exchange rate are frequently mentioned as an obstacle to growth as is the fact that such an obstacle may hurt democratic

13 '… it would be a mistake not to take the opportunity afforded by the major political transition to make significant reforms to the economic structure in each country. Politicians often have a short window of opportunity in which to succeed or fail—what was called the period of "extraordinary politics" when reforms can be accomplished with an ease that will later vanish'. (Amin et al., 2012, 13).

transitions.[14] Devaluations tend to damage all those whose consumption basket includes a significant component of imported goods—which is normally not the case for the poorer segments and the marginalised. Devaluation is likely to shift demand in favour of domestic agricultural products, and in this way shift income from cities to the countryside. It also improves the competitiveness of all manufactured exports, and of services such as tourism. If government income is at least in part linked to revenue from the export of raw materials, whose price is fixed internationally in dollars, devaluation also creates further fiscal space for the government. Conversely, devaluation is also an advantage to all citizens that have wealth or income denominated in foreign currencies: migrants' remittances may be encouraged and become more important, but crony capitalists who have piled up wealth in foreign accounts would also benefit. Finally, the government may gain or lose depending on whether public debt is denominated in the national or some foreign currency. Thus the net impact of using the exchange rate tool is difficult to predict a priori, but a case can be made that bold use of this tool in connection with political transition might be beneficial.

Reform of the banking sector can also be pursued relatively quickly. Banks should be invited to wipe their balance sheet clean of bad loans. Connivance between banks and crony capitalists must be broken as a first step in the direction of the restructuring of the banking sector and the reopening of credit opportunities to new, especially small-scale, entrepreneurs. Restructuring banks, changing their management especially by tapping the frequently considerable pool of national talent available in the diaspora, forcing recapitalisation when necessary and isolating non-performing debts in separate 'bad bank' structures would go a long way to turning a page in the political economy of democratising countries.

Thus, short-term policy tools are available and should be used boldly, while at the same time aiming at the longer-term objectives that the literature has very clearly identified. Yet, it will remain difficult to succeed unless the regional environment also evolves in the right direction. The dichotomy between rich and poor states in the region must be overcome through greater openness, and encouragement given to regional movements of capital and labour and

14 'The exchange rate in many countries is out of equilibrium, supported either by capital controls or by official reserve sales. Unlike other cases of major economic transition, Arab economies have not witnessed strong currency depreciations as yet. Without more exchange rate adjustments, however, the long-term fundamental reforms to encourage the private sector and increasingly open the economy to the rest of the world will not be successful'. (Amin et al., 2012, 83–84).

effective market integration. A degree of political convergence is a prerequisite for this, and democratic transitions are unlikely to succeed if they have to swim against the tide of regional authoritarianism.

References

Acemoglu, D., S. Naidu, P. Restrepo and J.A. Robinson (2014) *Democracy Does Cause Growth*, NBER Working Paper No. 20004 (Massachusetts: National Bureau of Economic Research) DOI: 10.3386/w20004.

Achcar, G. (2013) *The People Want—a Radical Exploration of the Arab Uprising* (Berkeley : University of California Press), 328 pages.

Alvaredo, F. and T. Piketty (2014) *Measuring Top Incomes and Inequality in the Middle East: Data Limitations and Illustration with the Case of Egypt*, Working Paper Series 832 (Cairo: Economic Research Forum), http://piketty.pse.ens.fr/files/Alvaredo Piketty2014ERF.pdf (accessed on 17 March 2016).

Amin, M., R. Assaad, N. al-Baharna, K. Dervis, R.M. Desai, N.S. Dhillon, A. Galal, Hafez Ghanem, C. Graham, and D. Kaufmann (2012) *After the Spring: Economic Transitions in the Arab World* (Oxford, Oxford University Press).

Atkinson, A.B. (2015) *Inequality—What can be done?* (Cambridge (Massachusetts): Harvard University Press).

Azmeh, S. (2014) *The Uprising of the Marginalised—a Socio-Economic Perspective of the Syrian Uprising*, LSE Middle East Centre Paper Series 6, November (London: LSE Middle East Centre) http://www.lse.ac.uk/middleEastCentre/publications/Paper-Series/UprisingoftheMarginalised.pdf (accessed on 31 March 2016).

Beinin, J. (2016) *Political Economy and Social Movement Theory Perspectives on the Tunisian and Egyptian Popular Uprisings of 2011*, LSE Middle East Centre Paper Series 14 January (London: LSE Middle East Centre) http://eprints.lse.ac.uk/65291/ (accessed on 1 April 2016).

Devarajan S. and L. Mottaghi (2014) 'Predictions, Perceptions and Economic Reality—Challenges of the seven Middle East and North Africa Countries described in 14 Charts' *MENA Quarterly Economic Brief*, August (Washington, D.C.: World Bank) http://elibrary.worldbank.org/doi/abs/10.1596/978-1-4648-0407-6.

Diwan, I. (2016) 'Economic Growth After the Arab Spring', *Project Syndicate*, March 4, https://www.project-syndicate.org/commentary/arab-spring-countries-economic-growth-by-ishac-diwan-2016-03 (accessed on 1 April 2016).

Ghanem, H. (2016a) *The Arab Spring Five Years Later—Toward Greater Inclusiveness* (Washington D.C.: Brookings Institution Press).

Ghanem, H. (ed.) (2016b) *The Arab Spring Five Years Later—Case Inclusiveness* (Washington D.C.: Brookings Institution Press).

Guardian (The) (2016) '*Germany tightens refugee policy as Finland joins Sweden in deportations*', January 29, http://www.theguardian.com/world/2016/jan/29/germany-tightens-borders-as-finland-joins-sweden-in-deporting-refugees (accessed on 5 April 2016).

Hakimian, H. (ed.) (2013a) *Inclusive Growth in MENA: Employment and Poverty Dimensions in a Comparative Context,* Femise Research Programme Research No. FEM 35, 16 June (London: Middle East Institute and Economics Department, SOAS) http://eprints.soas.ac.uk/17319/3/Inclusive%20Growth%20in%20MENA%20-%20Employment%20and%20Poverty%20Dimensions%20in%20a%20Comparative%20Context%20%28FEM3516_June%202013%29.pdf (accessed on 1 April 2016).

Hakimian, H. (2013b) 'The Search for Inclusive Growth in North Africa: A Comparative Approach' *Economic Brief* (Abidjan: African Development Bank) http://www.afdb.org/fileadmin/uploads/afdb/Documents/Publications/Economic_Brief_-_The_Search_for_Inclusive_Growth_in_North_Africa-_A_Comparative_Approach.pdf (accessed on 1 April 2016).

Hanieh, A. (2013) *Lineages of Revolt—Issues of Contemporary Capitalism in the Middle East* (Chicago : Haymarket Books).

Kamrava, M. ed. (2014) *Beyond the Arab Spring—The Evolving Ruling Bargain in the Middle East* (London: Hurst).

Khalaf, A. and G. Luciani (eds.) (2006) *Constitutional Reform and Political Participation in the Gulf,* (Dubai: Gulf Research Centre).

Luciani, G. (2016) *On the Economic Causes of the Arab Spring and its Possible Developments* in K. Selvik and B.O. Utvik (eds) *Oil States in the New Middle East—Uprisings and Stability* (Abingdon and New York: Routledge).

Mehlum, M., K. Moene and G. Ostenstadt (2016) 'Guest workers as a barrier to democratization in oil-rich countries' in K. Selvik and B.O. Utvik (eds) *Oil States in the New Middle East—Uprisings and Stability* (Abingdon and New York: Routledge).

Nugent, J.B., (2012) *Detecting Corruption and Evaluating Programs to Control It: Some Lessons for MENA* Working Paper n°738 (Giza, Egypt: Economic Research Forum) http://erf.org.eg/publications/detecting-corruption-evaluating-programs-control-lessons-mena/ (accessed on 1 April 2016).

Painter, A. and C. Thoung (2015) *Creative citizen, creative state: the principled and pragmatic case for a Universal Basic Income* (London: RSA), available on https://www.thersa.org/.

Piketty, T. (2013) *Le capital au XXIe siècle,* (Paris: Seuil).

Schiffbauer, M, A. Sy, S. Hussain, H. Sahnoun, P. Keefer, I. Diwan, D. Al-Kadi, D. Doemeland, and B. Rijkers (2015) *Jobs or Privileges: Unleashing the Employment Potential of the Middle East and North Africa,* MENA Development Report (Washington, D.C.: World Bank) http://documents.worldbank.org/curated/en/2014/06/19794535/jobs-or-privileges-unleashing-employment-potential-middle-east-north-africa (accessed on 31 March 2016).

Schuhmacher, T. (2016) *Back to the Future: The 'New' ENP towards the Southern Neighbourhood and the End of Ambition,* CEPOB Policy Brief No.1/16, January (Bruges: College of Europe) https://www.coleurope.eu/system/files_force/research-paper/schumacher_cepob_1-16.pdf?download=1 (accessed on 1 April 2016).

Selvik, K. and B.O. Utvik (eds.) (2016) *Oil States in the New Middle East—Uprisings and Stability* (Abingdon and New York: Routledge).

Springborg, R. (2016) 'Globalization and Its Discontents in the MENA' *Middle East Policy,* v. XXIII, no. 2 (Summer 2016). http://www.mepc.org/journal/middle-east-policy-archives/globalization-and-its-discontents-mena (accessed on 23 June 2016).

Verme, P., B. Milanovic, S. Al-Shawarby, S. El Tawila, M. Gadallah, A. El-Majeed and A. Enas (2014) *Inside Inequality in the Arab Republic of Egypt: Facts and Perceptions across People, Time and Space,* World Bank Studies (Washington, D.C.: World Bank) http://hdl.handle.net/10986/17583.

World Bank (2014) *The Unfinished Revolution: Bringing Opportunity, Good Jobs And Greater Wealth To All Tunisians,* Synthesis Development Policy Review, May (Washington, D.C.: World Bank). http://www.worldbank.org/content/dam/Worldbank/document/MNA/tunisia_report/tunisia_report_the_unfinished_revolution_eng_synthesis.pdf (accessed on 4 April 2016).

World Bank (2016) *The Economic Effects of War and Peace* MENA Quarterly Economic Brief, January (Washington, D.C.: World Bank) http://www.worldbank.org/en/region/mena/publication/mena-quarterly-economic-brief-january-2016 (accessed on 4 April 2016).

CHAPTER 2

Reflections on the Arab Uprisings

Samir Makdisi

Abstract

This chapter offers reflections on the Arab uprisings grouped under four headings: (1) the entrenchment of autocracy in the region, (2) the unravelling of autocracy, (3) the uncertainty of the transition process, and (4) the challenges of sustaining democratic transitions.

Among the primary factors underlying the general entrenchment of Arab autocracy, at least prior to the uprisings, are the relative abundance of oil resources and the region's multi-faceted conflicts, along with all their attendant disruptive foreign interventions.

Youth unemployment rising to very high levels and the persistence of deep economic inequality were important factors contributing to the uprisings. They were also reinforced by long frustrated aspirations for greater freedom and political participation on the part of social groups that have felt largely excluded from the benefits of economic development.

As of late 2016 the outcome of the uprisings remains highly uncertain especially with the rise to power of strictly fundamentalist groups and the ensuing armed conflicts that have come in their wake. The struggle between forces pushing for a move towards democracy and those pushing for the maintenance and/or regeneration of autocracy is presently in full play.

Transition experiences point to two fundamental challenges facing the consolidation of democratic transitions: firstly that the political victors be able to move in the direction of establishing genuinely representative and accountable political institutions. Secondly that they succeed in implementing an inclusive socio-economic strategy that not only focuses on growth and expanding employment opportunities but also eliminates 'elite capture' of the public sector.

1 Introduction

The Tunisian uprising of December 2010 ushered in what seemed to be a new political phase in the Arab world, namely the beginnings of the unravelling of Arab autocracy. It was followed by the Egyptian uprising in January 2011 and later the same year by uprisings in Syria, Libya and Yemen. However, five years

 | DOI 10.1163/9789004336452_003

on this trajectory is yet to take hold region-wide and prospects for democratic transitions in the foreseeable future remain highly uncertain. Tunisia may be forging ahead successfully along a democratic path, but Egypt's democratic course appears hesitant while in the other three countries the uprisings have turned into civil wars intertwined with outside military intervention, the case of Syria being especially tragic.

In the longer run, the uprisings may yet prove to be the catalyst that opened the door to a region-wide process of democratisation. However, as of late 2016—with a few exceptions, Lebanon and Tunisia among them—autocracy continues to reign, though of course in varying forms and to different degrees from one country to another.

With the objective of shedding some light on the political economy of potential democratic transitions in the Arab region this paper offers reflections on the uprisings grouped under four headings: (1) background—the entrenchment of autocracy in the region, (2) the unravelling of autocracy in a few of the Arab countries, (3) the uncertainty of the transition process towards democracy, and (4) the economic and political challenges of sustaining democratic transitions, once initiated. These reflections draw on published work of the author, referred to in the text.

While these reflections focus on the Arab region as a whole, we should remain cognisant of the fact that the underlying factors of the uprisings vary from one case to another, as does the role of domestic elements in undermining the autocratic order. These elements seem to have been more dominant and decisive in the cases of Tunisia and Egypt than in the other three cases. This in turn might have contributed to the apparent democratic success of Tunisia in the wake of its uprising, and the averting of armed domestic conflict in Egypt though the democratic process is yet to take hold.

2 On the Entrenchment of Arab Autocracy

A number of democracy indices are employed in the empirical literature. In this chapter we refer to two of them: the commonly used Polity IV index, which includes data going back many years, and the more recent and comprehensive The Economist Intelligence Unit (EIU) Democracy Index, which begins with 2006 (Tables 2.1 and 2.2 below). They reveal the general entrenchment of autocracy in the Arab region from the end of the Second World War, when most of the Arab countries became independent, up to the present time.

The Polity data include information only on the institutions of the central government and on political groups acting, or reacting, within the scope of

TABLE 2.1 *Polity IV scores across Arab countries.*

	1970	1980	1990	2000	2010	2011	2012	2013	2014
Libya	−7	−7	−7	−7	−7	−77	−77	−77	−77
Bahrain	—	−10	−10	−9	−5	−8	−10	−10	−10
Qatar	—	−10	−10	−10	−10	−10	−10	−10	−10
Saudi Arabia	−10	−10	−10	−10	−10	−10	−10	−10	−10
Syria	−9	−9	−9	−7	−7	−7	−9	−9	−9
Kuwait	−9	−10	−66	−7	−7	−7	−7	−7	−7
Egypt	−7	−6	−6	−6	−3	−2	−88	−4	−4
Morocco	−9	−8	−8	−6	−6	−4	−4	−4	−4
Jordan	−9	−10	−4	−2	−3	−3	−3	−3	−3
Algeria	−9	−9	−2	−3	2	2	2	2	2
Iraq	−7	−9	−9	−9	3	3	3	3	3
Lebanon	5	−77	−66	−66	6	6	6	6	6
Tunisia	−8	−9	−5	−3	−4	−88	−88	−88	7

SOURCE: POLITY IV DATA SERIES, VERSION 2014.

Note: The Polity IV scheme consists of six component measures that record the key qualities of executive recruitment, constraints on executive authority, and political competition. It also records changes in the institutionalised qualities of governing authority. The 'Polity Score' captures this regime authority spectrum on a 21-point scale ranging from −10 (hereditary monarchy) to +10 (consolidated democracy). They can also be converted to regime categories, for which a three-part categorisation is recommended: 'autocracies' (−10 to −6), 'anocracies' (−5 to +5) and 'democracies' (+6 to +10); there are also three special values— −66, −77 and −88—representing, respectively, periods of interruption (foreign occupation), interregnum (breakdown of central authority) and transition during which new institutions are being set up.

that authority. It does not include a consideration of groups and territories that are actively removed from that authority (i.e. separatists or 'fragments'; these are considered to be separate, though not independent, polities) or segments of the population that are not yet effectively politicised in relation to central state politics.

Numerous past and more recent analyses have addressed the question of lagging democracy in the Arab region compared to other regions (Table 2.3), or what has been termed Arab exceptionalism (see Salameh, 1994). These vary from a broad historical viewpoint to more focused analyses of specific underlying factors. Various historical, religious, social, ethnic, political, economic, and colonial explanations of this phenomenon have been posited. Space limitations

TABLE 2.2 *Ranking of Arab countries according to the EIU democracy index, 2010–2014.*

	2010 Rank	2010 Score	2014 Rank	2014 Score
Tunisia	145	2.79	79	6.31
Lebanon	86	5.82	98	5.12
Iraq	112	4.00	111	4.23
Mauritania	115	3.86	112	4.17
Morocco	116	3.79	116	4.00
Algeria	125	3.44	117	3.83
Libya	158	1.94	119	3.80
Kuwait	114	3.88	120	3.78
Jordan	117	3.74	121	3.76
Qatar	137	3.09	136	3.18
Egypt	138	3.07	138	3.16
Oman	143	2.86	139	3.15
Djibouti	154	2.20	145	2.99
Bahrain	122	3.49	147	2.87
Yemen	147	2.64	149	2.79
UAE	148	2.52	152	2.64
Sudan	151	2.42	153	2.54
Saudi Arabia	161	1.84	162	1.82
Syria	153	2.31	163	1.74

SOURCE: EIU REPORTS, 2011 AND 2014.

Note: The EIU index is a weighted average of 60 indicators grouped into five different categories: electoral process and pluralism, civil liberties, functioning of government, political participation, and political culture. In addition to a numeric score and a ranking, the index categorises countries as one of four regime types—full democracies (a score of 8–10), flawed democracies (6–7.9), hybrid regimes (4–5.9), and authoritarian regimes (0–3.9).

do not permit me to go into a review of this literature here.[1] I would simply like to refer to two factors that seem to be of primary importance in explaining the persistence of what has been termed the Arab democracy deficit, at least until

1 The following references are but a very small sample of writings starting with the early 1980s and representing differing viewpoints on this question: Center for Arab Unity Studies, 1983; Sharabi, 1988; Hudson, 1991; Kedourie, 1994; Salameh, 1994; Waterbury, 1994; Al Naqeeb, 1996; Harik, 2006; Bichara, 2006; Noland, 2008; Diamond, 2010; Amin et al., 2012; Chaney, 2012; Haseeb, 2013; Elbadawi and Makdisi., 2011; Aldashev et al., 2013.

TABLE 2.3 *EIU index across regions, 2010–2014.*

	EUI index 2010	EIU index 2011	EIU index 2013	EIU index 2014
North America	8.63	8.59	8.59	8.59
Western Europe	8.45	8.40	8.41	8.41
Eastern Europe	5.55	5.50	5.53	5.58
Latin America and Caribbean	6.37	6.35	6.38	6.36
Asia and Australasia	5.53	5.51	5.61	5.70
MENA	3.43	3.62	3.68	3.65
Sub-Saharan Africa	4.23	4.32	4.36	4.34
Total	5.46	5.49	5.53	5.55

SOURCE: EIU REPORTS, 2011 AND 2014.

the outbreak of the recent uprisings—the relative abundance of oil resources and the region's multi-faceted conflicts, including the unresolved Arab–Israeli conflict, along with all their attendant disruptive foreign interventions (see Elbadawi and Makdisi, 2017).[2]

The 'oil curse' effect—the trade-off, between economic welfare and political rights, associated with the relative abundance of oil resources—is well established in the literature (for a review, see Ross, 2014) though not necessarily a matter of universal agreement (Haber and Menaldo, 2011).[3] Nonetheless, at the political level its negative political impact on governance specifically in the oil rich countries is perhaps generally recognised. But at the economic level the influence of abundant oil wealth is more varied. While various beneficial

2 It is worth noting here that the persistence of autocracy in most Arab countries despite their notable socio-economic development since attaining independence after World War II does not seem to conform to the influential modernisation hypothesis that posits a positive correlation between development and democracy (Lipset, 1959 and 1960). By contrast, it appears to be generally more pronounced for the other developing regions of the world.

The modernisation hypothesis has its supporters as well as its critics who have advanced alternative theories of transition. Among its defenders, see, for example, Barro, 2015; Faria et al., 2014; among its critics, see Przeworski et al., 2000; Przeworski, 2004 and 2009; and Acemoglu et al., 2008 and 2009.

3 The authors argue that this oil and mineral reliance does not promote dictatorship over the long run even after taking into account a host of conditional effects suggested by the literature. This, however does not necessarily imply that there are no specific instances in which resource rents might have helped to sustain a dictatorship.

effects on development can rightly be pointed out (Luciani, 2012), recent empirical work has drawn attention to the required role of fiscal and monetary policies in countering its negative impact (e.g. the hindrance of economic diversification) thereby ensuring that oil resources are efficiently used for developmental purposes. This outcome, it is argued, would in large measure hinge on the efficacy and accountability of the institutions in place, notably fiscal institutions, keeping in mind that Arab fiscal institutions remain wanting in this regard (El Anshasy et al., 2015).

Equally important, perhaps more so, is the persistence of a conflictual regional environment. According to available data for the period 1990–2013 over 60 per cent of all Arab countries experienced at least one conflict, which makes the Arab region one of the most conflict-prone regions, accounting for around 17 per cent of world conflicts.[4] Of course at the centre of the region's conflictual environment is the unsettled but simmering Arab–Israeli conflict, which goes back to 1948 and does not have a parallel in other regions, at least in recent history.

Indeed, conflicts are found to have a uniquely negative effect on the democratisation process in the Arab region (keeping in mind that this effect can vary significantly from one country to another) partly because these conflicts have been exploited by incumbent autocratic regimes to justify their rule and to escape the consequences of their national failures (for a detailed analysis of the conflict effect, see Elbadawi and Makdisi, 2017). The Palestinian question remains unresolved while the settlement of civil wars in the pre-2010 period did not lead to a significant change in the political regimes of the war-torn countries involved. The outcome of the post-uprising civil conflicts is yet to be determined.

By contrast, in other regions of the contemporary world civil conflicts have mostly been followed by a move towards democracy, noted reversals notwithstanding (Jai Kwan, 2008), a contrast that appears to support the argument for the Arab region's exceptionalism.

3 On the Unravelling of Autocracy in a Few Arab Countries

Whatever the immediate triggers for the Tunisian and Egyptian uprisings, a gamut of interacting economic, political and other underlying factors have been building up over the years for a push towards a democratic space in the

4 See Uppsala Conflict Data Program (UCDP) (2016). The UCDP defines conflict as 'a contested incompatibility that concerns government and/or territory where the use of armed force between two parties, of which at least one is the government of a state, results in at least 25 battle-related deaths'.

region, initiated, as it turned out, by the successful overthrow of the Tunisian autocracy. However—as noted in the following section—given existing regional realities, how successful additional democratic breakthroughs in the region are, at least in the shorter run, remains to be seen.

In the economic domain two important factors underlying the uprisings are unemployment, increasing over the years to very high levels especially of youth unemployment, and the persistence of deep economic inequality (Hakimian, 2013; Bibi and Nabli, 2010), especially—as noted below—after the process of privatisation of the national economies started to take a strong hold. Accompanying these factors are the long frustrated aspirations for greater freedom and political participation on the part of social groups that have felt largely excluded from the benefits of economic development. Such aspirations have been reinforced by greater openness, both within the Arab region and towards the outside world—a result of the technological advances in information, and in consequence by a growing awareness of the attractions of democracy.

In the period following the break-up of the Soviet Union, the gradual shift in the development paradigm, from a nationalist developmental strategy based on a public sector oriented economy to a market economy, had major consequences. For all the economic benefits of this shift the private sector failed to generate the sufficient number of employment opportunities that state and public sector institutions had previously provided (no matter how inefficiently), especially for young people. Analysts attribute this failure primarily to misguided policies—often uneven, hesitant and incomplete—and to weak institutional performance characterised by cronyism and corruption (Ansani and Daniele, 2012).[5]

Whatever the causes of faltering Arab growth, in the period 2005–2010 Arab youth unemployment reached high levels averaging more than 25 per cent and it continued to rise in both 2011 and 2012 (the highest rate among various developing regions. See International Labor Organization (ILO), 2013). This growing unemployment rate tended to weaken regimes' hold on power and their authoritarian bargain—that is to say, their ability to trade off public goods and other economic benefits for political rights and participation—more so in non-oil-producing than in oil-rich counties. As some writers have put it, the Arab social contract started to unravel (Amin et al., 2012).

Furthermore, the declining economic role of the state has helped promote the growth and empowerment of independent civil society organisations that traditionally press for economic and political reforms. The Arab ruling classes

5 Institutional performance, it has been argued, plays a determining role in explaining differences in outcomes with regard to per capita income (Acemoglu and Robinson, 2008).

have attempted to counter this trend by co-opting both business and intellectual elites and by forging partnerships between highly placed government officials and business tycoons, who basically engage in rent seeking activities. In practice, this has meant that a few groups have been favoured, receiving the larger part of the benefits of growth to the relative exclusion of the majority of the populace; this phenomenon, in turn, has bred growing resentment. While the trend in income inequality may not have changed significantly in recent decades (Hakimian, 2013),[6] disillusionment with economic prospects has led to what has been termed 'unhappy growth' (Amin et al., 2012).

The impact of greater openness, both within the Arab region and with the outside world, on the weakening of the authoritarian bargain is perhaps self-evident. It helps civil society organisations, including those run by students, women and other social groups, to press harder for political reform. And, as amply demonstrated by the recent uprisings, deep-seated ambitions—not only with regards to socio-economic advancement but also to greater freedom and political participation—exist in large segments of the populace that have felt disenfranchised and largely excluded from the benefits of economic development.

The unexpected success of mass, street mobilisation in both Tunisia and Egypt acted as a spark for similar mass movements in other Arab countries: the younger generations in particular pressed successfully for the dismantling of the autocratic regimes of both countries, via mostly peaceful means including intensive use of rapidly spreading social networks.

These uprisings of Arab youth were influenced by two underlying factors. Primarily they had lost faith in the role of traditionalist, reformist political parties, which had proved incapable—for whatever reason—of acting as agents of political change and therefore had to be left behind. But also, they were influenced by the ripple effects of the important democratic changes that have taken place in other regions of the developing world.

Nonetheless, the region's democratic prospects remain highly uncertain, a matter to which we now turn.

---

6 The authors of the work cited point out that data tend to place the MENA region's income distribution levels between those of Africa and Asia. Overall, the region has moderately high levels of inequality: some countries, such as Egypt, are on the lower end of the scale of inequality, with an income distribution closer to the Asian pattern; others, such as Iran, have fairly high inequality, closer to African levels. A key finding is that despite huge structural changes in these economies, income distribution has not changed by much. Over the last few years, there have been indications of a worsening tendency, but the trend is not noticeable when compared to worsening income distribution in fast-growing Asian countries.

4 On the Uncertainty of the Transition towards Democracy

As already noted, of the five Arab countries where uprisings have taken place[7] only one, Tunisia, appears to be moving towards a genuine democracy as attested by the approval of a modern constitution in January 2014, and the free parliamentary elections of October 26 and presidential elections on December 21 of the same year, and by the generally relatively peaceful transfer of power among its major political contestants.

In Egypt the army ousted the elected president—Mohamed Morsi, a member of the Muslim Brotherhood—on July 3, 2013 after massive demonstrations and street confrontations between opponents and supporters of the Brotherhood. The result of the presidential elections that followed in June 2014, won by the head of the army, Abdelfattah al-Sisi, is described by some writers as a return to a modified Mubarak type regime. Despite the adoption of a new constitution in early 2014 and the parliamentary elections that took place in October 2015 (characterised by a relatively low turnout) and were completed in December of the same year, authoritarian or exclusionary forms of governance continue to exist; the process of overcoming them and moving towards a genuine democracy is yet to take place (See El Mikawy et al., 2017).

The uprisings in the other three countries have turned into civil wars and regional conflicts with confessional and/or ethnic overtones that, as of late 2016, have yet to be settled. In particular, the Syrian civil war has attracted armed fundamentalist groups (especially DAISH (Islamic State in Iraq and the Levant—ISIL) and Al Nusra) that oppose the regime, but also armed parties from neighbouring countries that support it, notably Lebanon's Hizbollah. The fundamentalists have come to control large segments not only of Syria but also Iraq, in turn widening the scope of the conflict and triggering foreign military interventions: firstly, US aerial bombing in support of Kurdish units fighting ISIL in northern Syria, and a year later (end September 2015) wide-ranging Russian aerial bombing in support of the regime. The Yemen civil war that erupted in early 2015 witnessed, in March of that year, the beginning of an aerial bombing campaign by a Saudi-led coalition in support of Yemeni parties fighting the 'Houthis' and their allies, a grouping that has its own regional supporters and that had earlier managed to seize power and establish control over the capital and a large part of the country. Libya, after the fall of the Gaddafi regime (a collapse that Western aerial bombing helped bring about), failed to

7 Bahrain has witnessed many popular demonstrations demanding political reform, but so far, with the assistance primarily of Saudi Arabia, the regime has succeeded in suppressing reform demands while thwarting any potential popular uprising.

make a stable transition and in 2014 a renewed civil war broke out between rival organisations seeking control of the country or parts of it.

Thus, while the uprisings have shaken the foundations of autocracy in parts of the Arab world and initially gave rise to a glimmer of hope for regional democratic change, the civil conflicts that have subsequently emerged have further strengthened the region's conflictual environment. In consequence, fed by emerging sectarian divisiveness, and in particular the rise to power of strict fundamentalist groups, the negative impact of conflicts in the region on the process of democratisation has further intensified, posing the threat of democratic reversals in those countries that managed to break out of the grip of entrenched autocracies.

What might explain the rise to power of strict fundamentalist groups that—in brutal fashion—employ religion as an instrument to achieve their political goals, lies outside the purview of this paper.[8] Unless ISIL and similar sectarian movements are contained and reversed, their ascendancy will represent an unprecedented threat to any potential transitions towards democracy. In fact, were fundamentalist parties to dominate the political scene in any post-uprising phase, it would be difficult to envision such transitions, both in individual countries and region-wide.[9]

Tunisia apart, the failure, so far, of democratic transitions to take hold in the wake of the uprisings will hopefully constitute only a passing, albeit a tragic, phase that will yet pave the way for a stable democratic change in the Arab world—however gradual, hesitant or difficult that change might prove. The experience of other regions in this regard, as outlined below, is instructive.

What should be kept in mind is that once the process towards democratisation begins to unfold on a solid basis in the region, it will tend to gain added momentum, positively affecting neighbouring countries that are yet to democratise. The reason for this is that societies located in democratic

8 In this regard, a number of questions would need to be addressed: Do these groups represent a response on the part of poorer segments of the population to political and economic exclusion? Are they simply the product of a strict fundamentalist ideology, and/or certain fundamentalist regimes and/or foreign powers that initially wished to use them for their own ends? Do they constitute a response to past Western colonialism and continued interventions in the affairs of the region? Or can, perhaps, a combination of all these and other factors explain their rise to power; a rise that has occurred to such an extent that the US and other Western countries, whatever their possible initial roles in fostering these groups, have come to consider them a threat to their own national interests.

9 Some writers caution that whereas Islam is compatible with democracy, Islamist fundamentalism is not: Islamist movements may embrace election ballots but merely as a political exigency while continuing to reject the concept of political pluralism that underlies democratic governance (see Tibi, 2008).

neighbourhoods become more likely to move towards democratic transitions: the significance of resource rents as a constraint to democratic transition in democratic regions greatly diminishes, even for highly resource-endowed societies (Elbadawi and Makdisi, 2017). Hence it can be argued that were the current Arab uprisings to eventually swell into a major regional phenomenon, that phenomenon might even spread to those societies that are highly resource-endowed and so far have remained unaffected.[10]

Moreover, as has been pointed out, for any given region the greater the number of countries that succeed in moving towards a consolidated democracy the less important is the potential threat of reversal (e.g. see Poast and Urpelainen, 2015).

The region is thus at a point in its post-uprisings phase where the struggle between the forces pushing for a move towards democracy and those pushing for the maintenance or regeneration of autocracy is in full play.[11] Of primary concern is that once a substantive move towards democratic governance is established, as in the case of Tunisia, various political and economic challenges would need to be successfully addressed in order to ensure a viable transition—a matter we will now take up.

5 On the Political and Economic Challenges of Sustaining Democratic Transitions

The experiences of other regions teach us that in the wake of democratic breakthroughs the consolidation of a democracy is not necessarily a foregone conclusion. Numerous reversals have taken place, though at a decreasing rate over the decades since 1960 and with notable variations from one region to another

10 A number of writers have written on the potential region-wide spread of democracy in the wake of the uprisings. For example, Haseeb (2013) points out that the emergence of an Arab democracy wave hinges on a set of four factors that, 'when co-incident are *decisive*, and these are: breaking the "barrier of fear"; non-violent resistance; sufficient national cohesion and popular sentiment; and the (positive) stance of the armed forces vis-à-vis the uprisings'.

11 It has been argued that the Arab Spring was made possible when the accumulated economic and political failures of the Arab political order led to a convergence of visions on the part of the Islamist and secular elements in society, notably in Tunisia and Egypt. Their failure to maintain consensus on a common platform of a viable social contract has contributed to the emergence of an authoritarian counter revolution. (El Affendi, 2017).

(Kapstein and Converse, 2008).[12] Equally, the transition towards democratic governance may not be accomplished quickly but may go through phases of various forms of partial democracy as a prelude, over time, to more advanced forms of democracy.[13]

The experience of countries that have successfully consolidated their democratic transitions indicates major politico-institutional and socio-economic challenges that need to be met for this objective to be achieved.

At the politico-institutional level, a major challenge is the willingness and ability of the political victors in countries that mange to break the hold of autocratic rule to establish, or move in the direction of establishing, genuinely representative, accountable and transparent political institutions. Ideally these would guarantee basic human rights, primarily freedom of expression and free choice, and provide an opportunity for citizens to participate in the political process, institutionalising their right to make choices and challenge public policies, and to hold governments accountable. And therefore the issue of what type of institutions are in place and who is framing and enforcing policy decisions become paramount.[14]

---

12 According to the authors of the work cited, of the 123 democratisations that took place during the period 1960–2004, 67 gave rise to democratic regimes that survived 2004, while the remaining 56 episodes had ended in a return to authoritarianism by the end of that year. Among those democratisations that were reversed, several later underwent second, third, or even fourth episodes of democratisation. Although fewer than half (47%) of the first-time democratisations were sustained, the survival rate of second-time democratisations approaches two-thirds (63%). Four of the six cases of fourth-time democratisation survived through to the end of 2004. These trends are closely aligned with the improving success rate of all democratisations over time. They point out that political institutions play the crucial role in democratic consolidation, especially institutions that place effective constraints on executive power.

13 The classifications adopted in both Polity IV and the EIU Democracy Index refer to political regimes that lie in-between autocracies and democracies. In a recent study by Mukand and Rodrik (2015) on the political economy of the liberal democracy, the authors point out it is characterised by three kinds of rights: property (elite interest), political (majority interest) and civil (minority interest). They explain why in the West liberal democracies came to be established while in the developing world most democracies that have emerged are electoral democracies that provide property and political but not civil rights.

14 Recent research, focusing on oil-rich countries, has drawn attention to the critical role of monetary and fiscal institutions in promoting the development desired, and specifically in countering the negative economic effects of abundant oil revenues. For analyses of this issue see the papers presented at a workshop organised by the Economic Research Forum in Kuwait, under the title 'Monetary and Fiscal Institutions in Resource–Rich

The political path to enforcing democratic reform (e.g. constitutional revisions, organisation of elections, etc.) will differ from one country to another (see UNDP, 2011). What matters is that genuine democratic institutions become established and operable and secure, whereby the toppled elite is not merely replaced by a new elite with a similar pattern of behaviour. Under these circumstances we need not fear an initial electoral success of particular politico-religious groups. Their initial success can later be democratically contained, if not reversed, especially if they fail at governing.

Developments in Tunisia demonstrate this question in a very encouraging way. The successful election of the National Constituent Assembly in October 2011 was an important step in the country's transition process. The Islamist Ennahda party emerged as the most important single political party, capturing around 40 per cent of parliamentary seats. But it agreed to join a coalition government whose main task was to guide the process of moving towards a new constitution. Despite ensuing political crises, social unrest and an economic slowdown, a successful national dialogue among the competing political parties, including Ennahda, eventually led to the adoption of a modern constitution and the transfer of power to an independent technocratic government. The peaceful legislative and presidential elections that took place in October–December 2014 demonstrated that Tunisia had been undergoing a successful democratic transition, though major political and economic challenges lie ahead (see Boughzala and Ben Romdhane, 2017).

In contrast, in the case of Egypt the move to establish accountable political institutions and a space for democratic political competition in the wake of the uprising has so far been, at best, only partially successful. As a recent paper argues (El Mikawy et al., 2017), while the constitution passed in 2014 respects social and economic rights, it continues to sanction an authoritarian bargain whereby security precedes freedoms. The fact that certain institutions such as the military continue to enjoy an autonomy that shields them from real political accountability renders uncertain the future of liberal democracy in the country.

At the socio-economic level what would be required is the design and implementation of a broad based and what has come to be referred to as inclusive strategy, one that should create expectations that growth, expanding employment opportunities, and equity will play a major role in the transition to a new economy (see Makdisi, 2015). This strategy would imply modernising the public sector and, importantly, eliminating its 'elite capture' with a view to ensuring that emerging political and business interests in the transition phase

Arab Economies' (November 4–5, 2015), http://erf.org.eg/events/monetary-and-fiscal-institutions-in-resource-rich-arab-economies/ (accessed on 7 April 2016).

are not capable of obstructing the implementation of policies supportive of inclusive growth.[15] At the same time, developmental experiences teach us that the extent to which developmental policies work depends on particular local, historical or institutional contexts.

Reconciling the objectives an all-inclusive strategy, basically implementing policies that at once promote growth and macro-economic stability while attending to the basic socio-economic needs of citizens, is of course not an easy task, especially when one considers the various social pressures and expectations that emerge during the transition process. Indeed, the record of democratic transitions elsewhere shows that such changes resulted, not infrequently, in economic recessions that either derailed or potentially could have derailed the process of substantive political reform. But, as noted above, if they are to succeed, it is a task that transition countries cannot avoid undertaking, with the determination that emerging political institutions assume the required supporting role. Of note are studies showing that transition countries that succeeded in implementing socio-economic reform have forged ahead economically more than those that failed to do so (Amin et al., 2012).

Chile offers a good example of a transition country that has been able to address the needs of the less privileged while implementing policies that have achieved growth and stability. Governmental policies supported low-income households, promoted education and allowed for investments in local health services and housing. Importantly, the government's social development programmes were accompanied by tax reform including putting in place a progressive income tax system. Increased social spending was, thus, matched by new sources of tax revenue (UNDP, 2011). A major lesson of the Chilean experience is that mobilising the resources necessary for financing the increased spending required if long neglected social needs are to be satisfied is of crucial importance for the maintenance of economic stability while addressing these needs. In this context it would be incumbent on the responsible authorities to avoid wasteful social spending that does not serve its intended purpose. Egypt's subsidy programmes are a case in point. Despite a high level of subsidy spending on safety net programmes, these programmes did not benefit the less privileged nor significantly address income and human poverty issues, though attempts have recently been made to improve their efficacy (El Mikawy et al., 2017).

Indeed, as recent research has shown with regards to Tunisia (e.g. Boughzala and Ben Romdhane, 2017), it would seem that the consolidation of the country's

15 As pointed out by some researchers, developmental opportunities are constrained not only by available resources and access to finance and trade but also by the established interests of the ruling elite rooted in existing political institutions (Currie-Alder et al., 2014).

nascent democracy could very well depend on the success of the responsible authorities in coping with the country's existing socio-economic problems. Specifically, this implies the authorities' ability to formulate and implement a coherent economic strategy that responds to key economic and social demands, mainly those of the young people that led the revolt. In particular, policy priorities should include creating new employment opportunities and implementing inclusive development strategies that, among other objectives, aim at narrowing regional disparities while (as the Chilean experience demonstrates) generating the financial resources required to maintain economic stability. If such policies do not succeed, Tunisia could risk a period of retrogression, though given the country's human potential and its recent history, the probability of such a risk being realised seems low.

6 Conclusion

Given that the Arab uprisings are not yet a region-wide phenomenon, a fundamental political change towards democratic governance in any one individual country will necessarily face negative regional pressures emanating from the still existing, non-democratic regional neighbourhood. Similarly, negative external interventions could disrupt a potential democratic process in the region that may be viewed by the intervening powers as being contrary to their regional interests. As long as a highly conflictual regional environment continues to prevail, its corrosive impact will continue to manifest itself, one way or another, on political developments in the region.

These influences will not necessarily impede the process of moving towards democracy initiated by the dismantling of autocracy in any given individual country, as in the case of Tunisia, but they could help derail that process, as has been happening in the other countries where uprisings have taken place.

References

Acemoglu D. and J. Robinson (2008) 'The Role of Institutions in Growth and Development', Commission on Growth and Development. Working paper No.10 (Washington D.C.: World Bank), http://siteresources.worldbank.org/EXTPREMNET/Resources/489960-1338997241035/Growth_Commission_Working_Paper_10_Role_Institutions_Growth_Development.pdf (accessed on 7 April 2016).

Acemoglu, D., S. Johnson, J. Robinson, and P. Yared (2008) 'Income and Democracy', *American Economic Review* 98(3), DOI: 10.1257/aer.98.3.808808-42.

Acemoglu D., S. Johnson, J. Robinson, and P. Yared (2009) 'Reevaluating the modernization hypothesis'. *Journal of Monetary Economics,* Vol. 56(8), DOI: 10.1016/j.jmoneco.2009.10.002.

Aldashev, G, J.-P. Platteau and. P. Sekeris (2013) 'Seduction of Religious Clerics and Violence in Autocratic Regimes—with special emphasis on Islam' (MS).

Al Naqeeb Khaldun (1996) *The Struggle Between Tribe and Democracy* (in Arabic), (London: Dar al-Saqi).

Amin, M., R. Assaad, N. al-Baharna, K. Dervis, R.M. Desai, N.S. Dhillon, A. Galal, Hafez Ghanem, C. Graham, and D. Kaufmann (2012) *After the Spring: Economic Transitions in the Arab World* (Oxford, Oxford University Press).

Ansani, A, and V. Daniele (2012) 'About a Revolution. The Economic Motivations of the Arab Spring', *International Journal of Development and Conflict,* 3(3), DOI: 10.1142/S2010269012500135.

Barro R, (2015) 'Convergence and Modernization', *Economic Journal,* 125(585), DOI: 10.1111/ecoj.12247.

Bibi, S. and M.K. Nabli (2010) "Equity and Inequality in the Arab Region". ERF Policy Research Report PRR33, Economic Research Forum, Cairo, Egypt. http://erf.org.eg/wp-content/uploads/2016/04/PRR33.pdf (accessed on 6 December 2016).

Bichara A. (2006) *The Arab Question: Introduction to an Arab Democracy Manifesto,* (Beirut: Center for Arab Unity Studies) (in Arabic).

Boughzala, M. and S. Ben Romdhane (2017) 'Transition from Autocracy to Democracy in Tunisia, Factors Underlying the Tunisian Uprising and the Prospects for Consolidating the Transition to Democracy', in Elbadawi, I and S. Makdisi (eds.), *Democratic Transitions in the Arab World* (Cambridge: Cambridge University Press).

Center for Arab Unity Studies (1983) *The Crisis of Democracy in the Arab world,* proceedings of a conference held in Limassol, Cyprus (in Arabic).

Chaney, E. (2012) 'Democratic Change in the Arab World, Past and Present', unpublished mimeo, Department of Economics, (Cambridge, Massachusetts: Harvard University).

Currie-Alder B., Kanbur R., Malone D.M., and Medhora R. (2014) *International Development. Ideas, Experience, and Prospects* (Oxford: Oxford University Press).

Diamond L. (2010) 'Why Are There No Arab Democracies?' *Journal of Democracy,* 21(1), http://www.journalofdemocracy.org/sites/default/files/Diamond-21-1.pdf (accessed on 7 April 2016).

El Affendi, A. (forthcoming) 'Overcoming Induced Insecurities: Stabilising Arab Democracies after the Spring' in Elbadawi, I. and S. Makdisi (eds.), *Democratic Transitions in the Arab World* (Cambridge: Cambridge University Press).

El Anshasy, A., K. Mohaddes and J.B. Nugent (2015) 'Fiscal Institutions and Macroeconomic Management in Resource-Rich Arab Countries', paper presented at a conference of the Economic Research Forum on 'Monetary and Fiscal Institutions in Resource-Rich Arab Economies', Kuwait, November 4–6.

Elbadawi, I. and S. Makdisi (2017) 'Explaining Democratic Transitions in the Arab World' in Elbadawi, I. and S. Makdisi (eds.) (2011) *Democratic Transitions in the Arab World* (Cambridge: Cambridge University Press).

Elbadawi, I. and S. Makdisi (eds.) (2011) *Democracy in the Arab World, Explaining the Deficit* (London and New York: Routledge).

Elbadawi, I., M. Goaied and M. Ben Taher (2015) 'Fiscal-Monetary Interdependence and Exchange Regimes in Oil-Dependent Arab Economies', paper presented at a workshop of the Economic Research Forum on 'Monetary and Fiscal Institutions in Resrouce-Rich Arab Economies', Kuwait, November 4–6.

El Mikawy, N., M. Mohieddin and S. El Ashmaouy (2017) 'Egypt: Pathways from Authoritarianism To Democracy: A Protracted Transition' in Elbadawi, I. and S. Makdisi (eds.) , *Democratic Transitions in the Arab World* (Cambridge: Cambridge University Press).

Faria H.J., HM Montesinos-Yufa and DR Morales (2014) 'Should the Modernization Hypothesis Survive Acemoglu, Johnson, Robinson, and Yared? Some More Evidence', *Econ Journal Watch*, http://econjwatch.org/file_download/799/CompleteIssue-Jan2014.pdf#page=18 (accessed on 5 April 2016).

Haber, S. and V. Menaldo (2011) 'Do Natural Resources Fuel Authoritarianism? A Reappraisal of the Resource Curse' *American Political Science Review*, 105(01), 1–26, DOI: 10.1017/S0003055410000584.

Hakimian, H. (ed.) (2013) *Inclusive Growth in MENA: Employment and Poverty Dimensions in a Comparative Context,* Femise Research Programme Research No. FEM 35, 16 June (London: Middle East Institute and Economics Department, SOAS) http://eprints.soas.ac.uk/17319/3/Inclusive%20Growth%20in%20MENA%20-%20Employment%20and%20Poverty%20Dimensions%20in%20a%20Comparative%20Context%20%28FEM3516_June%202013%29.pdf (accessed on 1 April 2016).

Harik I. (2006) 'Democracy, "Arab Exceptionalism", and Social Science', *Middle East Journal*, 60(4), 664–84, DOI: 10.3751.60.4.12.

Haseeb, K. El-Din (2013) 'The Arab Spring Revisited', in K. El-Din Haseeb (ed). *The Arab Spring: Critical Analyses* (London and New York: Routledge) 4–16.

Hudson M. (1991) 'After the Gulf War: Prospects for Democratization in the Arab World', *Middle East Journal*, 45(3), http://www.jstor.org/stable/4328313.

International Labor Organization (ILO) (2013) *Global Employment Trends 2013: Recovering from a second jobs dip* (Geneva: ILO), http://www.ilo.org/global/research/global-reports/global-employment-trends/2013/WCMS_202326/lang--en/index.htm (accessed on 5 April 2015).

Jai Kwan J. (2008) 'Mission Impossible? Democracy Building in Post-Civil War Societies' (Chicago: Midwest Political Science Association Annual Meeting), http://

government.arts.cornell.edu/assets/psac/sp08/MissionImpossible_PSAC.pdf (accessed on 5 April 2015).

Kapstein, E.B. and Converse, N. (2008) 'Poverty, Inequality, and Democracy. Why Democracies Fail', *Journal of Democracy,* 19(4), http://www.journalofdemocracy.org/poverty-inequality-and-democracy-why-democracies-fail (accessed on 5 April 2015).

Kedourie, E. (1994) *Democracy and Arab Political Culture* (London: Frank Kass).

Lipset, S.M. (1959) 'Some Social Requisites of Democracy: Economic Development and Political Legitimacy'. *American Political Science Review,* 53(1).

Lipset, S.M. (1960) *Political Man. The Social Bases of Politics* (New York: Doubleday).

Luciani, G. (ed.) (2012) *Resources Blessed, Diversification and the Gulf Development Model* (Berlin: Gerlach Press).

Makdisi, S. (2015) 'The Unraveling of Arab Autocracy: Socioeconomic Factors in Context' in Ali Kadri (ed.) *Development Challenges and Solutions After the Arab Spring* (London: Palgrave Macmillan), DOI: 10.1057/9781137541406.

Mukand, S. and D. Rodrik, (2015) 'The Political Economy of Liberal Democracy' NBER Working Paper No. 21540, DOI: 10.3386/w21540.

Noland, M. (2008) 'Explaining Middle Eastern Political Authoritarianism I: The Level of Democracy', *Review of Middle East Economics and Finance,* 4(1), DOI: 10.2202/1475-3693.1057.

Poast, P. and J. Urpelainen (2015) 'How International Organizations Support Democratization. Preventing Authoritarian Reversals or Promoting Consolidation' *World Politics,* V. 67(1), 72–113, DOI: 10.1017/S0043887114000343.

Przeworski, A. (2004) 'Economic Development and Transitions to Democracy' March, (MS), http://politics.as.nyu.edu/docs/IO/2800/transwp.pdf (accessed on 5 April 2015).

Przeworski, A. (2009) 'The Mechanics of Regime Instability in Latin America' *Journal of Politics in Latin America,* 2009(1), 5–36, https://www.ciaonet.org/attachments/14870/uploads (accessed on 5 April 2015).

Przeworski, A., J.A. Cheibub, M.E. Alvarez and F. Limongi (2000) *Democracy and Development: Political Institutions and Material Well-being in the World, 1950–1990* (Cambridge: Cambridge University Press).

Ross M. (2014) *What Have We Learned about the Resource Curse?* (Los Angeles), DOI: 10.2139/ssrn.2342668.

Salameh, G. (ed.) (1994) *Democracy without Democrats, the Renewal of Politics in the Muslim World* (London: I.B. Tauris).

Sharabi, H. (1988) *Neopatriarchy: A Theory of Distorted Change in Arab Society* (New York: Oxford University Press).

Tibi, B. (2008) 'Islamist Parties: Why They Can't Be Democratic', *Journal of Democracy,* 19(3), DOI: 10.1353/jod.0.0000.

United Nations Development Programme (UNDP) (2011) *Pathways to Democratic Transitions. Summary Report on Country Experiences, Lessons Learned and the Road Ahead, International Forum Report,* Cairo June 5–6, http://www.eg.undp.org/content/dam/egypt/docs/Publications/Docs%20Governance/Pathways_1110_Cairo%20Report%20WEB_FINAL.pdf (accessed on 5 April 2016).

Uppsala Conflict Data Program (UCDP) (2016) *UCDP Conflict Encyclopedia* (Uppsala University Department of Peace and Conflict Research) http://www.ucdp.uu.se (accessed on 6 April 2016).

Waterbury, J. (1994) 'Democracy Without Democrats? The potential for political liberalization in the Middle East', in G. Salameh (ed.) *Democracy Without Democrats? The Renewal of Politics in Muslim World* (London: I.B. Tauris).

CHAPTER 3

Rethinking the Rentier Curse

Adeel Malik

Abstract

The Middle Eastern political economy has long been studied through the prism of the resource curse—that is, how resource riches undermine the region's economic and political development. While many of the region's pathologies are rooted in an economic structure heavily reliant on external windfalls, the existing literature tends to overstate the role of oil. This research note develops the case for a broader conceptualisation of rents that includes not just windfalls from hydrocarbons, but also rents derived from aid, remittances and government manipulation of the economy. Reliance on these rent streams is the 'original sin' that perpetuates underdevelopment. Discussions of Arab political economy should therefore be framed as part of a broader enquiry into the relationship between rents and development. This requires, in turn, a deeper understanding of business–state relationships and the role of regional linkages in development.

1 Introduction

This chapter highlights the centrality of 'unearned' income streams, typically described as rents, for understanding the political economy of the Middle East. Many of the region's pathologies—including unemployment, a bloated state, a weak private sector or limited political evolution—are ultimately rooted in an economic structure heavily reliant on external windfalls, whether derived from oil, aid or remittances. Questioning the exclusive focus of the prevailing literature on oil, I develop the case for a broader conceptualisation of rent streams that includes, besides oil, rents derived from foreign aid, remittances and government regulation. These non-oil rent streams can also be both sizeable and significant in their impact.[1] Regulatory rents that result from market

1 Empirical studies suggest that natural resource rent is typically 10–20% of the GDP of developing countries although it can be significantly higher, especially in hydrocarbon-rich economies (Auty, 2001). Aid streams tend to be relatively stable and can have somewhat disappointing impacts, but there is disagreement whether this reflects Dutch Disease effects (Rajan and Subramanian, 2011), rent seeking (Boone, 1996) or political instability (Islam,

DOI 10.1163/9789004336452_004

subversion are particularly important in understanding the business–state relationship and its bearing on political economy. Reliance on these windfalls is the 'original sin' of development in the Middle East and North Africa (MENA). The story of Arab development is therefore a story of how these rent streams shape paths of political and economic development. I argue that the Middle East's resource curse can simply be viewed as part of a broader rent curse.

The basic analytical frame used in the literature is the celebrated—but increasingly contentious—paradigm of the *Rentier State Theory* (RST), which argues that unearned revenue streams, external to a country and accruing mainly to the government, shape that country's political and economic character.[2] The upshot: resource-rich societies are systematically condemned to having underdeveloped political structures. A key mechanism behind this adverse connection between natural resources and democracy is the fiscal independence of the state from taxation, which relieves it from intense pressure for accountability (the famous dictum, 'no representation without taxation'). Direct access to resource revenues also allows state elites to buy political consent through repression and patronage. The principal function of a rentier state is the allocation or distribution of rents, which tilts incentives away from production to predation, stifling competitive structural change that could otherwise have produced a social structure more favourable to democratisation—independent classes and horizontal alignments in society (Beblawi and Luciani, 1987; Ross, 2001).

As a general typology of resource-rich states, the RST captures many salient features of rentier states. For a long time it has served as a leading explanation for weak political institutions in oil-rich countries. Its deep influence on public debate is best illustrated by New York Times journalist Thomas Friedman's famous observation that in resource-rich countries 'the price of oil and the pace of freedom always move in opposite directions' (Friedman, 2009). The broad claims of the theory resonate with the actual MENA experience. Resource rents have enabled ruling elites to expand instruments of both patronage and

2005). In the period 1995–2004, remittances averaged 3.6% of GDP (Barajas et al., 2009), typically ranging between 2% and 10% but rising above 15% in seven countries, including Jordan. Although remittance flows tend to be stable and diffusely distributed, their net impact is disputed (Rajan and Subramanyan, 2011).

2 Rents are defined as 'supernormal profits, or the excess over the return on capital, land, and labour, when these factors of production are put to their next best use' (Dunning, 2008, 6). Beblawi and Luciani (1987) describe four conditions of a rentier state: (a) size and scale of the rent streams relative to the economy, (b) external source, (c) limited involvement of the population in the state's production activities, and (d) accrual to the government of a rentier state.

control. Without oil rents, it is difficult to sustain the region's repressive military structures, its bloated public sector, pervasive subsidies, and the 'cradle to grave' welfare systems. Whether through co-option or coercion, oil wealth has allowed states to subdue possible challengers, create new economic elites and bind old merchants in a relationship of dependence. In short, rarely can any facet of MENA political economy be studied without a deep understanding of how oil shapes the state–society relationship.

There is growing realisation that, while RST paints a good broad-brush caricature of resource-rich societies, it falls short of fully capturing the nuances, contexts and dynamics. Scholars have therefore called for refining and qualifying the claims and predictions of RST by studying the role of initial historical conditions, dynastic family politics, the micro-politics of development, and emergent forms of capitalism in the Gulf (Dunning, 2008; Hertog, 2010; Herb, 2009; Gray, 2011). Much of this literature can be read as simply an exercise in refinement, rather than an outright rejection of the theory. While agreeing with the broad thrust of this literature, this research note insists on developing a wider political economy of rents and development, which takes into account the nature, composition and deployment of rents. I argue that there is a need to transcend the continuing predilection for tracing the impact of oil on development. Oil revenues in MENA are complemented with other unearned income streams from aid, remittances and government regulation, which together constitute a broader challenge of 'rentierism'.

While oil rents clearly dominate the external revenue flows in MENA countries, the impact of other rents derived from foreign aid and remittances is insufficiently explored. Furthermore, far more emphasis has been placed on the role of external rents, whereas domestically generated rents from government manipulation of the economy are largely neglected by dominant approaches to studying MENA political economy. Such rents are critical, however, in the region's labour-abundant economies, where—given the relative scarcity of oil rents—domestic rents from economic protection play a prominent role in generating elites' commitment to regime continuity. Perhaps the best example of the importance of such rents is the pervasive use of non-tariff barriers in North African economies. Restrictive trade policy is used to privilege businesses connected to the regime or other insiders who are given control of the protected enclaves of the economy. In turn, the regime is able to secure a binding commitment to the maintenance of authoritarian order.

Another important dimension—largely omitted from dominant narratives—is the importance of the external anchor in sustaining authoritarianism in the Middle East. Existing theoretical accounts have been largely focused on how domestic recycling of resource rents buys the political acquiescence of key constituencies at home. While this is admittedly the core political economy dimension pertaining to the political economy of oil, another crucial dimension, at least in the Middle Eastern context, is the manner in which resource rents are externally recycled to build a support base abroad. As this research note will show, such recycling can take many forms and is often geared as much towards securing geopolitical returns as towards economic returns for overseas investments. As exporters of hydrocarbons, many MENA countries are highly integrated into global commodity and finance circuits. The external and domestic structures of power are therefore co-constituted in such domains.

All of this underscores the need to unpack the complex architecture of authoritarianism in resource-rich societies. The rentier experience in the Middle East is broader and deeper than uni-linear and deterministic oil-based accounts would have us believe.

The remainder of this article is structured as follows: Part 2 furnishes a brief background of the relationship between natural resources and development. Part 3 proposes a broader conceptualisation of rent streams and emphasises the role of the external recycling of rents. Part 4 provides a brief conclusion.

2 Natural Resources and Development in the Middle East

Before delving into the analysis of various rent streams it is useful to briefly review the relationship between natural resources and development. Ever since the discovery of oil, hydrocarbons have defined the Middle East's development experience. A quick review of the existing evidence suggests that the MENA region shares with other developing countries the basic pathologies associated with a resource curse. Arab economies have experienced a middling growth performance with substantial volatility of macroeconomic outcomes. The symptoms appear all too familiar: weak private sector, unproductive investment in white-elephant projects, pervasive rent seeking and a large and oversized public sector. Government spending (especially on subsidies and public employment) has remained surprisingly resilient in the face of fluctuating oil prices. The relationship between oil and development in MENA is well documented (Yousef, 2004; Elbadawi, 2005; Nugent and Pesaran, 2007). Rather than offering a comprehensive summary, I will highlight only the salient aspects of this literature.

Behind these generic patterns lies considerable diversity in individual development experiences. It is customary to classify the MENA region along two dimensions: labour and resources. The political economy dynamics of the resource-rich, labour-scarce countries of the Gulf are distinct from more labour-abundant economies in the region (some of which are oil-rich, such as Algeria, while others are oil-scarce, such as Egypt and Syria). Classifying the region by rent endowments, it is initially useful to divide these economies into capital-surplus oil exporters; capital-scarce oil exporters; and resource-poor, labour-surplus economies. During the first oil boom (1973–80) all three types of economy favoured the public sector for allocating rents and developed patronage systems that undermined markets and competitive structural change. However, the development strategies and the nature of underlying rent streams differed across countries.

- The capital-surplus oil exporters of the Gulf deployed their sizeable oil rents to co-opt political support by providing generous welfare. This has led to the rapid absorption of resource rents through high government consumption. It has also been accompanied by perverse outcomes: stable autocracies, pro-cyclical fiscal policy, labour market distortions, patronage-driven private sectors, and a high dependence on resource rents.
- The capital-deficient economies are labour-abundant with relatively modest resource rents per capita in comparison to Gulf countries. Some of these (e.g. Algeria and Iran) deployed rent to initiate state-led industrialisation behind high, protective tariffs, but largely failed to create competitive industrial strength. Like other oil exporters these economies also created systematic welfare entitlements. Importantly, oil rents are combined here with regulatory rents through the manipulation of the economy. This has led to rent seeking, unproductive investment, weak private sectors and greater resistance to reform.
- The resource-poor economies might be expected to achieve more rapid political and economic development due to their lower resource rents, but this ignores sizeable rents derived from foreign aid, worker remittances and regulation. In fact, in the first two to three decades following independence, Yemen and Syria both derived one-fifth of their respective GDPs from hydrocarbon exports, while Egypt generated aggregate rents in excess of 20–30 per cent of GDP. Morocco, Tunisia, and Jordan sustained sizeable rent streams until oil prices collapsed in the mid-1980s, after which they accelerated economic diversification but resisted opening up politically.

The labour surplus economies witnessed declining rents in the 1980s—resulting from falling oil prices and dwindling inflows from foreign aid and remittances. With growing debt-to-gross domestic product (GDP) ratios, economic reform became a policy imperative. Several MENA countries introduced privatisation and economic liberalisation on a limited scale. This was done in such a way as not to disrupt the status quo. Neo-liberal reform generated opportunities to exploit new rent streams through lucrative contracts and licenses in banking and telecommunications. These rents were allocated to consolidate elite coalitions and to reorganise political power. Overall, economic reforms failed to dismantle pervasive entry barriers and anti-competitive practices.

The second oil boom, which began with the oil price surge in the 1990s, led to a sizable windfall (MENA oil revenues grew fourfold during the period 2000–07). Most oil exporting governments initially responded prudently to the windfall revenue, through higher savings levels, slower domestic absorption, and a greater reliance on markets. During the aforementioned period, total MENA debt fell from 55 to 17 per cent of GDP. Oil exporting nations began to set aside a larger proportion of their current account surpluses in sovereign wealth funds (SWFs). Arguably, in several MENA countries, especially in the Gulf, the private sector has shown greater agency and independence. Despite this evidence of a steeper learning curve, however, the second oil boom did not redefine the rent-dependent model of development.

Public expenditure has accelerated since 2005 due to a growing commitment to salaries, subsidies, and infrastructure projects. Typically, roughly half of the extra hydrocarbon revenues have been deployed in resource-rich MENA states, with public spending noticeably higher in capital deficient economies, such as Iran. Public spending continues to be the primary driver of private investment in oil-rich MENA states, but returns on these investments (especially those on infrastructure) are typically low (Noumba Um et al., 2009). It is therefore unsurprising that the income per capita gains of regional oil exporters were mainly attributable to gains in the terms of trade, with limited contribution from non-oil GDP (Arezki and Nabli, 2012). It is pertinent to explore if social learning has any role to play in explaining differential policy responses to the two oil booms that the Arab resource-rich economies (RREs) witnessed, in the early 1970s and the first decade of the new millennium.

A key difference, relative to the 1970s, is that spending on infrastructure was relatively more restrained during the second oil boom. There was also a more robust saving response. Learning from the fiscal challenges of the 1980s, most Arab RREs have devised explicit strategies to set aside a growing proportion of their resource windfalls for the future. SWFs emerged as important saving and investment vehicles during the second oil boom. Apart from facilitating overseas investments, these savings are coming to the rescue of Arab RREs in the present climate of low oil prices. The question, however, remains: is the recycling of petrodollars fundamentally different across the two oil booms? Apart from the differential savings response, the nature and direction of investment also displays interesting differences. At home, Gulf Cooperation Council (GCC) countries have invested more in rail infrastructure,[3] and in educational and financial institutions.

The destinations of overseas investments are also more diversified, with greater cross-border investment in Asian and MENA countries. But, at least in Qatar and Abu Dhabi, the pattern of prestige acquisitions abroad has continued and, in some cases, even intensified. In some sense, SWFs and their associated investments represent merely a change of form rather than one of substance. As investment vehicles, SWFs continue to be directed towards prestige projects at home and brand acquisitions abroad. Although investments have gradually become more diversified in terms of their destinations, few are oriented towards promoting development in the region. There are also lingering questions about the transparency of SWFs. Their operations are unusually opaque, with little public knowledge of their investment strategies. Many SWFs lack clear withdrawal rules. Even when specified, these rules are not consistently implemented. As a result, despite being a promising instrument, SWFs have not been entirely successful in imposing fiscal constraints on the sovereign. As the brief review in this section has suggested, despite small changes on the margin, the old development model is alive and well. Oil rents continue to drive the region's core trajectory of political and economic development. However, as the following section will argue, oil rents are only one large component of the region's complex structure of rentierism.

3 From Resource Curse to Rent Curse

While the Middle East's resource riches are often held culpable for the region's perverse political economy, the role of oil can easily be overstated. It is also difficult to explain the adverse performance of relatively resource-scarce Arab countries (the likes of Syria, Jordan and Egypt). Despite the absence of vast quantities of oil, many of these nations share the resource-curse symptoms of their oil-rich neighbours. This is partly explained by the significance of non-oil rent streams that mimic the effect of oil, and help to shape a similarly adverse political economy. At least three such revenue streams are noteworthy in MENA economies that are relatively labour abundant and resource scarce: aid, remittances, and rents from government regulations. The first of these—foreign aid—is a geopolitical rent that can replicate resource-curse symptoms. By virtue of its strategic location, the average MENA state derives greater aid

3 Gulf Business, 11 January 2015, http://gulfbusiness.com/2015/01/gcc-rail-projects-see-investments-worth-200bn/#.VfXGqhFVhBc (accessed on 17 March 2016).

rents than the average low-income country or sub-Saharan African state. Over the last fifty years the MENA region has received roughly three times more net aid per capita than Latin America. Despite being home to a significantly greater proportion of poor people, South Asia received only USD 6 per capita in net foreign assistance during the last decade, compared to USD 43 per capita in MENA.

MENA economies engulfed in the Palestinian–Israeli conflict are particularly large aid recipients (Jordan and Lebanon receive the highest level of net aid per capita—USD 128). The figure for Egypt, while significant by international standards, does not take into account the additional stable rent stream in the form of US military aid (USD 1.5 billion annually). An average North African state receives more net aid (in per capita terms) than an average low-income country. Since 2011 aid flows have skyrocketed in Arab Spring countries, rising to USD 158 in Egypt and USD 86 in Tunisia (once more in per capita terms). In the wake of its political crisis, in 2013 Egypt secured aid pledges worth USD 12 billion. Interestingly, these aid windfalls are shared even by countries with precarious oil exports (e.g. Iraq, Bahrain and Oman).

A second potentially important source of rents is remittances from expatriate workers. The salience of these rents is again evident from the fact that the MENA region has the highest ratio of remittances to GDP of all the developing regions (4 per cent compared to 1–1.5 per cent in Latin America and sub-Saharan Africa). Jordan and Lebanon derive roughly 20 per cent of their respective GDPs from expatriate worker remittances. The ratio is similarly high, by international standards, in Yemen, Egypt and Morocco. Unlike oil and aid, remittances are well dispersed among recipients, leading to more ambiguous political effects. Although remittance flows, together with foreign aid, are statistically correlated with authoritarian stability, they can also weaken patron–client linkages and create an independent political space (Ahmed, 2012). The mechanisms behind these statistical correlations are unclear, however. It is surmised that remittances can influence government spending decisions, tilting them away from essential public goods, and that they can also relieve the political pressure emanating from excessive unemployment.

The economic effects are similarly ambiguous. While remittances can improve financial intermediation, they can also trigger Dutch Disease effects, depressing growth in the long term (Rajan and Subramanian, 2011). By providing the necessary foreign exchange cushion, remittances can shield countries from economic crises, thereby weakening incentives for economic reform. In MENA, a key feature of both aid and remittances is their high correlation with oil prices. This is easy to understand: oil rents are recycled in the region through financial support for poorer neighbours and the creation of jobs for

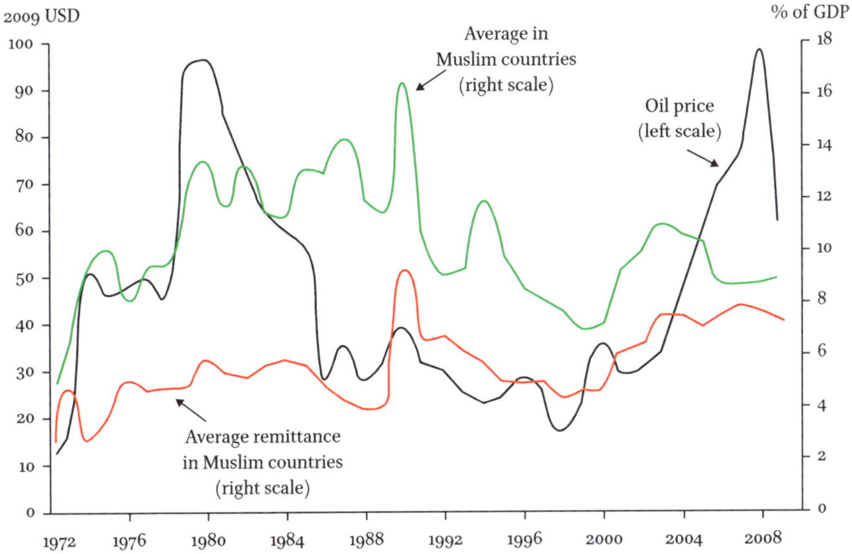

FIGURE 3.1 *Inter-linked capital flows: Oil, aid and remittances (1972–2008)*
SOURCE: AHMED (2012).
Note: Oil price (left scale)—USD per barrel

unskilled migrants from labour-surplus countries. The oil price is, therefore, a fundamental driver of these cross-border financial flows. As Figure 3.1 shows, aid to Muslim non-oil producers (in percentage of GDP) tracked quite closely with oil prices until 2002. A similar trend is observable for remittances.

The third rent stream, with particularly pernicious effects on political economy, is generated through government manipulation of the economy.[4] Arab markets are among the most protected in the world. In Arab countries domestic economic activity is routinely governed by monopoly concessions, price controls, procedural regulations and a raft of arbitrary trade barriers. Effectively, these barriers assign elites control of vital access points to the economy, generating rent streams that support 'networks of privilege' deemed essential for regime survival. Arguably, the need for such rent streams is most acutely felt in labour-abundant countries with more extended distributional commitments. This provides an important explanation for why non-tariff barriers remain both more pervasive and persistent in labour-abundant MENA economies. In fact, in terms of trade restrictiveness, MENA's labour-surplus economies leave all other regions, including sub-Saharan Africa, behind.[5]

4 These rents are often generated through government intervention that changes relative prices.
5 See Figure 7 in Malik and Awadallah (2013, 16).

Such policy-induced rents can be significant even in resource-rich countries. In most Arab RREs little is known about the number and strength of those with veto rights with regards to major fiscal policy decisions. The activities of many public sector enterprises also remain off the fiscal radar screen, with such quasi-public spending believed to be particularly important in Algeria, where public sector banks are repeatedly recapitalised through outright cancellations of their debts, purchase of non-performing loans (NPLs), and liquidity injections. Such transfers are often sophisticated ways of transferring rents to elite groups in society, groups without whose support the authoritarian order is difficult to sustain. In the GCC countries many popular instruments of patronage, such as land sales and tax benefits, are not accounted for in fiscal terms but are crucial forms of rent transfers to elite constituents. In fact, the literature on the business–state relationship in the Gulf has long recognised the ways in which a private sector that is structurally dependent on the state bolsters authoritarian stability (see Hertog, Luciani and Valeri, 2013).

Selective economic reform itself provides an important mechanism through which rents are generated to reconfigure elite alliances. Most North African countries have suffered from the familiar 'partial reform syndrome' that has remained a persistent feature of African economies (Van de Walle, 2001). Selective liberalisation of trade, finance and services has helped to generate new rent streams. The growth of the financial sector provides an important illustration of this point and deserves a separate mention.

3.1 *Finance and the Rentier Structure*

The financial sector acts as an important domain in which regulatory rents can be generated. This is particularly true in MENA's labour-abundant economies where the state has retained a domineering presence in the sector. These economies also stand out for the greater prominence of state-owned banks (SOBs) and specialised credit institutions (SCIs). Another feature of these countries' banking systems is the high share of non-performing loans. As a share of gross loans, non-performing loans in Algeria's government banks stood at 12.6 per cent in 2014. As the lead banker for the public sector, the financial sector is often used to safeguard oligarchic interests masquerading as claims by state enterprises. Partly as a consequence of excessive state involvement, there is also a greater 'informalisation' of the financial sector. Although capital flows are generally liberalised across the region, financial systems in labour-abundant RREs still exhibit some form of financial repression. With its pervasive exchange controls, which maintain negative real interest rates on dinar assets, Algeria presents clear evidence of financial repression.

Arguably, the banking sector in GCC countries can be considered comparatively 'well-developed, profitable and efficient' (Creane et al., 2003). With few exceptions, the banking sector in these economies extends reasonably high levels of credit to the private sector, when considered as a share of GDP. The region has one of the highest deposits-to-GDP ratios in the world. In most countries financial systems are also deep, as measured by the M2-to-GDP ratio.[6] Although more developed when measured by conventional yardsticks, the financial structures of GCC economies are structurally weak. Although the GCC economies are immune from direct interventions in the financial sector, their banking systems face high reserve requirements, and interest rates are sometimes explicitly or implicitly capped. Even privately owned banks sometimes work as disguised state-owned banks. Overlapping patterns of ownership of banks and firms further blurs the boundary between the public and the private. Relatedly, the banking sector is predominantly owned by the government and there is also a high lending exposure to connected actors. The non-bank financial sector is generally underdeveloped, with only a nominal presence for equity, insurance and bond markets (Snaije's chapter in this volume comments on this in more detail). The financial sector also remains exposed to volatility induced by fluctuations in the oil market. Like many Latin American oil exporters, external shocks and financial fragility are a fact of life in Arab RREs.

All of this is an invitation to look at the political economy of finance behind the shallow differences in the organisation and structure of finance between resource-rich and resource-scarce countries. While, in principle, financial markets are needed to facilitate inter-temporal consumption and business investment, their distributive function often trumps the productive logic in highly centralised, extractive regimes. In the MENA context, Henry and Springborg (2010, 108) provide an apt reminder that the 'banking system is a major asset for these regimes as long as insiders hold the levers of financial power, for they then extend the regime's reach and patronage networks into the private sector'. The manner in which finance extends the rentier structure is perhaps best illustrated by considering dynamics. All across MENA the financial sector has suffered from a weak pace of reform. With the exception of Africa, most regions have made more significant progress on financial development than has the Middle East. Even within MENA, the Arab oil exporters have been extremely slow reformers (Creane et al., 2003).

6 The M2 is defined as the sum of currency outside banks, demand deposits other than those of the central government, and the time, savings, and foreign currency deposits of resident sectors other than the central government (see http://data.worldbank.org/indicator/FM.LBL.MQMY.GD.ZS).

Such reluctance to reform is rooted in an adverse political economy where control of finance helps to sustain the disjunction between the economy and society, a hallmark of rentier states. Whatever limited reform has taken place has been neutralised to offset such reform's adverse political consequences. Rather than supporting a consistent and predictable process of liberalisation, most MENA states have engaged in partial liberalisation, which has permitted regimes to protect their interests. Foreign banks have usually been allowed to operate only if they agreed to broker deals with regime insiders. Such selective liberalisation of the financial sector has generated new rents for insiders. This is the familiar story of North Africa. In the resource-rich countries of the Gulf, the liberalisation of the financial sector was used as a politically safe avenue for economic diversification. This is most evident in GCC countries, where the need for diversification is most acutely felt. In Bahrain the assets of wholesale banks equal 480 per cent of GDP; those of retail banks equal 270 per cent of GDP (IMF, 2013). However, this regime of high finance does not pose a political threat since the bulk of lending is geared towards connected parties and real estate. Thus, even where depleting oil reserves have incentivised a move towards diversification, real estate, construction and financial sectors have been the preferred avenues for that diversification. This diversification strategy is politically more palatable, since it allows for controlled forms of accumulation.

The above discussion on finance underscores the complexity of the rentier structure in Arab economies, of which oil is only one—albeit important—component. Taken together, it is the totality of the rentier experience—rather than oil alone—that is potentially most damaging to Middle Eastern political economy. The resource curse is, in fact, a variant of a broader rent curse that can also manifest itself in resource-poor economies through dependence on foreign aid, remittances and regulatory rents. This has an important implication for how we analytically categorise these economies. Given that some of the oil wealth is recycled in the region through aid and remittances, the traditional distinction between oil and non-oil countries lacks analytical utility. The boundaries between the resource-rich and the resource-poor economies of MENA are indeed more fluid than often perceived.

3.2 *External Recycling of Rents*

Another neglected dimension of the mainstream analysis of rentier states pertains to the deployment of resource rents. The rentier analysis is largely concerned with the domestic cycling of rents that help to buy off key segments of society. While clearly a dominant concern, such rent distribution to domestic constituencies is only one major component of the distributive regime. It is complemented by a significant outflow of rents to appease strategically important external constituencies. The political economy implications of this external rent recycling are largely understudied. Arab RREs are not just exporters of hydrocarbons; they are also net exporters of capital. While overseas investments are a natural response to the limited absorptive capacity of the domestic economy, the export of capital is also partly geared towards aligning the interests of external constituencies with domestic political continuity. Resource-rich Arab states face the imperative of sharing their resource wealth, not just with their citizens, but also with key external constituencies.

Trillions of dollars are invested abroad in the acquisition of foreign companies and banks, the purchase of company shares, and in infrastructure projects, US treasury bills, and other means. The foreign assets of Saudi Arabia's financial system, including the Saudi Arabian Monetary Agency (SAMA) are estimated to stand at 130 per cent of the country's GDP. Such investments by sovereign wealth funds and high net worth individuals are not purely driven by economic returns but, equally, by a geopolitical logic that treats these investments as instruments for buying leverage in important foreign capitals. Closer to home, the Arab oil-exporting nations have also routinely acted as a lender of last resort for neighbours who are financially struggling. In fact, the resource-rich countries of the Gulf are effectively financing the social contracts of Yemen, Egypt and Jordan. These external commitments include oil and budgetary support for regional allies, and the escalating cost of regional military engagements. The fiscal cost of these growing external commitments is ultimately driven by the need to sustain the authoritarian pact at home. In fiscal terms, these can be described as contingent liabilities in the geopolitical domain.

Ultimately, high net foreign assets are also a natural outcome of specialisation in a highly internationalised commodity that inserts the region into global commodity and finance circuits. This globalisation of commodity and finance is, in turn, intertwined with the formation of classes at home (Hanieh, 2011). Capital connects not just financial markets but also Khaleeji elites who are both mobile and have a personal interest in a liberalised capital regime. The political significance of capital mobility has received attention in comparative politics, but largely in a localised context. Asset mobility has been described, in the democratisation literature, as a crucial intervening variable. It has been argued that democratisation may be less threatening to the elites when assets are mobile, since this can lower the risk of redistribution (Boix, 2003). Arab countries furnish contrasting evidence of this, however. Here, capital mobility can bolster authoritarian structures through the interplay between the domestic political and geopolitical arenas. This remains a largely under-studied domain of political economy.

It is in this context that the regime of near perfect capital mobility maintained in most Arab RREs should be situated.[7] Such unhindered movement of cross-border capital flows carries a larger political significance hitherto unappreciated by the resource-curse literature. From a purely macroeconomic standpoint, the regime of perfect capital mobility springs from a pragmatic concern for draining excess liquidity from the system and preventing the dangers of Dutch Disease evident in so many other resource-rich contexts. It is also inherently tied to preserving the credibility of the fixed exchange rate regime, which is also ultimately tied to regime legitimacy too. But there is also a complementary logic for capital mobility, a logic that is rooted in an underlying political economy that is excessively dependent on the import of labour from developing countries and the export of capital to developed markets. If low-skilled, foreign workers are important for sustaining the segmented labour regimes in GCC states, capital mobility is needed to facilitate outward remittance flows. This labour market arrangement is clearly significant from a political economy standpoint, since reliance on cheap foreign labour acts as an insurance against the possibility of class struggles emanating from labour politics (Herb, 2009).

4 Conclusion

In this research note I have tried to advocate a broader conceptualisation of rents that goes beyond a simple insistence on the role of hydrocarbon rents in shaping Middle Eastern political economy. I have argued that authoritarian structures in MENA are underpinned through a broader edifice of rents, which are both external and internal. Amongst internal rents, aid and remittances play a significant role in many Arab societies, ranging from Lebanon to Egypt. Despite their limited scale in comparison to oil rents, their impact in terms of political economy is often significant. Importantly, rents generated domestically through government manipulation of the economy play a crucial role in connecting the fate of business classes to the prevailing political order. All across the region, rulers often act as businessmen. For independent merchants, it is difficult to thrive outside the royal circle (Hertog et al., 2013). Domestic economic rents not only provide lucrative deals to insiders; they also generate elites' commitments to the ruler. This is one reason why such rents are more prevalent in MENA's labour-abundant economies where oil rents are either insufficient or unable to meet the more extensive distributional

7 Algeria and Libya provide important exceptions to this.

commitments of the regime. While the importance of these individual rent streams is recognised in the literature, their combined significance for MENA political economy is underappreciated.

Another important characteristic of the region's rentier structures relates to the external deployment of rents. The political economy significance of such deployment has been largely ignored by previous analyses. As MENA is a resource-rich region *par excellence*, most hydrocarbon exporters in the region maintain sizeable current account surpluses, enabling them to project their financial and diplomatic power abroad. Through their overseas investments and purchases, Arab exporters buy significant geopolitical influence, which—in turn—helps to bolster authoritarian structures at home. Expansive economic and financial engagement with the outside world provides interesting clues to the external recycling of rents, an activity that helps to build durable foreign commitment for the domestic political order. Just as the recycling of domestically generated economic rents creates binding commitments from the elites, several types of capital outflows are guises through which rents are distributed to core external constituencies to buy firm commitment to ruling families.

Given the significance of the non-oil rent streams, this article has argued that the Middle East appears to suffer from a broader rent curse. The oil curse is just a variant of the overall rent curse that MENA economies are trapped in. Concentrated economic and political structures in the Middle East are therefore essentially tied up with the creation, capture and distribution of these rents. A focus on the broader rentier structure allows us to frame the political economy of the Middle East within the emerging paradigms linking rents and institutional development. In fact, as argued by North, Wallis and Weingast (2012), it is difficult to evaluate any social order without a consideration of the nature, concentration and deployment of rents. With their consequent role in restricting economic opportunity, rents fundamentally define the scope and possibility of political action. Importantly, in the Middle Eastern context, well-entrenched rentier structures are crucial for understanding why authoritarian regimes are so durable despite occasional challenges to their rule. As the North African uprisings have painfully revealed, it is easier to remove regime leaders than to eliminate the rentier structures that feed the associated elite coalitions.

References

Ahmed, F. (2012) 'The Perils of Unearned Foreign Income: Aid, Remittances, and Government Survival', *American Political Science Review*, 106(1), 146–165, DOI: 10.1017/S0003055411000475.

Arezki, and M. Nabli (2012) *Natural Resources, Volatility and Inclusive Growth: Perspectives from Middle East North Africa*, IMF Working Paper 12/111, (Washington, D.C.: IMF), https://www.imf.org/external/pubs/cat/longres.aspx?sk=25891.0 (accessed on 18 March 2016).

Auty, R.M. (2001) *Natural Resources and Economic Development* (Oxford: Oxford University Press).

Barajas, A., R. Chami, C. Fullenkamp, P. Montiel and M.T. Gapen, (2009). *Do Workers' Remittances Promote Economic Growth?*, 09/153 Working Papers, (Washington, D.C.: International Monetary Fund)

Beblawi, H and G. Luciani (1987) *The Rentier State* (London: Croom Helm).

Boix, C. (2003) *Democracy and Redistribution* (New York: Cambridge University Press).

Boone, P. (1996) 'Politics and the Effectiveness of Foreign Aid', *European Economic Review* 89(1), pp. 22–46.

Creane, S., R. Goyal, A. Mobarak, and R. Sab (2003) *Financial Development in the Middle East and North Africa* (Washington, D.C.: IMF), http://www.imf.org/external/pubs/ft/med/2003/eng/creane/ (Accessed on 18 March 2016).

Dunning, T. (2008) *Crude Democracy: Natural Resource Wealth and Political Regimes* (Cambridge: Cambridge University Press).

Elbadawi, I.A. (2005) 'Reviving Growth in the Arab Region', *Economic Development and Cultural Change*, 53(2), 293–326, DOI: 10.1086/425375.

Friedman, T.L. (2009) 'The First Law of Petropolitics', *Foreign Policy*, October 16, http://foreignpolicy.com/2009/10/16/the-first-law-of-petropolitics/ (accessed on 18 March 2016).

Gray, M. (2011) 'A theory of "Late Rentierism" in the Arab States of the Gulf', Georgetown University School of Foreign Service in Qatar, Center for International and Regional Studies, *Occasional Paper* (*CRIS*), 7:1–50, https://repository.library.georgetown.edu/bitstream/handle/10822/558291/CIRSOccasionalPaper7MatthewGray2011.pdf?sequence=5 (accessed on 19 March 2016).

Hanieh, A. (2011) *Capitalism and Class in the Gulf* (London: Palgrave Publishers), 258 p.

Henry, C. and R. Springborg (2010) *Globalization and Politics of Development in the Middle East.* (Cambridge: Cambridge University Press), 382 p.

Herb, M. (2009) 'A Nation of Bureaucrats: Political Participation and Economic Diversification in Kuwait and the United Arab Emirates', *International Journal of Middle East Studies*, 41(03), DOI: 10.1017/S0020743809091119.

Hertog, S. (2010) *Princes, Brokers and Bureaucrats: Oil and the State in Saudi Arabia* (Ithaca NY: Cornell University Press).

Hertog, S., G. Luciani and M. Valeri (2013) *Business Politics in the Middle East* (London/New York, Hurst/Oxford University Press).

IMF (International Monetary Fund) (2013). *Bahrain: Financial Sector Assessment* (Washington, D.C.: IMF).

Islam, M.N. (2005) 'Regime Changes, Economic Policies and the Effect of Aid on Growth' *Journal of Development Economics* 41 (8), 1467–1492, DOI: 10.1080/002203805 00187828.

Malik, A. and B. Awadallah (2013). 'The Economics of the Arab Spring' *World Development*, 45: 296–313, DOI: 10.1016/j.worlddev.2012.12.015.

North, D., J. Wallis, and B. Weingast (2012) *Violence and Social Orders: A Conceptual Framework for Interpreting Human History* (Cambridge: Cambridge University Press), 346 p.

Noumba Um, P., S. Straub and C. Vellutini (2009) 'Infrastructure and Economic Growth in Midlde East and North Africa', *World Bank Policy Research Working Paper 5105*, (Washington, D.C.: World Bank), DOI: 10.1596/1813-9450-5105.

Nugent, J.B., Pesaran, M.H. (2007). *Introduction Explaining Growth in the Middle East. Contribution to Economic Analysis* (Vol. 278), 1–30 (Amsterdam: Elsevier).

Rajan, R.G. and A. Subramanian (2011) Aid, Dutch Disease and Manufacturing Growth, *Journal of Development Economics*, Volume 94(1), 106–118, DOI: 10.1016/ j.jdeveco.2009.12.004.

Ross, M. (2001) 'Does Oil Hinder Democracy?' *World Politics*, 53(03), 325–361, DOI: 10.1353/wp.2001.0011.

Van de Walle, N. (2001). *African Economies and the Politics of Permanent Crisis, 1979–1999*. (Cambridge: Cambridge University Press), 306 p.

Yousef, T. (2004) 'Development, Growth and Policy Reform in Middle East and North Africa since 1950', *Journal of Economic Perspectives*, 18(3), 91–115, http://www.jstor .org/stable/3216808.

CHAPTER 4

A Brief Political Economy of Energy Subsidies in the Middle East and North Africa

Laura El-Katiri and Bassam Fattouh[1]

Abstract

Energy subsidies are among the most pervasive and controversial fiscal policy tools used in the Middle East and North Africa (MENA). In a region with few functioning social welfare systems, subsidised energy prices continue to form an important social safety net, albeit a highly costly and inefficient one. In the MENA region's oil and gas producing countries, low energy prices have also historically formed an important element of an unwritten social contract, where governments have extracted their countries' hydrocarbon riches in return for citizens' participation in sharing resource rents. While it is clear that energy subsidy reform will not be the only variable at play, its potential socio-economic dividends are important factors for enabling some common regional objectives—sustainable fiscal policies, fiscal space to invest in key areas, and a more efficient and equitable distribution of scarce resources—to be achieved, helping to promote a more stable political status quo in the long term. If accommodated by effective mitigation measures, reforming energy subsidies in the MENA region's middle-income economies could be a powerful tool for governments—addressing those very profound socio-economic grievances that have contributed to the outbreak of political protest and, in some cases, to an intensification of domestic infighting over political control. In this paper, we look at some of the MENA region's potential avenues for reform. While the past has demonstrated the political difficulty of reforming energy prices, recent experience also shows that the reform of energy subsidies can be achieved, if accompanied by a set of enabling factors.

1 Introduction

Energy subsidies are among the most pervasive and controversial fiscal policy tools in the Middle East and North Africa (MENA). Their reform continues to be difficult, from a political, economic and social perspective, due to the original objectives of these measures—such as the need to protect the interests of

1 A version of this article was published as working paper (https://www.oxfordenergy.org/wpcms/wp-content/uploads/2015/02/MEP-11.pdf).

 | DOI 10.1163/9789004336452_005

low-income households and to foster domestic industrial growth. In a region with few functioning social welfare systems, subsidised energy prices continue to form an important social safety net, albeit a highly costly and inefficient one. In the MENA region's oil and gas producing countries, low domestic energy prices have also historically formed an important element of an unwritten social contract, where governments extract their countries' hydrocarbon riches, in return compensating their citizens through a variety of direct and indirect channels, including subsidies and other welfare benefits (El-Katiri et al., 2012; El-Katiri, 2013a). Energy subsidies hence play a pivotal role in a complex state–citizen relationship, a relationship that has come under increasing scrutiny in many Arab countries since the onset of the Arab uprisings in 2010.

The four years or more since protests erupted in Tunisia in December 2010, and the widespread regional unrest later summarised under the popularised term the 'Arab Spring', have placed the issue of greater socio-economic justice at the heart of MENA politics. In a way this has complicated, and in many cases delayed, overdue energy pricing reforms in a number of regional economies, as governments have feared that rising living costs would only intensify popular turmoil. On the other hand, despite being widely perceived as a fundamental economic and social benefit, energy subsidies form an important part of the socio-economic problems, and of the vastly distorted economic incentives, that plague the economies of the MENA region. The reform of energy pricing systems is also a complex process, which often requires structural changes to ownership and control over some of the most crucial assets of the state in the Middle East—oil, gas and electricity, together with their accompanying distribution infrastructure and networks. In lower- and middle-income countries, measures for reforming energy prices, if not accompanied by appropriate mitigation measures (such as a more effective and transparent social safety system), have an adverse effect on the disposable incomes of the poor and the aspiring middle classes.

There are also intra-regional differences behind the drivers of reform. The fiscal pressures associated with energy subsidies are a primary driver for reform in many of the region's lower- and middle-income countries, particularly those in need of financial support from international institutions such as the World Bank and the International Monetary Fund (IMF). But the recent decline in international oil prices (since the second half of 2014), coupled with rising fiscal break-even prices in many oil-exporting countries, has also provided relatively strong incentives for the wealthier oil and gas producers to consider their respective domestic energy-pricing frameworks. This is in addition to the long-term consequences that many oil producers face as they continue to divert increasing volumes of oil and gas away from export markets to satisfy rapidly growing domestic demand, at prices far below world market levels.

In this paper, we look at some of the MENA region's potential avenues for reform. While the past has demonstrated the political difficulty of reforming energy prices, recent experiences in several MENA economies also show that the reform of energy subsidies can be achieved, if accompanied by a set of enabling factors. The rest of the paper proceeds as follows: Section 2 provides a brief background on energy subsidies in the MENA region; Section 3 looks at some of the reform experiences in the region; Section 4 concludes.

2 A Brief Background on Energy Subsidies

2.1 *Issues with Measuring Energy Subsidies*

Energy subsidies are neither straightforward to define nor simple to measure; this tends to complicate any meaningful debate around them. There is no commonly agreed definition of what constitutes a subsidy, and this fact—in part—is reflected in the continued inability of major international organisations such as the World Bank, the United Nations Development Programme (UNDP), and Organization of the Petroleum Exporting Countries (OPEC) to agree on common terms.[2] A widely used definition considers a subsidy as:

> ... any measure that keeps prices for consumers below the market level or keeps prices for producers above the market level, or that reduces costs for consumers and producers by giving direct or indirect support.
>
> DE MOOR and CALAMAI, 1997, 1

It is clear from the above definition that many governments' actions can be categorised as involving assistance, including subsidies (in-kind, cash or credit, or relating to tax or procurement). Some of these are *on-budget* or *explicit subsidies* that constitute explicit transfers made by the government to either the producer or the consumer receiving the subsidy, registered in the state's budget. For instance, a government may mandate that a public utility set the selling price below the cost of production. The government then finances that public utility's losses by transferring funds from the general budget.[3] Energy

2 IEA et al. (2010) notes the existence of a major disagreement among international organisations concerning the choice of the reference price, and that consequently 'a commonly agreed definition of subsidies has proven a major challenge in the G-20 context and countries have decided to adopt their own definition of energy subsidies'.

3 The budget records of many countries (including Egypt) show how this concept underlies the measurement of subsidies in the economy.

subsidies can also be cross-financed between different energy user groups. *Cross-subsidies* occur when tariffs below the cost of production are charged, to household users for instance, and the revenue shortfall is offset by increasing industrial/commercial sector tariffs above cost levels. Countries such as Lebanon, Yemen, Egypt, Libya, and Syria all charge their industrial customers considerably higher electricity prices than charged to residential customers, suggesting some form of cross-subsidisation.[4]

But there is also the question of the benchmark against which domestic prices should be compared. For instance, the national oil company can be mandated to sell petroleum products to the domestic market at below international prices but above production costs. In this case, the national oil company does not incur financial losses, and hence the government does not need to make an explicit transfer to compensate for those losses. Nevertheless, there is still an implicit cost involved, which represents the *opportunity cost* (the economic rent/revenue wasted by the failure to sell oil at higher, market prices). This entails a transfer from the government to the final consumers, even though such a transfer does not appear explicitly on state oil companies' records or in the government budget. If this foregone revenue had been collected, it could have been used by the government in a variety of ways, including to reduce the budget deficit and the size of the public debt; to increase expenditure in more productive areas such as infrastructure, education or health; by redistributing it directly to its people through cash transfers; or to reduce, where applicable, taxation (Gupta et al., 2003). *Implicit subsidies* are less transparent and more difficult to calculate. They typically occur in oil producing countries, where mostly state-owned oil companies produce, refine and market petroleum products.

Based on the price-gap approach—which measures the gap between the subsidised price and a benchmark price to reflect the opportunity cost (defined as the supply cost of an energy product including transport and distribution costs)—a recent IMF report estimates pre-tax energy subsidies in the MENA region as having reached USD 237 billion in 2011, equivalent to 48 per cent of world subsidies, 8.6 per cent of regional GDP, and 22 per cent of government revenue (Sdralevich et al., 2014). These figures, however, should be treated with caution given the many caveats to using the price-gap approach in some contexts. Issues such as the production of joint products (for instance crude oil, natural gas, and natural gas liquids (NGLs)), the availability of spare capacity in some Arab oil-producing countries, and the ability of key Arab oil

4 Since in all these countries public utilities do not recover their costs, this form of cross-subsidisation is nevertheless imperfect, and does not prevent the sector from systemic loss making.

exporters to influence international oil prices could affect the measurement of subsidies.[5] A recent study by the IMF broadens the definition of an energy subsidy to:

> … [a post-tax energy subsidy, which arises] when consumer prices are below supply costs plus a tax to reflect environmental damage and an additional tax applied to all consumption goods to raise government revenues.
>
> COADY ET AL., 2015, 1

Based on this definition, global energy subsidies are estimated at a massive USD 5.3 trillion for 2015, or 6.5 per cent of global GDP, despite the recent fall in the oil price. This higher estimate of global energy subsidies results from the inclusion of components such as local air pollution, global warming, and other (non-internalised) domestic externalities in the post-tax energy price.

2.2 *Energy Subsidies and MENA Fiscal Stability*

As has become evident throughout the first decade of the twenty-first century, energy subsidies constitute a significant fiscal burden. With rising world market prices for oil and natural gas since the turn of the new millennium, the MENA region's parallel surge in domestic demand has translated into a rapid growth in fiscal expenditure on energy subsidies in importing countries such as Morocco, Egypt, Jordan, Syria, and Lebanon. Egypt's expenditure on energy subsidies reached a staggering USD 21 billion (EGP 143.7 billion) in the financial year 2013/14—a figure equivalent to 19.5 per cent of total government spending, or almost the entire value of aid received by Egypt from Middle Eastern donors since mid-2012.[6] Yemen's energy subsidy bill for 2013/14 was most recently estimated to be around USD 3.5 billion, a third of government expenditure and in excess of the country's budgeted deficit of USD 3.2 billion in that fiscal year (MEES, 2014h; Ghobari and El Gamal, 2014). The recent fall in the oil price comes as a welcome relief to these oil importers, but such relief could prove temporary, given that the future trajectory of oil prices remains highly uncertain.

---

5 A report notes that the price-gap method has limitations, which apply particularly in the case of countries with large endowments of energy resources (IEA et al., 2010).

6 MEES (2014a); authors' estimates of Gulf and Turkish aid paid to Egypt since the Morsi regime assumed power until February 2014 (around USD 24.5 billion). It is important to note that in measuring energy subsidies, Egypt only considers the actual expenditure on subsidies and not the opportunity cost. Based on the opportunity cost, the size of the subsidy would be much higher.

A parallel problem related to current energy pricing in oil and gas producing countries—and in countries, such as Egypt, that are net importers of some fuels—is the medium- and long-term effect that current pricing policies have on these countries' own domestic production, and hence on their future revenue streams. Low domestic energy prices in many oil and gas producing countries provide a poor incentive for independent oil and gas companies to invest in new exploration and upstream development projects. Natural gas is the energy source most affected by domestic pricing policies—reflected in the poor fiscal terms offered to oil and gas companies considering investment opportunities. This will become increasingly important as a larger proportion of Middle East oil and gas becomes more expensive to produce. The development of gas reserves has hence lagged decades behind the Middle East's massive gas resource endowment undermining the long-term supply potential of the region.

The MENA economies' exceptionally high reliance on oil and natural gas—tradable fossil fuels whose world market prices fluctuate significantly—has also made the region highly vulnerable to international commodity price cycles. Energy subsidies have also been shown to be strong, procyclical 'destabilisers' in oil- and gas-importing countries across MENA, as government spending on subsidies increases during economic boom times along with rising demand, and declines as economic activity falls (Sdralevich et al., 2014, 21–22; IMF, 2013, 37–40). Several studies have demonstrated the negative consequences of procyclical spending in developing economies (Lane, 2003; Abdih et al., 2010; Kaminsky et al. 2004; Erbil, 2011), including the effect of commodity cycles on political stability over the medium and long term.[7]

2.3 *Energy Subsidies and Social Equity*

The widespread use of energy subsidies in developing countries continues to be widely defended on the basis of social security and ensuring access to energy. However, energy subsidies are largely inequitable as they naturally accrue most to the largest users—energy-intensive industries and middle- to high-income households.[8] Petroleum product subsidies in particular benefit primarily the urban middle class, and households that can afford a car. In a recent study, the IMF found that the poorest quintiles in Egypt, Jordan, Mauritania, Morocco, and Yemen receive only about 1–7 per cent of total diesel subsidies, while the richest quintiles receive subsidies to the tune of 42–77 per cent of

7 E.g. Collier and Hoeffler (1998).

8 This also, where applicable, relates to natural gas/LPG. Kerosene, by contrast, tends to be proportionately consumed most by lower-income households, although substantial leakages exist to higher income groups. See e.g. Alderman (2002); Clements et al. (2003); Coady et al. (2006); Hope and Singh (1999).

the total. In Egypt, the poorest 40 per cent of the population receives only 3 per cent of direct gasoline subsidies, 7 per cent of natural gas subsidies, and 10 per cent of diesel subsidies (Sdralevich et al., 2014).

Energy subsidies, many of which leak to higher income groups and industries, could otherwise have been invested in alternative channels—free public health and education, infrastructure improvements, or alternative tax reductions for small and medium-sized businesses. All these would provide substantially higher social and economic returns than perceived citizen benefits bound to energy consumption. Separate funds could have been spent targeting low-income households more effectively, for instance, through comprehensive social safety nets. In some MENA countries, the size of energy subsidies relative to other forms of expenditure is staggering.[9] In Egypt, total government expenditure on energy subsidies in 2008 equalled combined expenditure on health and education; as did fuel subsidies in Jordan prior to the country's 2008 reform of fuel prices. Yemen's budgeted expenditure on fuel subsidies in 2008 amounted to more than 34 per cent of total government expenditure—more than one and a-half times the expenditure on education and health combined (Breisinger et al., 2011).

The widespread use of energy subsidies also affects the rate of investment in the energy sector in parts of MENA; the quality of coverage of different energy services, including fuel supply and electricity, consequently affects social groups differently. Caps on government subsidies paid to producers, or flat payment subsidies, often may not fully compensate domestic oil/gas producers, refineries, importers and distributors, and electricity producers for their incurred losses, and may undermine the rate of return on their investment. When funds are diverted away from state-owned enterprises and oil marketing companies and distributors, these companies will not be able to upgrade their internal capabilities, invest in new infrastructure, or shift to modern, cleaner, and more efficient technologies. The result is often the provision of low-quality services to end users, most visibly in the region's electricity sector.

Recurring power outages have characterised electricity provision throughout wide parts of MENA, typically due to decade-long underinvestment in electricity generation and in transmission and distribution networks. In many parts of the Levant and the Gulf, this situation is further exacerbated by a culture

9 The IMF reports that in about half of MENA countries, total pre-tax energy subsidies were higher than capital spending in 2011. In all oil exporters, total pre-tax energy subsidies exceeded spending on education and on health, while in Egypt, Jordan, and Lebanon spending on total pre-tax energy subsidies was higher than spending on capital, health, or education. In 2008, Egypt dedicated 11.93% of its gross annual expenditure to education, 5.94% to health, and an estimated 17.85% to fuel subsidies. Fattouh and El-Katiri (2012b).

of non-payment of utility bills by some parts of the population. Recurring blackouts, seen in recent years across many parts of the Levant, Iraq, Egypt, and perhaps most paradoxically in several Gulf Cooperation Council (GCC) member states (Bahrain, Kuwait, Oman, Qatar, Saudi Arabia, and the United Arab Emirates (UAE)), are just one of the most visible consequences of lagging new investment and insufficient capacity across many parts of MENA. These blackouts proportionally affect middle-income households and small businesses significantly more than any other energy-consumer group. Long waiting times for new electricity connections for private households and businesses are often the consequence, resulting in annual losses in foregone business activity and backup costs for the economies concerned (World Bank, 2008).

For some of the poorest parts of MENA, however, the consequences of underinvestment and a lack of electricity grid access are staggering. Lack of electrification in remote areas can be seen primarily in Yemen and in some rural parts of Morocco. In Yemen, little more than half the population has access to electricity, as the chronically underfunded state utility has insufficient funds to invest in expanding the country's electricity grid and generation capacity (Breisinger et al., 2011; El-Katiri and Fattouh, 2011). Of those households with electricity access, which are entirely concentrated in the wealthier former North, nearly 70 per cent are on 'lifeline rates', supposedly enabling electricity access for low-income households. Yemen's case painfully illustrates the highly regressive nature of energy subsidies.

Continued significant fuel price differences between neighbouring countries in MENA, owing to different subsidy regimes, have also incentivised large-scale fuel smuggling across borders. Fuel smuggling has been of particular concern among neighbouring countries in the Levant, such as Syria, Jordan, and Lebanon; between Egypt and the Palestinian territories; across the closed borders between Algeria and Morocco and between Tunisia and Libya (resulting from the 2011 uprisings) (Algerie DZ, 2008; France 24, 2011); into and from Iraq and neighbouring countries; and from and to Yemen (Wahab, 2006; Ibrahim, 2011). Iran, with (up to end-2010) some of the world's lowest prices for fuel, has suffered from endemic cross-border fuel smuggling to all its neighbours, a problem also incurred by other Gulf States (Arab Times, 2011). Fuel smuggling not only contributes to illegal contraband trade at the expense of the domestic economy, but in many cases substantially exacerbates existing fuel shortages in subsidising countries, as seen most recently in Yemen (MEES, 2014h; Ghobari and El Gamal, 2014).

2.4 *Energy Subsidies and Domestic Energy Consumption*

While high revenues and foreign assets are currently shielding many of the MENA region's larger oil and gas exporters in the short term, energy exporters face a longer-term challenge related to the way in which their current pricing policies affect their domestic energy consumption. The pivotal role played by national hydrocarbon resources in the development of many large MENA oil and gas producers has deeply affected the way energy features as a critical component in the citizen–state relationship. Oil wealth has facilitated much of the modern-day socio-economic development in the region, particularly that of the very oil-rich Gulf monarchies. Rather than engaging in more democratic forms of government, many of these countries' traditional political systems are based on the state's central role as a distributor or allocator of wealth in return for political legitimacy (Luciani, 1987; El-Katiri, 2013a).

The perceived abundance of energy resources, guaranteed by the state, and coupled to the state's role as a provider for its citizens, has historically been enshrined in some of the world's lowest prices for fuel, natural gas, and electricity. These in-kind citizen benefits, which also fuelled many oil producers' industrial expansion towards energy-intensive industries during the 1960s and 1970s, are supplemented by often generous welfare systems that have become an effective element in these states' political stability over several decades.

Low domestic energy prices have led to a surge in regional energy consumption—beyond the influence of such factors as economic and population growth. With regional energy consumption having more than quadrupled in less than 30 years (authors' calculations based on World Bank, 2014), the MENA region is now one of the world's fastest growing energy markets, and is forecast to become the second most important driving force of global energy demand after Asia in the period to 2040 (IEA, 2011; EIA, 2011). Saudi Arabia is already the world's twelfth-largest energy consumer, and the sixth-largest consumer of oil and natural gas, with oil consumption alone having more than doubled over the past ten years (based on BP and EIA statistics). Other large regional oil and gas producers in the Gulf follow this pattern, albeit with smaller populations, and are leading the world's league tables in terms of per capita living standards.

The fiscal problems arising from current consumption patterns that remain tied to current pricing policies in MENA's oil and gas producers in the long term are related to the way in which most of these states finance their spending. Many of these countries do not tax their domestic citizens, but finance themselves to an overwhelming extent on the basis of export revenues for their valuable oil and natural gas resources—the level of this dependence ranges from around 60 per cent of total government revenues in Qatar to over 90 per cent in countries such as Libya, Iraq, Kuwait, and Saudi Arabia (Fattouh and El-Katiri, 2012a, 3). A further increase in already generous welfare handouts (for background, see El-Katiri, L., 2013a; El-Katiri, M., 2013; Gause III, 2013) has also allowed the oil- and gas-rich Gulf monarchies to avoid Arab Spring-style political upheaval. This modus operandi works as long as sufficient volumes of hydrocarbon exports are available. However, some studies have shown that under the business-as-usual scenario (where domestic demand keeps increasing at a robust pace and the GCC governments fail to diversify their economies) export capability could be eroded, leading to a collapse of these countries' revenue base, with detrimental political consequences.[10] Recent falling oil prices, if they persist, will make the need for an adjustment of spending patterns (including a reform of energy subsidies) increasingly urgent.

The MENA region's low energy prices have also had many unintended consequences, including the very high and (countering trends virtually everywhere else in the world) rising energy intensity of MENA economies, meaning that more energy per unit of economic output is needed in these economies than anywhere else in the world.[11] This is partly because the concentration of economic activity around energy-intensive industries in MENA's oil-producing countries has diverted much investment from other economic sectors. However, the high energy intensity of MENA economies is also due to inefficiencies in energy use across the region.[12] A recent ABB study, comparing energy efficiency rates in power generation across a range of countries globally, shows that MENA energy producers such as the UAE, Libya and Saudi Arabia are among the world's least energy-efficient countries in terms of domestic power generation

10 Simulations of Saudi Arabia's domestic oil demand, such as those conducted by Chatham House and Citibank, show the potential for Saudi Arabia—under a business-as-usual scenario—to exhaust its own domestic reserve base in just 15–20 years, turning itself ultimately into a net importer of oil, unless alternative policy options are pursued. (Lahn and Stevens, 2011; Daya and El Baltaji, 2012). See also El-Katiri, L. (2013b).

11 Total primary energy consumption per dollar of GDP (an indicator of energy intensity) over the past three decades has declined in all parts of the world, with the exception of MENA. Energy intensity growth rates in several MENA economies, including the UAE, Saudi Arabia and Oman, have risen particularly fast, more than tripling in the UAE and Saudi Arabia since 1980. This growth is not a Gulf phenomenon alone, however; energy intensity in several other economies, including Jordan, Egypt and Syria, also increased by more than a third over the same time period. Egypt and several Mashreq economies—including Jordan—whose industries are generally less energy intensive, still require over 40% more energy per unit of economic output than do some of the world's less energy-intensive economies, such as Denmark or Spain. Fattouh and El-Katiri (2013).

12 In a recent article, Prince Abdulaziz Bin Salman Al-Saud argues that 'Although this growth in demand is partially attributed to the industrial growth and growing economic prosperity in the kingdom, a rather significant portion of it results from the inefficient use of energy; deeming this accelerated growth unsustainable. Whereas the vast majority of countries have managed to lower the energy intensity of their economies, the kingdom's energy intensity increased significantly over the last two decades. Hence, it is a strategic imperative for the kingdom that energy efficiency becomes a major topic for all decisions related to an increase in demand for fuel and feedstock'. (Al-Saud, Prince Abdulaziz Bin Salman, 2014, 4).

(ABB, 2014). However, MENA's net-importers of energy, including Jordan, Lebanon and Morocco, fare little better, comparing unfavourably to other developing economies, including those in Latin America. Similar conclusions apply to the region's rapidly growing transport sector, where average fuel consumption per vehicle across the Middle East is more than twice the average of countries without fuel subsidies.[13]

Low energy prices for regionally produced oil and natural gas have also affected the composition of the MENA economies' domestic energy mix. While these economies have historically not faced the same incentives as consumer countries in Europe and North America to diversify their domestic energy mix away from fossil fuels (for domestic energy security reasons) they may well have overlooked the economic potential of alternative energies such as renewable energy sources and nuclear power, given the influence of some of the world's lowest domestic prices for fossil fuels (El-Katiri, 2014; El-Katiri and Husain, 2014). As a result, the MENA economies remain dependent on oil and natural gas for a staggering 95 per cent of their domestic energy needs; more than any other region in the world (El-Katiri (2014) based on World Bank (2014) data). Their lack of diversity in domestic energy sources has left many MENA energy importers exceptionally exposed to commodity price cycles and to surging world market prices for oil and natural gas.

Recent evidence from Kuwait shows that a realignment of prices at, or closer to, the market price level confers a benefit on current and future generations of Kuwaitis (in terms of fiscal savings) that outweighs the impact of raising consumers' electricity and water prices to market price levels.[14] Such studies also underline the tremendous potential for economic savings to be made, including through the reduction of deadweight loss.

3 Reforming Energy Subsidies in MENA

Although energy subsidies are an inefficient and regressive distribution method, their reduction or elimination is a delicate economic and political task that

13 Notably, the Middle East region in this context includes Iran, which until 2010 was widely cited as the single largest subsidiser of domestic fuels in the world. (Bressand et al., 2007).

14 See Fattouh and Mahadeva (2014). The authors show that in the market price scenario with consumer prices at about ten times current levels, there is a total fiscal cost of about a third of the value of fuel input used in the power sector (or about 1.5% of GDP), entirely due to the cash transfer. This, however, is just less than a fifth of the fiscal cost of the current low-price regime, and in principle represents a massive saving. The net benefit of moving to market prices is 6.3% of GDP.

requires considerable skill and political will. Without appropriate compensatory programmes and without effective state capacity to provide public goods such as public transport networks and social welfare for the poorer segments of a society, energy price increases following reform will impact real incomes and could become a very potent source of public anger and social unrest. Notably, energy pricing reform affects not only the poor, but also the MENA region's aspiring middle class, and the region's industries. This is all the more concerning for oil and gas producing countries, whose industrial base is often highly energy intensive, and for whose populations the ownership of a car is a critical sign of social progress.

The economic lock-in effect of energy subsidies in MENA countries is further reinforced by strong coalition-building by groups who benefit from current pricing systems—in particular industrial groups, but also members of current sociopolitical elites, who tend to have little interest in supporting public spending reforms. The Arab Spring affected the region's political climate, deterring meaningful reform of domestic energy pricing policies across the MENA region due to widespread government concern that the fear of rising living costs, associated with subsidy reform, could stir up further popular discontent. Nevertheless, reform efforts have become much more common in MENA than expected, providing a wealth of experience around the 'how and when' of regional subsidy reform (Sdralevich et al., 2014, 44–55).

3.1 *Gradual Reform Efforts in the Levant and North Africa*

Fear of incitement of a popular backlash has kept those MENA countries that were largely unaffected by Arab Spring-style unrest cautious of energy pricing reform. In spite of remaining largely unaffected by street protests, in comparison with countries such as Egypt and Tunisia, Morocco and Jordan both rolled back reforms following the ousting of the Tunisian and Egyptian presidencies in 2011 and the outbreak of political protest across many other parts of the region. Both Morocco and Jordan are IMF debtors who, a few years previously, had initiated tentative reforms to reduce domestic energy subsidies. Jordan had, for instance, made several attempts to reform the domestic prices of food and energy—in 2008 its government announced a programme of domestic energy price liberalisation. However, the reform stalled and was reversed in January 2011, when the government decided to cut food and fuel prices in response to political protests seen in neighbouring countries. In an unexpected gesture of cross-regional solidarity between Arab monarchies, the wealthy GCC states extended an invitation to the kingdoms of Morocco and Jordan to join the Gulf Cooperation Council, and subsequently increased their level of assistance to both countries, in the form of advantageous loans and unconditional development aid. This helped both countries initially withstand calls from international lending organisations for further fiscal reforms (MEES, 2011; MEES, 2012a; MEES, 2013; MEES, 2014e).

A year on from the Arab Spring, however, domestic energy subsidy reform was back on the agendas of several North African and Levantine energy importers. Jordan's rapidly rising fuel imports—partly due to declining gas imports from Egypt, which has since been struggling to supply its own domestic market—subsequently contributed to a skyrocketing energy subsidy bill that eventually reached 40 per cent of total government spending. Faced with limited room for manoeuvre, the Jordanian government was forced to curb public spending significantly—including that on fuel subsidies—as part of a USD 2.05 billion standby arrangement with the IMF; one aim of this arrangement was to help the kingdom recover from the economic strains associated with the mass inflow of Syrian refugees, a result of the political crisis in neighbouring Syria (MEES, 2012c). But Jordan's reform efforts were not exclusively externally driven; the repercussions of the Arab Spring had made fiscal reforms practically unavoidable if political and economic stability were to be maintained. This was a small but significant turning point in the way in which many governments have since come to see energy subsidy reform.

Jordan's November 2012 decision to gradually lift all petroleum product subsidies—later followed by the lifting of LPG and electricity subsidies—was painful, and faced considerable opposition both in parliament and on Amman's streets. Street chants denouncing the Jordanian king led to a series of confrontations between protesters and the police. Having withstood this initial opposition, Jordan has since progressed with its reforms, following a gradual drying-up of popular opposition to them. The government's response included a series of television and newspaper interviews underlining the government's need to reduce the burden of subsidies, or otherwise 'face catastrophe and insolvency'.[15] In an effort to mitigate the effects of fuel price increases on Jordanian families, the government announced that within a week of the reform poor Jordanian households (below an annual household income of USD 14,100 (Jordanian dinar (JOD) 10,000)) would receive a direct cash handout of USD 99 (JOD 70); in effect around 70 per cent of the population would receive cash transfers. Electricity tariffs for individual economic sectors and high-income households have been increased a further three times since May 2012—part of a strategy to ensure the return of the National Electric Power Company NEPCO, Jordan's national electric power company, to cost recovery over the medium term.

15 Prime Minister Abd Allah al-Nusur said, 'If the move [had been] delayed, we would have faced a catastrophe and insolvency'. (MEES, 2012c).

The interim results of the reform have been largely positive; alongside other fiscal reforms, energy subsidy reforms helped reduce the Jordanian government's deficit from 14.5 per cent of GDP in 2011 to around 8.3 per cent of GDP in 2014. As a result, Jordan's access to lending from international capital markets has markedly improved (IMF, 2014a).

Morocco decided to freeze energy prices in 2011 in spite of the high and rising level of global oil prices and the country's dependence on imported energy for virtually all of its domestic energy needs. The move came largely as a direct response to popular protests in neighbouring North African countries and to—in small numbers and for a short period of time—protests on its own streets. This decision soon led to a rapidly ballooning energy subsidy bill. By the end of 2012, Morocco's energy subsidy bill had become

> … almost the size of the overall fiscal deficit, as much as spending on investment, and more than the spending on health and education combined.
>
> IMF, 2014b, 16

An initial round of energy price rises reduced the cost of subsidies by nearly half to—still—around USD 4.1 billion, or 10 per cent of government spending in 2013 (MEES, 2014f). Agreeing with the IMF to reduce the fiscal burden of subsidies in return for a USD 6.2 billion IMF Precautionary and Liquidity Line in August 2012, Morocco announced far-reaching domestic pricing reform for petroleum products between late 2013 and early 2014. Morocco's case is interesting as it is one of the few MENA countries that not only raised prices for domestic fuel products, but actually linked them on a permanent basis to international prices. Price adjustments are made twice monthly by the Ministry of General Affairs and Governance, independently from the ministries of Energy and of Electricity.[16]

In order to avoid any political backlash from this reform effort (having faced mass popular protests during the 1980s when it attempted to raise prices for basic foodstuffs), Morocco implemented a comprehensive and fairly well-orchestrated communication strategy to accompany the reform. This included public TV and radio discussions, newspaper articles, advertisements, and debates explaining in remarkable and easily understood detail the economic reasons for the reform of prices, the different reform steps, the reason for linking prices to a regularly reviewed international price index, and the multiple

16 For the law governing this arrangement, see Royaume du Maroc (2013).

benefits of reform to society as a whole[17] (including the availability of more money for investment elsewhere[18]). The government also assured the population of what benefits would remain: electricity prices, already among the region's highest, initially remained unchanged, but were increased in July 2014 (nearly a year after the indexation system was launched) as part of the government's restructuring of the Office National de l'électricité (ONE); while LPG, used primarily as a cooking and heating fuel in Moroccan households, remains heavily subsidised.

The reform clearly targeted those people who, supposedly, could afford higher prices: industrial consumers, factories, and car drivers. Finally, the government emphasised that price indexation offered a fair deal on both sides: prices could increase, but would also fall when international prices decreased. The Moroccan reform effort was not met with a public outcry, and subsequently went largely unnoticed by international media. Key to enabling this notable success has been two consecutive governments that, despite varying party interests, were willing and able to build the necessary coalitions to enact the price increases, despite opposing views within their own ranks. The country's moderate Islamic party, the Parti de la justice et du développement (PJD), has notably been instrumental in rallying support for the reform, both within government and among the population. Morocco's total subsidies—including food, which had peaked in 2012 at 6.6 per cent of GDP, fell to around 3.9 per cent of GDP in 2013 (Verme et al., 2014).

3.2 *Yemen's Failed Reform Efforts*

Yemen illustrates the converse case, of domestic pricing reform efforts that have largely failed over several years. While these policies have been revised over time, in the most recent conflict they have proven to be additionally destabilising in an already heated political situation. By the end of 2010, subsidies for liquid fuels, LPG, and electricity had usurped around a third of state spending, more than the country's combined spending on health and education (Fattouh and El-Katiri, 2012b, 49). Yemen's subsidies overwhelmingly benefited the country's urban upper and middle classes, who have access to transport,

17 For an example of how the French-speaking urban middle classes were targeted, see Agueniou (2013).

18 A study of some past Moroccan publications aimed at younger audiences illustrates the government's line of argument. In *Jeune Afrique*, Ahmed Lahlimi, head of Morocco's High Planning Commission, cited the volume of petroleum product subsidies across several North and sub-Saharan African countries, concluding '*C'est effectivement problématique car cela représente autant d'investissements en moins pour le pays*'. (Author's translation: '["These amounts of expenditure on fuel subsidies"] are highly problematic since they represent foregone investment') (Ballong, 2010).

energy, and infrastructure links. Even today, around half the country (primarily the former South and the geographically remote provinces across Yemen's northern borders) lacks infrastructure; formal, price-controlled markets; and the ability to access the country's highly subsidised electricity grid.[19] Yemen's severely deteriorating domestic security situation prior to and following the onset of the Arab Spring has led to a further deterioration in the country's finances. An increasing number of attacks on its oil and gas infrastructure have halted the country's hydrocarbon exports, adding to pre-existing domestic fuel shortages (MEES, 2014i; Saeed, 2014; MEES, 2014g).

Having had to import rising volumes of fuel products to cover shortfalls in domestic production, fiscal pressure on Yemen reached unprecedented levels; in a hasty and ill-prepared reform effort in July 2014, the country was forced (under intense pressure from lenders) to raise domestic energy prices. Amidst political turmoil, daily demonstrations in the streets of Sanaa and continued violent conflict between tribal groups and the central government in several provinces (many of which remain isolated from any electricity or fuel supply), the government's decision to raise domestic energy prices was seen as a further failure by the state to provide for its citizens (Abdullah, 2014). Yemen's weak central state has subsequently been unable to withstand pressure from non-state groups—notably the Houthis—for a swift reversal of initial reform efforts (Security Council, 2014). This underlines the difficulty, if not impossibility, of reforming energy pricing once a state has failed fiscally and politically and has lost its credibility, and once its citizens' faith in its capabilities has collapsed.

Yemen's case also illustrates the enormous challenges that the region's weak states face in implementing subsidy reform. With the complex interrelationship between energy subsidies and economic efficiency, and the difficulty of communicating the value of suffering short-term pain (removal of energy subsidies) versus the desirability of achieving long-term gain (economic growth) to their populations, weak states are clearly in no position to reform energy subsidies. Even more so when they are faced with the need to respond to fiscal pressures, rather than being in a position to present a credible set of reforms that are aimed at improving people's livelihoods over the medium and long term. This difficulty, experienced by Yemen, is reflected in other contexts. For instance, Al-Khatteeb and Istepanian describe the fear of reform in the case of Iraq, writing:

> There was and still remains a general fear among the Iraqi officials that any radical economic reforms, such as the elimination of subsidies for basic necessities like kerosene, cooking gas, electricity, and food rations

19 El-Katiri and Fattouh (2011, 30–40) give an overview of access to electricity and different fuels across Yemen's provinces and income groups.

> would be faced with strong opposition by the public and might cause widespread rioting, destabilizing an already fragile political process.
>
> AL-KHATTEEB and ISTEPANIAN, 2015, 4

3.3 *Egypt's 2014 Five-to-Midnight Reform*

Egypt offers an interesting counterexample to the Yemeni case. Having experienced political turmoil as part of the Arab Spring through not one but two subsequent changes of government, in addition to transitory government and years of instability, Egypt has nevertheless carried out a series of fuel and electricity price reforms since the election of President General al-Sisi. Fiscal pressure resulting from the country's spending on subsidies has been the main factor pushing Egypt's new government to engage in these reform efforts, despite the risk of popular unrest.[20]

While Egypt's July 2014 price hikes on most petroleum products were steep (up to 70 per cent price increases overnight),[21] they have also been fairly successful in reducing the country's spending on oil subsidies (down to less than 7 per cent of total government spending in the planned budget for 2015/16, from a figure of 20 per cent back in 2012/13) (MEES, 2015).[22] However, whilst spending on oil subsidies has fallen, spending on electricity subsidies has risen. Initial figures suggest that electricity subsidies are set to cost Egypt an estimated USD 3.42 billion (EGP 24.6 billion) for the fiscal year 2014/15, up 85 per cent on the 2013/14 figure of USD 1.84 billion (EGP 13.3 billion), though somewhat down on the original 2014/15 budget figure of USD 3.78 billion (EGP 27.2 billion) (MEES, 2015). The process of phasing the subsidy out is thus likely to be lengthy, although the government has been ambiguous on the timing and nature of future price rises.[23] In addition, Egypt's declining natural gas production has meant that the country has had to import growing volumes of internationally sourced LNG, while natural gas continues to be sold to domestic consumers at prices far below the import cost.

---

20 For a background to Egypt's unfolding energy problem during the first decade of the twenty-first century, see Darbouche and Mabro (2011).

21 Diesel prices increased by 64%, gasoline 80 by 77%, and gasoline 92 by 41%. However, these prices are still very low by international standards. See MEES (2014b).

22 Naturally, the decline in international prices for oil has also contributed towards this reduction in spending on subsidies.

23 According to the *Financial Times* the Egyptian government plans to phase out electricity subsidies over five years. The case of products is less clear, but the Minister of Planning has been quoted as saying that 'In five years fuel will be offered at 80 per cent of its real cost to sections of the population which are deemed to need subsidies, the rest will pay market prices'. (Saleh, 2014).

These recent reform measures are bold by any standard, especially so in light of the political and social instability still engulfing Egypt, and reveal the extent of fiscal pressures and the limited choices faced by the Egyptian government. Defying many analysts' predictions, these price hikes, though very steep, have not resulted in mass protests and civil unrest.[24] Part of the reason for this relates to timing. The reform measures were announced following a wave of nationalist fervour that saw President al-Sisi assume power, with strong support from his base for the onslaught against the Muslim Brotherhood. The violent crackdown on both the brotherhood and public protests may also have discouraged people from demonstrating. With hopes for a more stable future, for many Egyptians the prospect of paying higher prices for energy was arguably the lesser evil compared with the disastrous economic consequences of yet more political turmoil. The al-Sisi government may also have benefited from a much higher level of credibility than previous governments, promising a fairer socio-economic system and tying the reform of fuel and electricity prices to the unmistakeable need for financial resources to be used on essential services such as health and education. President al-Sisi, and Prime Minister Ibrahim Mahlab have been key proponents of the reforms, and have been personally engaged in communicating their necessity, using a series of media interviews to emphasise the need for common sacrifices in order to make Egypt 'great again' (Al Bawaba, 2014; Mubashir Misr, 2014).

While such factors can partly explain the muted response on the streets, the energy reforms' success will depend on the government's ability to introduce measures to mitigate the impact of high energy prices for the most vulnerable groups in society. Some such measures have, indeed, been introduced—the government freezing the prices of publicly distributed bread, rice, sugar, tea, flour and oil. The government has also expanded the food subsidy system, applying discounts to the prices of additional products such as meat and chicken. The price of LPG (widely used by low-income households) was not raised in the latest wave of reforms. Yet despite these mitigating measures, there is deep frustration among Egypt's low- and middle-income households related to the higher costs of living due to the price hikes. There is also scepticism about the government's ability to translate savings made thanks to the reforms into real benefits for the population (Rashwan, 2014).

Although the Egyptian government can be relieved that its initial reform steps did not cause mass protests, the road is long and key challenges remain.

24 There have been some small-scale protests and strikes (taxi drivers), but these were not widespread and did not threaten to destabilise the existing political system. (Fahim, 2014).

Experience in other countries shows there is always the risk that the pace of reform slows down, or even that reforms are reversed. The government therefore needs to strengthen its currently highly ineffective social protection schemes and safety nets. For instance, in the case of ration cards, the World Bank has found that eligibility criteria (such as being retired or a public sector employee) are not pro-poor, leaving poor Egyptians less eligible for a high-subsidy ration card than are non-poor Egyptians. Also, these regressive eligibility criteria are not well enforced—more than two-thirds of those holding high-subsidy ration cards do not meet the requisite criteria to do so.[25] The Egyptian government also has to establish credible commitments, including measures in areas such as public transport and infrastructure investment, laying the ground for the sound implementation of future price reforms.

Another issue to consider in the Egyptian case is the continued level of regulatory intervention in energy markets as a whole, given that Egypt has been adjusting prices on an ad hoc basis with no apparent plan in mind for future reform steps. One rationale for the current wave of reforms is that it will provide the government with the fiscal space needed to increase investment in public infrastructure and improve key services. In the absence of regular price adjustments, however, fluctuations in international energy prices may quickly erode current fiscal gains, further reducing the funds available for mitigation measures and public investment. For instance, the savings Egypt has made in the area of oil subsidies have partly resulted from the collapse of international oil prices since July 2014. Higher prices would reverse some of these savings and could force the government to adjust prices by engaging in highly visible political interventions, rather than by applying an automatic mechanism that helps reduce fuel subsidies.

3.4 *The Iranian Reform Experience*

Iran's targeted subsidy reform, initiated in 2010, is one of the most interesting cases the region has to offer. It is all the more significant as it has been conducted by a large oil and gas producing state that has, in the past, been perceived to be the most immune to calls for the rationalisation of domestic energy prices. The reform followed more than a decade of political controversy with regards to Iran's domestic oil prices, which were then among the lowest in the world. Surging domestic demand for energy, following more than a decade

25 Households in the top quintile receive subsidies of around 20% on the rationed products, compared with less than 16% for the lowest quintile. In terms of coverage, a third of the poor do not have ration cards, excluding them from the benefits of ration card subsidies. (World Bank, 2005).

of international sanctions that had severely affected Iran's ability to produce from its enormous reserve base, had left the world's largest reserve holder of natural gas reliant on top-up imports to avoid power shortages and load shedding. Iran's domestic subsidy burden, measured on the basis of opportunity cost, was estimated to be around USD 100 billion by 2010, an amount that exceeded the country's annual revenues from oil exports—at the time—of USD 70–80 billion (Guillaume et al., 2011, 4; Energy Compass, 2011; Tabatabai, 2011).

Iran's initial energy subsidy reform step, in December 2010, was estimated to have removed around USD 50–60 billion worth of subsidies (around 15 per cent of GDP) based on average 2010 international selling prices; this was achieved by dramatically raising the prices of such items as gasoline (300 per cent), natural gas (50 per cent), and diesel (900 per cent), virtually overnight (Energy Compass, 2011; Argus, 2013a). Within five years (coinciding with the country's Five-Year Plan) Iran's domestic energy prices should have risen to 90 per cent of their international market value. The architects of Iran's subsidy reform have been clear that price increases should be meaningful, in order to reduce demand effectively. Moreover, as outlined by some observers:

> … relatively small domestic price increases could be rapidly eroded in real term by domestic inflation, an increase in international prices, or exchange rate depreciation.
>
> GUILLAUME ET AL., 2011, 12

Finally, a front-loaded reform resulting in fast, large savings was a key requirement for the implementation of the Iranian government's single most important mitigation effort—a compensatory cash transfer system.

An essential part of Iran's strategy from the beginning was the redistribution, via cash grants, of proceeds generated by the reforms to different elements in the economy. Initial plans in 2010/11 included specific allocation targets: 30 per cent to domestic industries, in cash, to help them adjust to a gradually higher pricing environment (enabling energy efficiency-enhancing investments); 20 per cent to government institutions for similar adjustments; and 50 per cent to citizens, in the form of cash grants, to compensate households for generally higher living costs (Guillaume et al., 2011, 10). An initial plan to target lower-income households with these cash transfers proved unworkable, so the government moved on to a universal cash transfer system with sums paid per adult to the head of each household. The sum—on average USD 180 for a household of four during the first six months of the reform—amounted to around half of the nation's minimum wage: a substantial benefit, particularly for those on low incomes (Tabatabai, 2011, 15).

To further reduce the risk of widespread protest following these bold price rises, Iran's reform efforts were accompanied by a meticulously planned and executed public communication strategy, run by a government-appointed spokesman. Iranian news media (television, radio, websites and newspapers) and political, business, and social leaders and academics were all mobilised to speak in favour of the reform and to outline its many benefits to Iranian society. The campaign placed special emphasis on the background to the transformation—the enormous waste of Iranian natural and financial resources caused by the subsidy regime and the fact that the rich rather than the poor benefited most. The expected gains were also explained in detail—a universal cash transfer benefiting many poor households (Guillaume et al., 2011, 17–19; Tabatabai, 2011, 18–19). The entire communication strategy emphasised the shift of subsidies from products to people, a policy that would improve social equity, industrial competitiveness and economic diversification. To further counter the risks associated with the reform, the government widely advertised its policy of actively using monetary policy to counteract inflationary risks; prior to the reform, it also built up large stockpiles of basic goods to avoid bunkering and panic buying (Guillaume et al., 2011, 11).

Iran's subsidy reform has not been without complications. International sanctions (tightened significantly, and acting as a considerable restriction on oil exports since mid-2012), and the accompanying steep fall in the country's currency exchange rate, have created a surge in Iranian living costs and significantly complicated the efforts towards transformation; a second phase of the subsidy reform, planned for October 2012, has been suspended (MEES, 2012b).

In the run-up to presidential elections in 2013, the clear political value of Iran's cash transfer system also meant that the system—intended only initially to be universal—became a major issue in a political tug of war between different camps. Iranian politicians and oil and gas business leaders criticised the country for continuing to pay near-universal cash transfers that the system was increasingly unable to afford—the popularity of the scheme had seen the government keep handing out universal transfers at levels that soon exceeded the net savings it was making, with little left for other intended recipients such as industry.[26]

A new round of price increases, coupled with a reduction in monthly cash transfers to households, was initiated in early 2014, with the intention

26 Iran's Oil Minister, Bijan Namdar Zanganeh, has vociferously criticised Iran's cash transfer system, saying the Iranian oil and gas sector (from which the majority of revenues for the system come) could not afford to pay the handouts that were increasingly threatening domestic, upstream and refining companies' development projects (Argus, 2013a; Argus, 2013b).

of achieving combined savings of around USD 19.1 billion in the Iranian year 2014/15 (MEES, 2014c; MEES, 2014d).

A systematic evaluation of the impact of Iran's price reform on consumption is difficult due to the presence of various other factors including the intensification of international sanctions against the country in mid-2012; sanctions that have affected Iran's oil exports. Furthermore, demand for electricity, and for natural gas in particular, are highly supply-driven, implying that shortfalls in the supply of these commodities in some provinces may translate into reduced demand growth even where price effects would not have indicated a steep fall in consumption. Among Iranian observers, some general agreement has emerged that the initial energy price rises in 2010 reduced fuel product and natural gas demand significantly in the following months, although the effect in subsequent months is less clear (IOD, 2011; Amuzegar, 2012). The main lesson to draw from the Iranian case, however, is the political feasibility of even a radical reform process if it is accompanied by sufficient planning, and makes use of an approach that provides a credible reform framework in the form of government commitments to facilitating the switch towards greater energy efficiency, coupled to a well-designed mitigation scheme that offers cash, rather than in-kind, benefits.

4 Conclusions

The reform of energy subsidies in MENA remains an economically and politically delicate task, one from which many of the region's governments still shy away, for several reasons. The Arab Spring has added a further, interesting variable to the region's energy subsidy dilemma, for it has instilled in many of the region's governments an even greater fear of the Arab street, including in countries that have remained largely unaffected by the political turmoil that has unfolded across the region since late 2010. Initially a complicating factor that has significantly delayed plans for energy pricing reform in the region since that turmoil began, the lessons of the Arab Spring could also provide an important underlying measurement against which governments can systematically reassess the way they spend national resources within their domestic economies, and a way of both the poor and the middle class receiving a better deal than has been offered in the past.[27]

27 Some recent, country-focused papers have started to explore various avenues for change (Kandil, 2010; Verme et al. 2014; World Bank, 2011). Verme et al. (2014) specifically model the effect a further subsidy reduction, combined with a universal cash grant, could have on poverty levels in Morocco.

In the short term, however, rather than questions of wider social justice, the energy subsidy reform agenda in MENA will likely be dominated by questions of fiscal sustainability. The manner in which the fiscal burden of energy subsidies has spiralled out of control in recent years will render their reform increasingly unavoidable in a growing number of MENA economies—mainly energy importers and small-sized oil and gas producers such as Jordan, Lebanon, Egypt, Syria and Yemen. This is undoubtedly the most unsatisfactory path towards reform, and the long-term success of current policies—most of which have been implemented on an ad hoc basis under pressure from international lending organisations at times of severely compromised government capacity in a number of conflict-ridden MENA states—stands in marked contrast to the more desirable objective of comprehensively overhauling social security and equity issues throughout the MENA region. Striking the right balance between these parallel objectives will undoubtedly prove critical to determining the eventual success of energy subsidy reform, beyond mere fiscal savings for cash-strapped governments.

The importance of government credibility and capacity to mitigate the negative effects of energy subsidy reform on domestic customers has been made painfully clear in cases where energy price reforms have led to counterproductive outcomes, which has been the case—for example—in Yemen. The Yemeni case, as well as positive examples of reform efforts in countries such as Jordan, Morocco, Egypt and Iran, suggests that it is better to reform energy subsidies before a political or economic crisis point is reached. The fiscal discipline required for such endeavours may still prevent many MENA governments from initiating such comprehensive fiscal reform efforts proactively, and without immediate pressure from international lending bodies. In the medium and long terms, however, rationalising the way in which energy and fiscal resources are spent domestically will become an ever more critical element in ensuring the political and economic stability that these states ultimately seek.

The Iranian example is an important one, as it has demonstrated that a reform of domestic energy pricing can be economically and politically feasible for large oil and gas producers. Iran's unique features—including a large, heterogeneous population and geography, relatively large gaps between rich and poor, and additional complicating factors such as the presence of intensifying international sanctions—further strengthen the country's experience as a case in point. Many of the Gulf's other oil and gas producers—wealthy both in absolute and per capita terms—are equipped with even more powerful fiscal resources with which to enact the necessary mitigation measures to ensure a more rational use of their valuable oil and gas resources over the long term. In this context, the UAE's August 2015 move to deregulate domestic fuel prices sends an encouraging message in view both of the consistency with which the reform has been carried out, and the complete absence of any political turmoil during the first round of gasoline price increases (of up to almost 25 per cent) (The National, 2015). In view of the need for many more of the region's governments to accommodate the rising economic and political aspirations of their populations (which are becoming increasingly younger and better educated), the reform of energy pricing mechanisms, together with the provision of more effectively targeted benefits for their citizens, should arguably be an urgent priority for many MENA countries.

References

ABB (2014) *The State of Global Energy Efficiency. Global and Sectoral Energy Efficiency Trends*, Researched and written by Enerdata, ABB Ltd, www.abb-energyefficiency.com/assets/documents-download/ABB-Trends-in-global-energy-efficiency-2013.pdf (accessed on January 2015).

Abdih, Y., P. Lopez-Murphy, A. Roitman and R. Sahay (2010) *The Cyclicality of Fiscal Policy in the Middle East and Central Asia: Is the Current Crisis Different?*, IMF Working Paper No. 10/68, March, http://www.imf.org/external/pubs/ft/wp/2010/wp1068.pdf (accessed on 22 March 2016).

Abdullah, K. (2014) *Army breaks up protests as Yemen raises fuel prices*, Reuters, 30 July, http://uk.reuters.com/article/uk-yemen-budget-subsidies-idUKKBN0FZ1F020140730 (accessed on 22 March 2016).

Agueniou, S. (2013) 'Comment fonctionnera l'indexation des prix des produits pétroliers', *La Vie Éco*, 16 September (Casablanca: La Vie Eco Press) www.lavieeco.com/news/economie/comment-fonctionnera-l-indexation-des-prix-des-produits-petroliers-26546.html (accessed on September 2014).

Al Bawaba (2014) 'Ra'is al-wuzara' al-masri juhawilu tabrira ziadah asa'ar al-wuqud' ('Egyptian Prime Minister tries to justify fuel price rise', in Arabic), *Al Bawaba*, 5 July (Amman: Al Bawaba Middle East Limited).

Al-Khatteeb, L. and Istepanian, H. (2015) Turn a Light On: Electricity Sector Reform in Iraq. (Washinton DC: The Brookings Institution) Retrieved from http://www.brookings.edu/~/media/research/files/papers/2015/03/18-electricity-sector-reform-iraq-alkhatteeb-istepanian/alkhatteeb-istepanian-english-pdf.pdf (accessed on August 2015).

Al-Saud, Prince Abdulaziz Bin Salman (2014) 'A brief on Saudi Arabia's Energy Efficiency Program (SEEP)', *Oxford Energy Forum*, Issue 96, May, 4 (Oxford: The Oxford Institute for Energy Studies) https://www.oxfordenergy.org/wpcms/wp-content/uploads/2014/06/OEF-96.pdf (accessed on 21 March 2016).

Alderman, H. (2002) *Subsidies as a Social Safety Net: Effectiveness and Challenges*, Social Protection Discussion Paper Series, 0224 (Washington, DC: World Bank), http://siteresources.worldbank.org/SOCIALPROTECTION/Resources/SP-Discussion-papers/Safety-Nets-DP/0224.pdf (accessed on 22 March 2016).

Algerie DZ (2008) 'Contrebande d'essence entre l'Algérie et le Maroc', Algerie DZ, 2 July, http://www.algerie-dz.com/article14360.html (accessed on 22 March 2016).

Amuzegar, J. (2012) 'Iran's Subsidies Reform: A Year Later', *Middle East Economic Survey*, 30 January (Cyprus: Middle East Petroleum and Economic Publications).

Arab Times (2011) 'Subsidized fuel smuggling costs Kuwait KD 245m yearly', *Arab Times*, 17 November, (Kuwait: Arab Times).

Argus (2013a) 'Iran fuel subsidies under new scrutiny', *Petroleum Argus*, 28 October.

Argus (2013b) 'Iran oil industry feels pinch of subsidy reforms', *Petroleum Argus*, 19 November.

Ballong, S. (2010) 'Carburant: vers la fin des subventions', *Jeune Afrique*, 13 July (Paris: Jeune Afrique).

Breisinger, C., W. Engelke and O. Ecker (2011) *Petroleum Subsidies in Yemen: Leveraging Reform for Development*, IFPRI Discussion Paper 01071 (Washington, DC: IFPRI), March, http://citeseerx.ist.psu.edu/viewdoc/download?doi=10.1.1.226.7675&rep=rep1&type=pdf (accessed on 22 March 2016).

Bressand, F., D. Farrell, P. Haas, F. Morin, S. Nyquist, J. Remes, S. Roemer, M. Rogers, J. Rosenfeld and J. Woetzel (2007) *Curbing Global Energy Demand Growth: The Energy Productivity Opportunity*, McKinsey Global Institute, May, p. 15, http://www.mckinsey.com/~/media/McKinsey/Business%20Functions/Sustainability%20and%20Resource%20Productivity/Our%20Insights/Curbing%20global%20energy%20demand%20growth/MGI_Curbing_Global_Energy_Demand_full_report.ashx (Accessed on 22 March 2016).

Clements, B.J., S. Gupta and H.-S. Jung (2003) *Real and distributive effects of petroleum price liberalization: The case of Indonesia*, IMF Working Papers 03/204, (Washington, DC: International Monetary Fund), https://www.imf.org/external/pubs/cat/longres.aspx?sk=16882.0 (Accessed on 22 March 2016).

Coady, D., I. Parry, L. Sears, and B. Shang (2015), How Large Are Global Energy Subsidies?, WP15/105, (Washington DC: International Monetary Fund), https://www.imf.org/external/pubs/ft/wp/2015/wp15105.pdf (Accessed on 21 March 2016).

Coady, D.P., M. El Said, R. Gillingham, K. Kpodar, P. Medas and D. Newhouse (2006) *The Magnitude and Distribution of Fuel Subsidies: Evidence from Bolivia, Ghana, Jordan, Mali, and Sri Lanka*, IMF Working Paper, 06/247 (Washington, DC: International Monetary Fund), https://www.imf.org/external/pubs/ft/wp/2006/wp06247.pdf (Accessed on 21 March 2016).

Collier, P. and A. Hoeffler (1998) *On economic causes of civil war*, Oxford Economic Papers, 50 (1998), pp. 563–573, DOI: 10.1093/oep/50.4.563.

Darbouche, H. and R. Mabro (2011) 'Egypt's Natural Gas Market: So Far So Good But Where To Next?' in Fattouh, B. and J. Stern (eds.) *Natural Gas Markets in the Middle East and North Africa* (Oxford: Oxford University Press), pp. 125–161.

Daya A. and D. El Baltaji (2012) *Saudi Arabia May Become Oil Importer by 2030, Citigroup Says*, (New York: Bloomberg), 4 September, http://www.bloomberg.com/news/articles/2012-09-04/saudi-arabia-may-become-oil-importer-by-2030-citigroup-says-1- (accessed on 22 March 2016).

de Moor, A. and P. Calamai (1997) *Subsidizing Unsustainable Development*, Earth Council and the Institute for Research on Public Expenditure, p. 1., www.cbd.int/doc/case-studies/inc/cs-inc-earthcouncil-unsustainable-en.pdf (accessed on July 2012).

EIA (US Energy Information Administration) (2011) *International Energy Outlook 2011* (Washington DC: US Energy Information Agency).

El-Katiri, L. (2013a) 'The Guardian State and its Economic Development Model', *Journal of Development Studies*, 26 November, pp. 22–34, DOI: 10.1080/00220388.2013.849340.

El-Katiri, L. (2013b) *Energy Sustainability in the Gulf: The Why and the How*, OIES Paper MEP4, (Oxford: The Oxford Institute for Energy Studies) http://www.oxfordenergy.org/wpcms/wp-content/uploads/2013/03/MEP_4.pdf (accessed on July 2015).

El-Katiri, L. (2014) *A Roadmap for Renewable Energy in the Middle East and North Africa*, OIES Paper, MEP 6 (Oxford: The Oxford Institute for Energy Studies) http://www.oxfordenergy.org/wpcms/wp-content/uploads/2014/01/MEP-6.pdf (accessed on July 2015).

El-Katiri, L. and B. Fattouh (2011) *Energy Poverty in the Arab World: The Case of Yemen*, MEP 1 (Oxford: The Oxford Institute for Energy Studies) http://www.oxfordenergy.org/wpcms/wp-content/uploads/2011/08/MEP_1.pdf (accessed on July 2015).

El-Katiri, L. and M. Husain (2014) *Prospects for Renewable Energy in GCC States: Opportunities and the Need for Reform*, OIES Research Paper MEP 10 (Oxford: The Oxford Institute for Energy Studies) http://www.oxfordenergy.org/wpcms/wp-content/uploads/2014/09/MEP-10.pdf (accessed on July 2015).

El-Katiri, L., B. Fattouh and P. Segal (2012) 'Anatomy of an Oil-Based Welfare State: Rent Distribution in Kuwait' in: Held, D. and Coates-Ulrichsen, K. (eds.) *The Transformation of the Gulf States: Politics, Economics and the Global Order* (London: Routledge), pp. 165–186.

El-Katiri, M. (2013) *The Future of the Arab Gulf Monarchies in the Age of Uncertainties*, (Carlisle, Pennsylvania: U.S. Army War College Strategic Studies Institute), June.

Energy Compass (2011) 'Iran: Biting the Bullet', *Energy Compass*, 14 January.

Erbil, N. (2011) *Is Fiscal Policy Procyclical in Developing Oil-Producing Countries?*, IMF Working Paper, WP/11/171 (Washington DC: International Monetary Fund) https://www.imf.org/external/pubs/ft/wp/2011/wp11171.pdf (accessed on 22 March 2016).

Fahim, K. (2014) 'Egypt Cuts Tax Breaks for Fuel; Few Protest', *New York Times*, 17 July, http://www.nytimes.com/2014/07/18/world/middleeast/egypt-cuts-tax-breaks-for-fuel-few-protest.html?_r=0 (accessed on 22 March 2016).

Fattouh, B and L. Mahadeva (2014) *Price Reform in Kuwait's Electricity and Water Sector—Assessing the Net Benefits in the Presence of Congestion*, OIES Paper, MEP 9, (Oxford: The Oxford Institute for Energy Studies) http://www.oxfordenergy.org/wpcms/wp-content/uploads/2014/04/MEP-9.pdf (accessed on May 2015).

Fattouh, B. and L. El-Katiri (2012a) *Energy and Arab Economic Development*, Arab Human Development Report Research Paper Series, (New York: UNDP Regional Bureau for Arab States), http://www.arab-hdr.org/publications/other/ahdrps/ENG FattouhKatiriV2.pdf (accessed on May 2015).

Fattouh, B. and L. El-Katiri (2012b) *Energy Subsidies in the Arab World*, Arab Human Development Report Research Paper, (New York: UNDP Regional Bureau for Arab States) http://www.arab-hdr.org/publications/other/ahdrps/Energy%20Subsidies-Bassam%20Fattouh-Final.pdf (accessed on May 2015).

Fattouh, B. and L. El-Katiri (2013) 'Energy Subsidies in the Middle East and North Africa' *Energy Strategy Reviews*, 2:1, June 2013, pp. 108–115, DOI: 10.1016/j.esr.2012.11.004.

France 24 (2011) 'La contrebande vers la Libye assèche les pompes à essence dans l'Est algérien', (Paris: France 24), 11 August, http://observers.france24.com/fr/20110810-contrebande-vers-libye-asseche-pompes-essence-est-algerien-tebessa-penurie-essence-tunisie (accessed on 22 March 2016).

Gause F.G. III (2013) *Kings for All Seasons: How the Middle East's Monarchies Survived the Arab Spring*, Brookings Doha Center Analysis Paper (Washington DC and Doha: The Brookings Institution), http://www.brookings.edu/~/media/Research/Files/Papers/2013/09/24-resilience-arab-monarchies-gause/Resilience-Arab-Monarchies_English.pdf?la=en (accessed on 22 March 2016).

Ghobari, M. and El Gamal, R. (2014) *Army breaks up protests as Yemen raises fuel prices*, Reuters, 30 July, http://uk.reuters.com/article/uk-yemen-budget-subsidies-idUKKBN0FZ1F020140730 (accessed on 22 March 2016).

Guillaume, D., R. Zytek, and M.R. Farzin (2011) *Iran–The Chronicles of the Subsidy Reform*, IMF Working Paper, WP/11/167, (Washington, DC: International Monetary Fund), https://www.imf.org/external/pubs/ft/wp/2011/wp11167.pdf (accessed on 22 March 2016).

Gupta, S., B. Clements, K. Fletcher and G. Inchauste (2003) 'Issues in Domestic Petroleum Pricing in Oil-Producing Countries', in Davis, J., R. Ossowski and A. Fedelino (eds.), *Fiscal Policy Formulation and Implementation in Oil-Producing Countries* (Washington, DC: International Monetary Fund).

Hope, E. and B. Singh (1999) *Energy Price Increases in Developing Countries: Case Studies of Colombia, Ghana, Indonesia, Malaysia, Turkey, and Zimbabwe*, World Bank Policy Research Working Paper No. 1442 (Washington DC: World Bank), DOI: 10.1596/1813-9450-1442.

Ibrahim, L. (2011) *Syria to Raise Fuel-Oil Price to Limit Smuggling*, (New York: Bloomberg), 10 August, http://www.bloomberg.com/news/articles/2011-08-10/syria-to-raise-fuel-oil-price-to-limit-smuggling-thawra-says (accessed on 22 March 2016).

IEA (International Energy Agency) (2011) *World Energy Outlook 2011* (Paris: OECD/IEA), 696 p, http://www.worldenergyoutlook.org/weo2011/ (accessed on 22 March 2016).

IEA, OPEC, OECD, and World Bank. (2010) *Analysis of the Scope of Energy Subsidies and Suggestions for the G-20 Initiative*, Joint Report prepared for submission to the G-20 Summit Meeting Toronto (Canada), June 2010, https://www.oecd.org/env/49090716.pdf (accessed on 22 March 2016).

IMF (International Monetary Fund) (2013) *Regional economic outlook: Asia and Pacific* (Washington, DC: International Monetary Fund).

IMF (International Monetary Fund) (2014a) *Jordan. Article IV Consultation, Third and Forth Review under the Stand-By Arrangement, Request for Wavers of Non-observance of Performance Criterion and Applicability of Performance Criterion—Staff Report; Press Releases; and Statement by the Executive Director for Jordan.* IMF Country Report No. 14/152, June 2014, https://www.imf.org/external/pubs/ft/scr/2014/cr14152.pdf (accessed on 22 March 2016).

IMF (International Monetary Fund) (2014b) Morocco. *Article IV Consultation Staff Report; Press Releases; and Statement by the Executive Director for Morocco.* IMF Country Report No.14/65, March, https://www.imf.org/external/pubs/ft/scr/2014/cr1465.pdf (Accessed on 22 March 2016).

IOD (International Oil Daily) (2011) 'Price Hikes Squeeze Iranian Gasoline Demand', *International Oil Daily*, (New York, London: Energy Intelligence Group) 17 January.

Kaminsky, G.L., C.M. Reinhart and C.A. Vegh (2004) *When it rains, it pours: Pro-Cyclical Capital Flows and Macroeconomic Policies*, Working Paper 10780, National Bureau of Economic Research, www.nber.org/papers/w10780.pdf (accessed on September 2014).

Kandil, M. (2010) *The Subsidy System in Egypt: Alternatives for Reform*, Policy Viewpoint Series, (Cairo: The Egyptian Centre for Economic Studies (ECES)), December, http://www.eces.org.eg/MediaFiles/Uploaded_Files/%7B10D14532-9640-4DCE-A76E-EBAD724A51D4%7D_PVP25-Eng.pdf (accessed on 22 March 2016).

Lahn, G. and P. Stevens (2011) *Burning Oil to Keep Cool. The Hidden Energy Crisis in Saudi Arabia*, (London: The Royal Institute of International Affairs, Chatham House), December, https://www.chathamhouse.org/sites/files/chathamhouse/public/Research/Energy,%20Environment%20and%20Development/1211pr_lahn_stevens.pdf (accessed on 22 March 2016).

Lane, P.R. (2003) 'The cyclical behaviour of fiscal policy: evidence from the OECD', *Journal of Public Economics*, 87(12), pp. 2661–2675, DOI: 10.1016/S0047-2727(02)00075-0.

Luciani, G. (1987) 'Allocative versus production states: a theoretical framework' in Beblawi, H. and G. Luciani (eds.) *The Rentier State* (London: Croom Helm), pp. 63–82.

MEES (Middle East Economic Survey) (2011) 'GCC Endorses King 'Abd Allah's Call To Achieve Union' *Middle East Economic Survey*, 26 December.

MEES (Middle East Economic Survey) (2012a) 'Arab Fund Chief Pledges Continued Support In Wake Of Arab Spring' *Middle East Economic Survey*, 16 April.

MEES (Middle East Economic Survey) (2012b) 'Iran Suspends Subsidy Cuts, Slashes Budget', *Middle East Economic Survey*, 2 October.

MEES (Middle East Economic Survey) (2012c) 'Jordan's Energy Price Hike Triggers Protests', *Middle East Economic Survey*, 16 November.

MEES (Middle East Economic Survey) (2013) 'GCC Aid Flows To Bahrain And Morocco' *Middle East Economic Survey*, 1 March.

MEES (Middle East Economic Survey) (2014a) 'Egypt looks to Reform to Attract Investment, Boost Growth', *Middle East Economic Survey*, 18 July.

MEES (Middle East Economic Survey) (2014b) 'Egypt Price Hikes Push Inflation Rate to 10.6%', *Middle East Economic Survey*, 15 August.

MEES (Middle East Economic Survey) (2014c) 'Iran Advances Subsidies Reform' *Middle East Economic Survey*, 28 February, 57(09).

MEES (Middle East Economic Survey) (2014d) 'Iran Kicks Off Phase II Of Subsidy Reform', *Middle East Economic Survey*, 25 April.

MEES (Middle East Economic Survey) (2014e) 'Morocco Bags IMF, EU, Qatari Cash', *Middle East Economic Survey*, 1 August.

MEES (Middle East Economic Survey) (2014f) 'Morocco Targets Further Subsidy Reductions' *Middle East Economic Survey*, 21 March.

MEES (Middle East Economic Survey) (2014g) 'Yemen Mired In Fuel Subsidy Dilemma', *Middle East Economic Survey*, 23 May.

MEES (Middle East Economic Survey) (2014h) 'Yemen Oil Minister Replaced As Fuel Crisis Deepens' *Middle East Economic Survey*, 20 June.

MEES (Middle East Economic Survey) (2014i) 'Yemen: 2014 Budget Looks To Patch Holes In Violence-Fueled Revenue Slump', *Middle East Economic Survey*, 24 January.

MEES (Middle East Economic Survey) (2015) 'Egypt Lays Out Further Subsidy Cuts For 2015–16 But Overall Spending Up', *Middle East Economic Survey*, 26 June.

Mubashir Misr (2014) 'Al-Sisi jubariru ziadat al-asa'ar … wa juhadhiru min al-irhab' ('Al-Sisi justifies fuel price rise… and warns of terrorism', in Arabic), *Mubashir Misr*, 7 July.

Rashwan, N. (2014) 'Voices from Egypt: How will increased energy prices affect you?', *Middle East Eye*, 6 July, http://www.middleeasteye.net/news/voices-egypt-how-will-new-energy-prices-affect-you-1738307315 (accessed on 22 March 2016).

Royaume du Maroc (2013) Bulletin Officiel du 5 septembre, No. 1686, http://81.192.52.100/BO/FR/2013/BO_6184_Fr.pdf (accessed on September 2014).

Saeed, A. (2014) 'Ministry of Oil: Fuel subsidy partially to blame for shortage', *Yemen Times*, 6 May.

Saleh, H. (2014) 'Egypt sharply raises energy prices', *Financial Times*, 5 July, https://next.ft.com/content/08576d00-043f-11e4-ab6a-00144feab7de (Accessed on 22 March 2016).

Sdralevich, C., R. Sab, Y. Zouhar and G. Albertin (2014) *Subsidy Reform in the Middle East and North Africa Recent Progress and Challenges Ahead*, IMF Middle East and Central Asia Department (Washington, DC: International Monetary Fund), http://www.imf.org/external/pubs/ft/dp/2014/1403mcd.pdf (accesssed on 22 March 2016).

Security Council (2014) *Yemen: October 2014 Monthly Forecast*, UN Security Council Report, 30 September, http://www.securitycouncilreport.org/monthly-forecast/2014-10/yemen_11.php (accessed on October 2014).

Tabatabai, H. (2011) *The Basic Income Road to Reforming Iran's Price Subsidies*, Basic Income Studies, 6:1, pp. 1–24.

The National (2015) 'UAE fuel prices for August announced' *The National*, 28 July, (Abu Dhabi: The National) http://www.thenational.ae/uae/transport/uae-fuel-prices-for-august-announced (accessed on August 2015).

Verme, P., K. El-Massnaoui and A. Araar (2014) *Reforming Subsidies in Morocco*, Economic Premise 134 (Washington DC: World Bank), http://www-wds.worldbank.org/external/default/WDSContentServer/WDSP/IB/2014/02/06/000333037_20140206144354/Rendered/PDF/845160BRI00B0x382123B00PUBLIC00EP134.pdf (accessed on 22 March 2016).

Wahab, B.A. (2006) 'How Iraqi Oil Smuggling Greases Violence', *Middle East Quarterly*, Fall 2006, pp. 53–9, http://www.meforum.org/1020/how-iraqi-oil-smuggling-greases-violence (accessed on 22 March 2016).

World Bank (2005) *Egypt—Towards a More Effective Social Policy: Subsidies and Social Safety Net*, Social and Economic Development Group, NO. 33550-EG, 16 December, (Washington DC: World Bank). http://siteresources.worldbank.org/INTPSIA/Resources/490023-1171551075650/Egypt_PSIA_121605.pdf (accessed on 22 March 2016).

World Bank (2008) *Republic of Lebanon. Electricity Sector Public Expenditure Review*, Report No. 41421-LB (Washington DC: World Bank), http://siteresources.worldbank.org/INTMNAREGTOPENERGY/Resources/LebanonElectricityPER.pdf (accessed on 22 March 2016).

World Bank (2011) *Electricity Subsidies and Household Welfare in Jordan: Can households afford to pay for the budget crisis?*, Background paper for the Jordan Poverty Reduction Strategy (Amman: Hashemite Kingdom of Jordan) http://inform.gov.jo/LinkClick.aspx?fileticket=srsTqsT1lQM%3d&portalid=0&language=en-US (accessed on 22 March 2016).

World Bank (2014) Database of World Development Indicators, (Washington DC: World Bank), http://data.worldbank.org/data-catalog/world-development-indicators (accessed on January 2015).

CHAPTER 5

The Political Economy of Distribution in the Middle East: Is There Scope for a New Social Contract?

Steffen Hertog

Abstract

The majority of Arab political economies are characterised by a peculiar distributional system built on excess public employment and wide-ranging energy subsidies—features that exist in other developing countries but are more pronounced in the Arab world. This chapter provides an overview of this distribution regime, develops hypotheses regarding its historical origin, and analyses the political and economic distortions it creates. It builds on a wide range of literature on energy subsidies and on recent publications on (the weakness of) conventional social safety regimes. In its comparative analysis of public employment, it mostly relies on primary data.

The article proposes that the current distribution regime not only benefits insiders and creates multiple segmentation of labour markets, it also weakens links between business and citizens. There follows a discussion of the outlines of an alternative social contract based on less distortionary welfare systems, notably direct cash grants for citizens. In this, the text again draws on a well-developed literature on energy subsidy reform and on potential strategies for compensating for energy price increases. The article's main contribution to the literature lies in its analysis of public employment reform and its labour market implications and of the wider political economy implications of distributional reform. It spells out the potential impact of a more inclusive and less distortionary distribution and welfare regime on social stratification and on relations between state, business and citizens.

1 Introduction

If there ever was a social contract in the Arab world's low- to mid-income countries, it has frayed badly in recent decades—and, as the uprisings that have taken place since 2011 have shown, has in some cases altogether broken down. This is not because regimes have not tried to provide for their citizens: despite relatively low levels of economic development, most Arab countries have developed large ambitions to distribute resources among their populations in the

DOI 10.1163/9789004336452_006

post-second World War era. Compared to other economies in the developing world, Arab countries stand out in particular regarding the scale of government employment and the provision of subsidies, notably but not only on energy products.

This distributional regime has however proven fiscally unsustainable, economically distortionary and, most importantly, ineffective in reducing income inequalities as it has created insider–outsider dynamics and benefited the privileged most of all. It did not prevent socio-economic grievances from spreading in the run-up to 2011—and yet, as a first reaction to the regional uprisings, most regimes increased patronage through public employment or subsidies even more. Some Arab governments have recently tackled subsidy reforms in a piecemeal fashion. Wider-reaching thinking about which new type of social contract might replace the unfair and unsustainable old distributional regimes is lacking however. In fact, there is little encompassing analysis of the existing regimes of wealth (re)distribution to start with.

To contribute to filling these gaps, this contribution will provide an overview of the current distribution regime in core Arab countries in the Maghreb and the Mashreq, and will then discuss potential policy alternatives, with a particular focus on a regime of direct, unconditional cash grants. In the description of the status quo and the analysis of the distortions it creates, the text draws on a variety of detailed studies on Middle East and North Africa (MENA) energy subsidies and on more recent work on (the weakness of) conventional social safety regimes.

There is less literature on public employment, and no literature pulling the different aspects of distribution together in a comparative fashion. The political economy implications of current distribution patterns in particular have gone unanalysed; this contribution will propose that the current regime not only benefits insiders and creates multiple segmentation of labour markets, it also weakens links between business and citizens. A high-level descriptive overview and political economy analysis of the Arab welfare regime is hence the first main objective of the contribution.

In its subsequent discussion of an alternative social contract, the chapter can again draw on a well-developed literature on energy subsidy reform and on potential strategies for compensating for energy price increases, including cash grants. There is less literature on public employment reform and its economic implications, and practically nothing on the wider political economy implications of distributional reform. The chapter's second core contribution will hence lie in the latter area, focusing on the potential impact of a more inclusive and less distortionary distributional and welfare regime on social stratification, and on relations between state, business and citizens.

The contribution primarily focuses on non-Gulf Arab countries in the Maghreb and the Mashreq.[1] I have written a separate paper on rent distribution in high-rent countries around the world, of which the GCC monarchies are leading representatives (Hertog, 2014b). Many of the arguments presented here, however, apply in a modified fashion also to the Gulf Cooperation Council (GCC) countries; notably those on economic distortions, labour market segmentation and cash grants as a viable distributional alternative. While the fiscal situation is less pressing for GCC members, and there is correspondingly more leeway to experiment with alternative distribution regimes, the scale of subsidies and government over-employment and the resulting distortions are if anything more dramatic.

2 Current Distributional Structures

2.1 *Public Employment*

Public employment has been a critical tool of wealth distribution across the Arab world since independence. Populist-authoritarian republics in particular—such as Egypt, Syria and Algeria—have historically tried to guarantee government jobs for all nationals. This ambition has been scaled back since the 1970s, as the share of public employment has been stagnating and real public sector wages have declined. Yet in international comparison, most countries on which we have data retain a quite high proportion of government jobs to total employment (Figure 5.1).

Morocco is a conspicuous exception and is also, as we will see, the Arab country with the smallest subsidy provision. Among core Maghreb and Mashreq countries, Morocco stands out in having been less ambitious in both distribution and public service provision and in relying more strongly on private-driven development. As Figure 5.2 shows, however, public salaries represent a large share of the gross domestic product (GDP), which seems to reflect a concentration of resources on smaller cadres of better-paid public servants. In Egypt, by contrast, salaries are spread thin among a much larger government workforce. Altogether, however, Arab public salary expenditure—just like

1 The peripheral cases—Djibouti, Mauritania and Sudan—are not included systematically as their distributional regimes and histories of state-building differ from those of more central Arab countries. Similarly, Lebanon, although located in the middle of the Arab world, is included mostly as a contrast case that has not seen the ambitious state-building of other core Arab regimes.

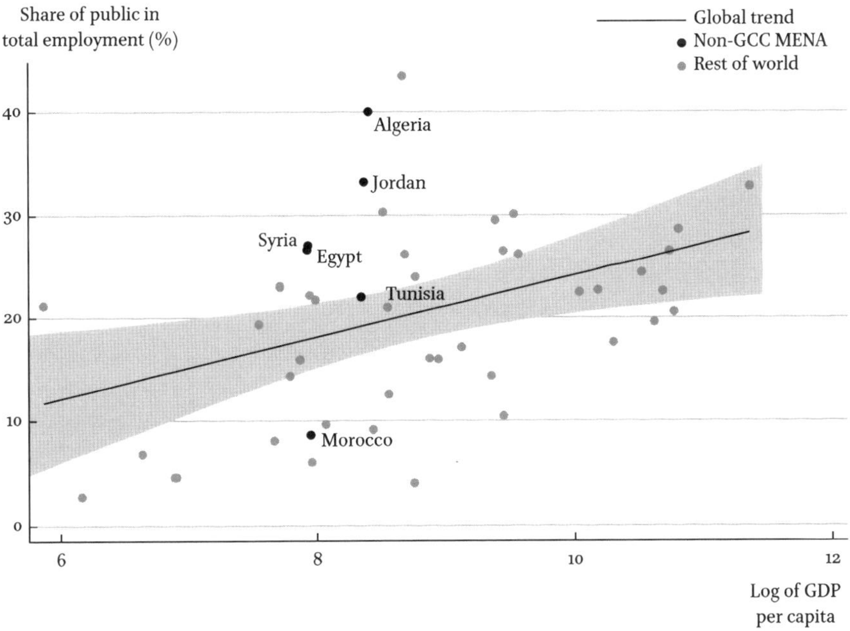

FIGURE 5.1 *Public employment shares in international comparison*
SOURCE: AUTHOR, CALCULATED FROM ILO, WORLD BANK DEVELOPMENT INDICATORS, AND NATIONAL DATA.
Note: GCC countries are left out of this graph, as the large-scale presence of foreign workers in the private sector makes a direct comparison of private and public employment problematic. We know however that in all cases bar Bahrain, more than half of citizens are employed by the respective governments (Hertog, 2014a).

employment numbers—lies above international averages (the exception of Lebanon in Figure 5.2 will be briefly discussed below).[2]

Although available data are patchy, in the cases where we have data, salaries in government, long-term stagnation notwithstanding, typically are higher than in the private sector, especially compared to the informal sector (Bodor, 2010; Yousef, 2004).[3]

2 In Egypt, the relatively low numbers might also be explained by the lack of accounting for employment costs in state-owned enterprises and potentially in the large military sector. In GCC countries, the low shares in GDP are an artefact of the large share of the oil sector in GDP (where few are employed); their share in non-oil GDP is much higher.

3 Another piece of evidence comes from the 2010–14 wave of the World Values Survey, which included 12 Arab countries, and which asked respondents both about their income and their employment status. While government employment appears to be on average better paid all over the world, WVS data shows that the average gap in the Arab world is twice as large as elsewhere.

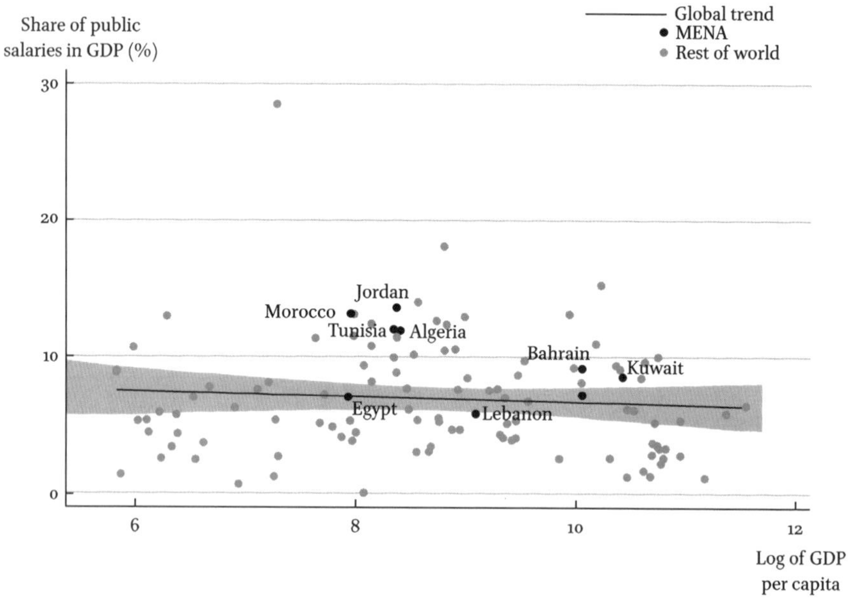

FIGURE 5.2 *Public salary expenses in international comparison*
SOURCE: AUTHOR, CALCULATED FROM ILO AND WORLD BANK DEVELOPMENT INDICATORS DATA.

Figure 5.3 shows that government subsidies and transfers, to the extent that they are recorded as government expenditure, also tend to be somewhat above the average for countries with similar incomes.

As accounting rules for subsidies are often unclear, and energy subsidies in particular are often under-reported, one can dispute how meaningful these figures are (energy subsidies are discussed separately below using International Monetary Fund (IMF) data). It is clear however that this budget item for the most part does not comprise conventional social safety systems in MENA, the volume of which is only estimated to be 0.7 per cent of GDP (Levin, Silva, and Morgandi, 2012).

2.2 *Subsidies*

While information on public employment is patchy, more research has been carried out on subsidies in the Arab world, particularly on energy subsidies. With energy subsidies that are on average 12 times higher than in the world at large according to 2011 IMF estimates, the region stands out even more—and this includes energy importers, where subsidies have a direct fiscal impact rather than the harder to define opportunity costs of energy subsidies for energy

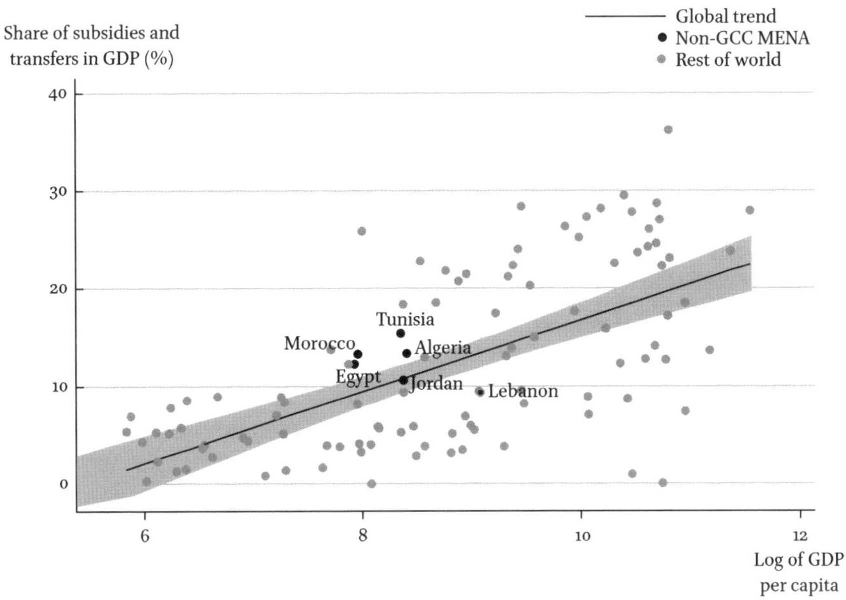

FIGURE 5.3 *Government subsidies and transfers in international comparison*
SOURCE: AUTHOR, CALCULATED FROM WORLD BANK DEVELOPMENT INDICATORS DATA.

exporters (Luciani, 2012). Among the core Arab countries, Morocco alone has managed to reduce energy subsidies to a fiscally manageable level (Figure 5.4). Although the 2011 figures are inflated by the high international energy prices of that year, Arab countries continue to devote much more resources to the provision of cheap energy than do most other developing countries.

The subsidies consist of cheap transport fuel, electricity and gas. Average diesel prices in MENA are lower than in any other region of the world and only half of US prices. Electricity subsidies average 2 per cent of GDP (Sdralevich et al., 2014).

Most MENA governments also continue to provide food subsidies that represent an average of almost 1 per cent of GDP and are considerably higher in formerly 'progressive' republics like Tunisia, Algeria, Egypt, Syria and Iraq.

2.3 *Historical Roots*

While this chapter cannot engage with the historical roots of Arab distributional systems in any detail, some preliminary remarks are in order: First, the historical protagonists of mass employment and subsidisation arguably were the Arab nationalist republics, whose populist-authoritarian leaders aspired to the creation of a new middle class and the removal of old bourgeois elites, and

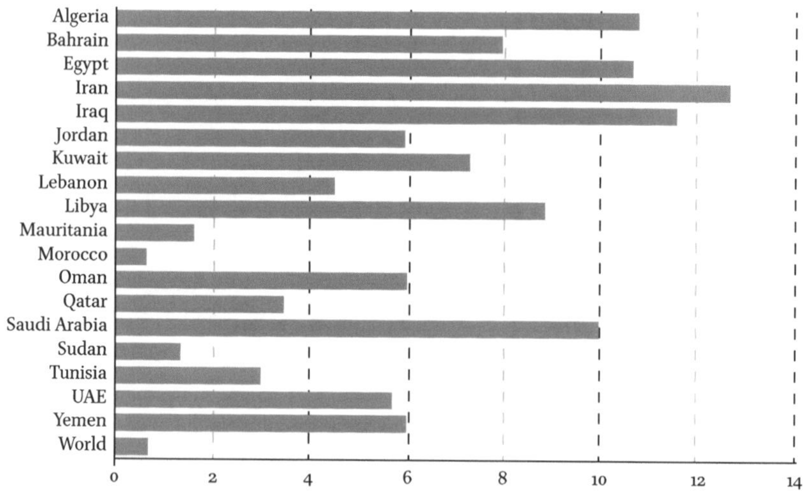

FIGURE 5.4 *Pre-tax energy subsidies as % of* GDP *in 2011*
SOURCE: IMF, 2013B.

who tried to leverage the state apparatus as the main driver of economic development (Henry and Springborg, 2010; Heydemann, 1999; Richards and Waterbury, 2007). The heavy statist legacy of these republics remains visible in the aforementioned employment and subsidy statistics but also in the heavy and cumbersome bureaucratic penetration of the lives of citizens and businesses, as evidenced by international statistics on government effectiveness and ease of doing business.

The stronger commitment to food subsidies among republics in particular reflects an agenda of redistribution. It is noteworthy that while Tunisia started to shed its socialist ambitions from the 1960s on and has gone further in liberalising than its former nationalist republican peers, it too retains large food subsidies as a core 'socialist' legacy.

It is likely that the populist-distributional policies of the nationalist republics put pressure on other countries in the region to play catch-up. The ideological competition between Arab nationalism and conservative monarchism from the 1950s on (Kerr, 1965) forced monarchies to step up their own distributional efforts—a decision visible in the GCC countries' employment and subsidy policies, but also in similar policies in much poorer Jordan, which was positioned at the fulcrum of regional ideological competition for much of post-second Wold War Arab history. Morocco, as a more peripheral monarchy with deeper historical roots, appears to have been under less pressure to play catch-up.

The one republic that never quite embarked on a path of nationalist statebuilding is Lebanon (Henry and Springborg, 2010). Despite considerable energy subsidies, it is also the country with the smallest distributional footprint in the region. Its unusually weak statehood however contributed to its descent into a civil war in the 1970s that itself was shaped by the ideological and power rivalries of the region. At least in the classical period of ideological rivalry in the region from the 1950s to the 1970s, distributional state-building may have been a condition of regime survival.

The availability of both natural resource and strategic rents in the region did of course help states to engage in over-employment and, especially, provision of cheap energy. As the experience of other regions shows, however, rents do not automatically generate such structures: sub-Saharan African or South East Asian oil states for example have much lower levels of energy subsidies and tend to have smaller state apparatuses.

2.4 *Lack of Other Social Safety Mechanisms*

While public employment and subsidies are costly and distortionary, most Arab governments offer comparatively little by way of social security policies. This might be another legacy of authoritarian-populist state-building, in which elites saw direct state employment as a tool not only of distribution but also of reshaping and controlling society—an objective for which mundane policies like unemployment assistance and income support grants for the poor were less suited. The tangible nature of directly provided, subsidised goods might also make them more attractive to authoritarian rulers.

As mentioned above, non-contributory social safety programmes only amount to an average of 0.7 per cent of GDP across the Arab world (Levin, Silva, and Morgandi, 2012). Those few programmes that do exist are, moreover, remarkably ineffective: World Bank research shows that they fail to reach two-thirds of individuals in the poorest quintile, a coverage rate that is less than half the world average, including in regions not generally associated with generous welfare benefits, like Latin America or Central Asia.

As with subsidies, ineffective targeting means that a considerable share of social safety resources actually go to the non-poor.[4] In every one of the 11 Arab countries included in the World Bank study, the size of general food and fuel subsidies dwarfs that of social safety spending. It appears that in the Arab world, public employment and subsidies function as a substitute rather than a complement for conventional welfare tools. As we will see, the Arab approach to sharing wealth is as costly as it is ineffective in realising objectives of equity

4 'The average nonsubsidy SSN program in the region distributes only 23 percent of its total benefits to the bottom quintile, while the corresponding figure for the average comparator programs in Latin America and the Caribbean and in Eastern Europe and Central Asia is 59 percent'. (Levin, Silva, and Morgandi, 2012, xxiv).

and poverty alleviation. It also appears path-dependent, in the sense that early decisions to distribute resources through particular channels have—even if the political reasons for these decisions might now be obsolete—proven hard to reverse, while decisions to deepen the existing pattern of distribution are taken more easily.

2.5 *Distortionary Economic Impacts*

Because Arab distributional regimes involve in-kind distribution rather than distributing money as is the case with most modern social safety nets, their distortionary economic impact is particularly pronounced. To the extent that government employment is surplus to requirements—and there is much anecdotal evidence that some of it is—it takes human resources out of the private labour market where they might be more productive. Due to higher wages and shorter working hours, the general preference for government employment is widespread among Arab citizens. As Figure 5.5 shows, in every single Arab country polled by Gallup, the majority of respondents prefer government over private employment. As one might expect, private sector preference is relatively strongest in the least distributive states—Lebanon, Morocco and Sudan.

A preference for government employment, and government recruitment based on formal credentials, arguably lead to educational decisions that are suboptimal for the private labour market. While it has become a much more remote prospect for most young jobseekers, educational systems are still geared to preparing participants for government employment, with an excessive focus on tertiary education and on subjects of limited relevance for the private economy (Adams and Winthrop, 2015; World Bank, 2008). Figure 5.6 shows, for example, that—according to UNESCO statistics—a disproportionate share of Arab students study arts and humanities subjects. This is unusual in the content of developing economies and probably best explained as a legacy of public sector oriented 'credentialism', where the formal level of education matters more than the subject studied (Salehi-Isfahani, 2012). Public sector overemployment also creates overhead costs that arguably represent a deadweight loss to society.

Distortions in economic behaviour are even more obvious in the field of energy subsidies. IMF research shows that the energy intensity of economic output in the MENA region is not particularly high in global comparative terms (although it is higher among oil exporting countries). Different from most other world regions, however, energy intensity has stagnated over the last decade among MENA oil importers and has increased among oil exporters, while it has declined in all other regions bar Latin America, which itself has seen a commodities boom. Low energy prices hence give no incentives for

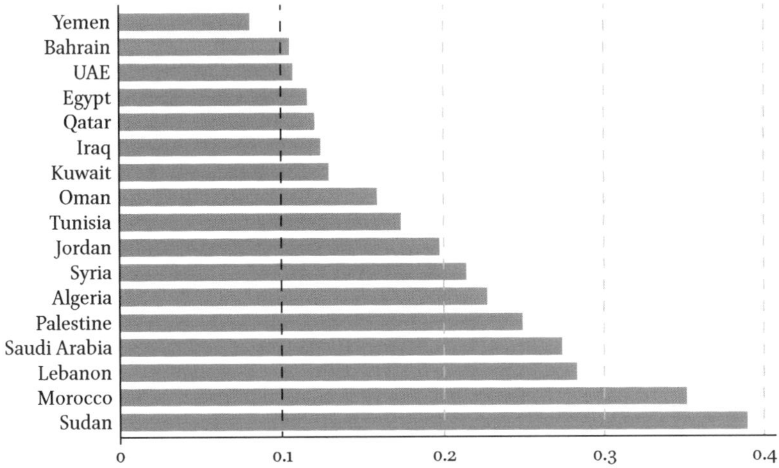

FIGURE 5.5 *Preference for government employment in the Arab region*
SOURCE: GALLUP/ISHAC DIWAN.
Note: Gallup poll, conducted in the Arab world in several waves, asking respondents whether for similar pay and conditions they would prefer to work for the government or private sector; 0 = preference for government, 1 = preference for private sector.

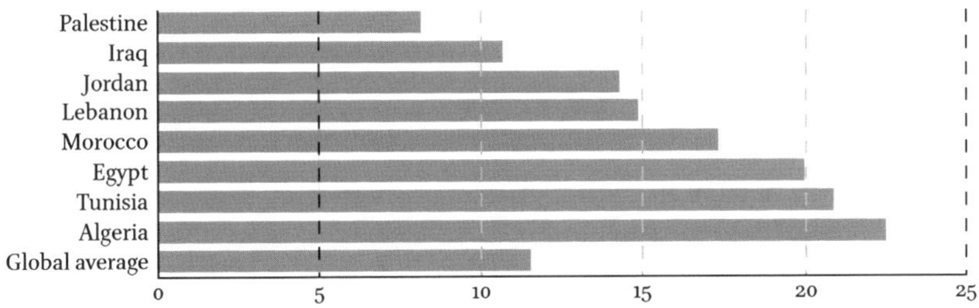

FIGURE 5.6 *Share of students in arts and humanities in select Arab countries*
SOURCE: UNESCO UIS DATA CENTRE (HTTP://DATA.UIS.UNESCO.ORG/)

energy conservation but instead lock in costly and increasingly unsustainable consumption structures. The IMF also documents the energy-intensive bias of Egyptian industry despite the fact that Egypt is a labour-surplus country; the IMF argues that low energy prices create a bias towards capital-intensive industries that fail to absorb the large numbers of jobseekers in the MENA region (Sdralevich et al., 2014, 23, 65).

Figures 5.7 and 5.8 show various countries' shifts in energy intensity from a longer perspective—from 1980 to 2010—with 2010 oil and gas rents per capita and year on the x axis. MENA countries are circled. We see that:

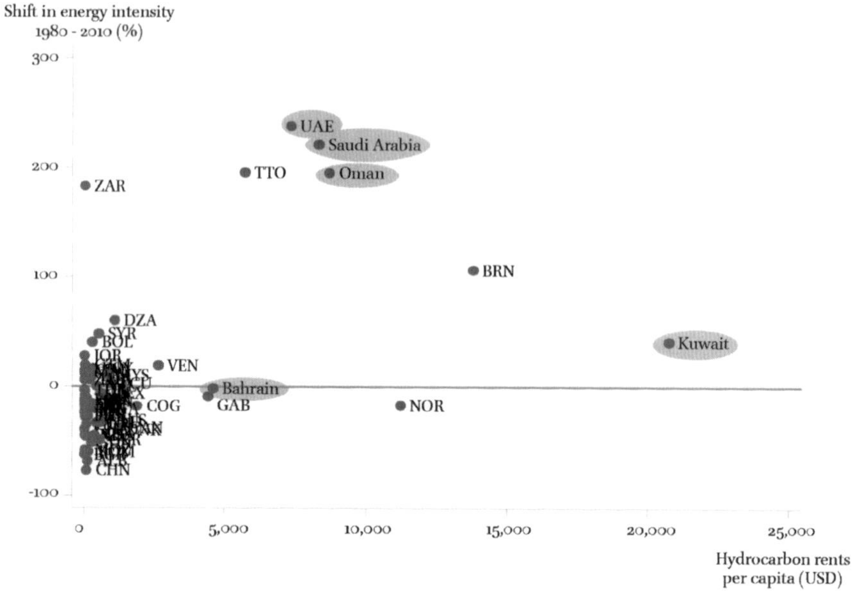

FIGURE 5.7 *Rents per capita and shifts in energy intensity (energy used per unit of* GDP*) 1980–2010*
SOURCE: AUTHOR, BASED ON WORLD DEVELOPMENT INDICATORS.

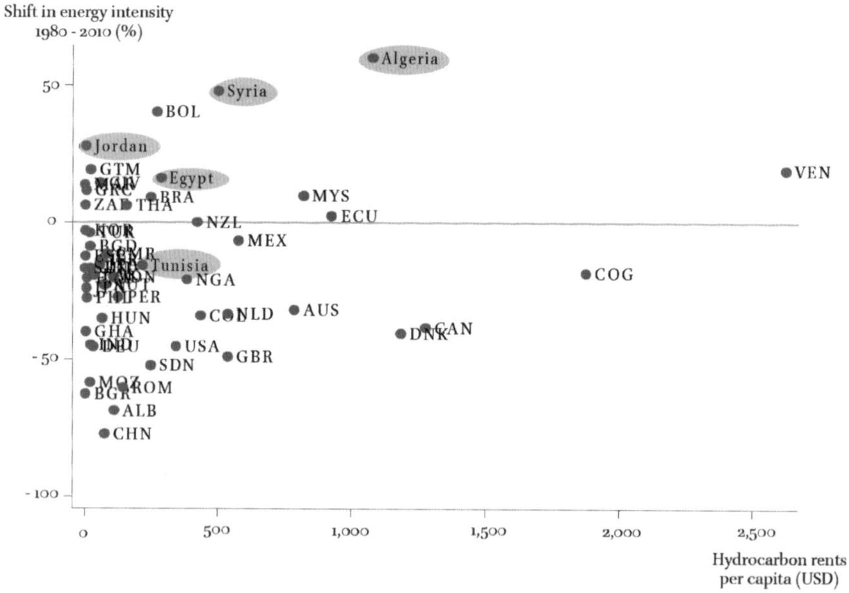

FIGURE 5.8 *Rents per capita and shifts in energy intensity since 1980 without high-rent countries*
SOURCE: AUTHOR, BASED ON WORLD DEVELOPMENT INDICATORS.

(a) High-rent countries around the world have generally experienced a decline in energy efficiency.
(b) Mid-rent countries have not experienced such a decline in general, but mid-rent cases in MENA (Algeria, Egypt, Syria) have, although less dramatic in scale.

Particularly in energy-importing countries, low electricity prices also tend to create undersupply and shortages, as energy producers—which are often state owned—struggle to recover their costs. Energy subsidies also lead to negative environmental externalities. Fuel subsidies in particular cause smuggling, while electricity subsidies undermine incentives to develop alternative energies, which in principle have significant potential in the hot and sunny MENA region.

While food subsidies are smaller in scale, they have also created distortions—perhaps most famously in Egypt, where at least until partial reforms in 2014, subsidised 'baladi' bread was so cheap that it was regularly used as animal fodder (*Reuters*, 2015).

3 How the Distributional System Creates Social Stratification

In addition to economic distortions, the current wealth-sharing regime also has undesirable and arguably unintended distributional consequences. These are well documented for energy, but less so for public sector employment.

3.1 *Labour Market Consequences*

Public employment is a scarce, lumpy, private good. Given the fiscal constraints of all but the very richest Arab countries (Kuwait, Qatar and the UAE), it has to be rationed. It tends to benefit the more educated, who are usually of a privileged economic background to start with (Assaad and Krafft, 2014; Dougherty, 2014). There is also a widespread perception that nepotism and corruption play a role in the allocation of public jobs (El-Gammal, 2013), which reflects such allocation's potential to be used as a discretionary tool of political patronage, and creates further inequities in access.

Excessive public sector employment has contributed to a triple segmentation of labour markets between public, formal private, and informal private—a structure that itself contributes significantly to inequality. To—among other aims—make private employment competitive with public employment, Arab governments have created fairly wide-ranging labour market regulations and high barriers to dismissal from formal private employment. As a result, however, all non-GCC Arab countries bar Jordan rank—according to the World

Economic Forum—in the bottom fifth of 144 countries with regards to 'labour market efficiency' (Jordan ranks 97th). While intended to protect employees, regulation has instead created a huge informal sector, which ranges in size from 25 to 45 per cent of non-GCC Arab economies (IMF, 2011, 45), and in which jobs are precarious and badly paid.

Together with the high share of government employment, this means that formal private employment—the mainstay of developed labour markets—remains a residual category across the Arab world. Arab public employment and labour market policies have, probably unintentionally, created an unequal 'double insider' system.

There are no estimates for the impact of public employment on income distribution in the Arab world, but given its scarce and relatively privileged nature it is likely to contribute to inequality, especially since it has been more strongly rationed from the 1970s on. It might not be coincidence that the cases with the strongest estimated increases in inequality since then appear to be republics that once made the more expansive distributional promises and relied more strongly on public sector employment, notably Egypt and Tunisia (Figure 5.9) (Syria, despite rampant crony capitalism, retained more of its statist economy until recently). While some of this inequality could result from the structural adjustment programmes these countries underwent, it is also clear that the rationing of public sector employment—and the resulting unequal access to opportunities—was a fiscal inevitability even in the absence of structural adjustment.

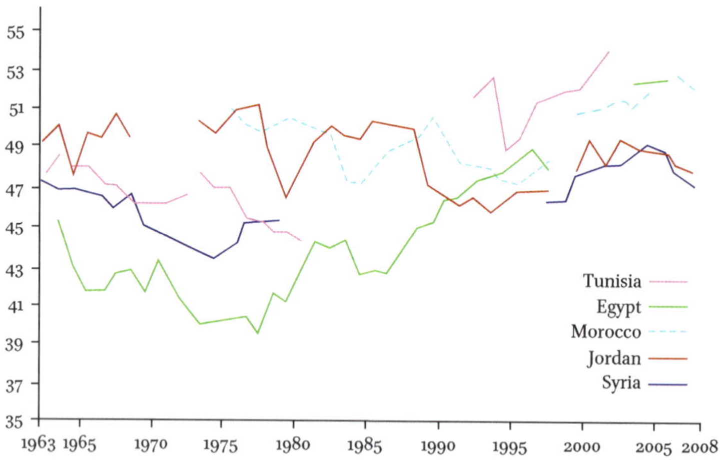

FIGURE 5.9 *Gini coefficients of selected Arab countries*
SOURCE: ESTIMATED HOUSEHOLD INCOME INEQUALITY DATASET, UNIVERSITY OF TEXAS INEQUALITY PROJECT

3.2 *Regressive Energy Subsidies*

The negative distributional consequences of subsidies are better understood and documented: it is widely known for example that most energy subsidies are regressive in that they benefit larger and richer consumers disproportionately. The IMF has shown that the bottom 40 per cent of the population receive only between 3 and 20 per cent of diesel and gasoline subsidies in eight different Arab countries. The regressive effects of LPG and electricity subsidies are somewhat less dramatic, but in no single case do the poor receive their proportional share. The picture for food subsidies is somewhat better; but even for these, many individual policies disproportionately benefit richer strata (Sdralevich et al., 2014).

The staggering opportunity costs of energy subsidies are illustrated by comparing them to government capital spending and education and health budgets. In many Arab countries, subsidies are larger than total capital spending, and in all 11 MENA oil exporters analysed by the IMF, subsidies in 2011 were larger than education and health budgets respectively, and sometimes larger than both budgets combined. Among oil importers, Jordan and Lebanon maintained energy subsidies that were larger than capital spending, education, and health, respectively; in Lebanon they were larger than the education and health budgets combined, while in Egypt they were larger than all three budget items combined (Sdralevich et al., 2014, 18).

3.3 *State, Business and Citizen in the Distributional System*

A subtle but potentially important political economy consequence of the Arab distributional regime is that it weakens the link between the business class and citizens: few citizens aspire to private employment and those who are privately employed often operate in the informal sector. At the same time, business remains state-dependent in many ways—through the provision of cheap energy but also due to high levels of administrative protection (World Bank, 2009). Together with a legacy of cronyism and corruption—themselves potentially facilitated by heavy state intervention, and over-staffed and unaccountable bureaucracies—this arguably explains the prevailing low trust placed in Arab businesses. According to the 2010–14 World Values Survey, 20 per cent of respondents in the ten non-GCC Arab countries polled have 'no trust at all' in big companies, compared with a figure of 10 per cent in the rest of the world. This likely helps to explain the lack of leadership that Arab business showed during, and has shown since, the regional uprisings.

At the same time, in eight out of ten non-GCC Arab countries—all bar Jordan and Morocco—public trust in government institutions, including the civil service, is lower than in other countries with comparable levels of development. This demonstrates that the region's comparatively expansive but lopsided welfare regime fails to generate political buy-in. While the state hence plays a dominant role, it does so in an ineffective way, failing both to steer the economy towards higher productivity and job creation, and to create equitable social outcomes or inspire public trust.

3.4 *Attempts at Change*

Whether seen from the standpoint of efficiency or of equity, there could hardly be a worse way of distributing wealth than through subsidised energy, particularly in the Arab region's energy-importing countries. Public sector employment as a tool of welfare is somewhat less economically irrational, but more distortionary of politically sensitive labour markets.

The above problems, albeit rarely looked at in an integrated fashion, are not unknown to regional policymakers. Facing increasing fiscal constraints, poorer Arab countries made some attempts at partial subsidy reform before 2011 (Sdralevich et al., 2014; IMF, 2013a; Devarajan et al., 2014). These however were abandoned with the uprisings. Instead, both old and new regimes relapsed into ingrained patterns of patronage spending, showing how deeply entrenched the old distribution regime has become. The post-Mubarak transitional government in Egypt ordered rises in subsidies and public sector salaries, and the transitional government in Tunisia new public sector jobs; while in Syria Assad has increased the heating oil allowance for public workers and augmented government salaries. The Jordanian government increased subsidies as well as salaries and pensions, while Morocco temporarily doubled its subsidy budget (Hertog, 2011).

These steps have proven unsustainable and have since been partially rolled back. Egypt, Jordan, Morocco, Tunisia and Yemen have initiated partial pricing reforms of transport fuels and electricity since 2012 (Sdralevich et al., 2014).

It is encouraging that most of these reform efforts have been accompanied by some form of compensatory policy. These include cash transfers to families below a certain income threshold in Jordan, plans to strengthen existing social safety nets in Morocco, a 'lifeline' electricity tariffs for small consumers and a new social housing programme in Tunisia, and expanded coverage of the Social Welfare Fund in Yemen. The reform process generally is piecemeal however and the compensation strategies often diffuse and not clearly enough linked to, and financed through, the savings achieved. Reforms are also limited to energy subsidies in particular, while public employment and labour market regulations remain untouched. The initiatives hence fall short of the big-picture thinking that is necessary for moving towards a new social contract and a distributional regime that are both more efficient and inclusive.

4 Potential Alternatives to Current Distributional Regimes

The unfairness, inefficiency and fiscal non-sustainability of the current systems are obvious. Most economists agree that the Arab world needs further energy subsidy reform and a thorough reform of the public sector, moving governments towards needs-based hiring and potentially a smaller public workforce. But the regional reform debate touching on these issues remains disjointed, focused on individual sectoral problems, and typically apolitical. The discussion of reform is seldom related to the underlying political economy of distribution that has been constraining reform options.

As a result, no answers are offered to how the frayed social contract embedded in existing regimes can be reshaped to become more economically and politically sustainable. If distribution structures are to be reformed, however, Arab citizens will require an alternative, inclusive welfare regime that goes beyond small-scale, sector-specific compensatory measures. Reforms that fall short of this are unlikely to be politically acceptable and are hence likely to remain piecemeal.

While some of the recent energy reforms in Arab countries have been accompanied by compensatory measures such as ration cards or cash grants for needy households, both reforms and compensation policies have been smaller scale and partial—and there has been no serious thinking devoted to how to make public sector reform politically palatable. There is a need for more ambitious thinking that combines a reduction of traditional forms of patronage with the creation of new wealth sharing and social security institutions that will foster a more inclusive, less economically distortionary social contract.

This contribution cannot provide a comprehensive answer in this search for a new contract—but it can hopefully contribute some larger-picture ideas that take into account not only economic but also social and political constraints to reform. In this spirit, the following section will propose direct, unconditional cash grants as a comprehensive alternative to subsidised energy and public sector over-employment. A move towards cash grants would both remove the economic distortions created by the current distribution system and provide a fairer and more inclusive wealth-sharing regime, helping to alleviate the deep socio-economic segmentation of Arab societies.

4.1 *The Long Run: Modern Social Security Systems*

As we have seen, most Arab governments have devoted considerable resources to existing patronage mechanisms. Even if only some of the savings derived from dismantling these structures were available to be spent on new welfare institutions, the resources at the disposal of governments would be considerable, and far above the current scale of social security provision.

In the long run, Arab countries should build up conventional social security mechanisms such as means-tested income support, unemployment assistance, unemployment insurance, and active labour market policies such as retraining and job placement services. In the short run, these are not an option, as putting them in place will require considerable capacity-building efforts. Compensation for any distributional reforms in the sectors of energy and public employment, however, will have to be immediate: both to protect the livelihoods of vulnerable populations and to make reforms politically feasible. Savings from reforms should be immediately 'ring-fenced' for social spending, to ensure they are not just frittered away and used to plug holes in national budgets.

What could instant social spending look like? There is one simple option that has been widely discussed for advanced countries and for resource-rich developing countries, but not to date for the lower-income parts of the Arab world: direct, unconditional cash grants for all adult citizens. These would be particularly easily justified and implemented in the Arab world's oil-rich states. But the potential windfall from distributional reform in most of the hydrocarbon-poor Maghreb and Mashreq countries makes them a serious option there too.

4.2 *The Short Run: Cash Grants to All Citizens*

Universal, unconditional cash grants have been debated at some length as the most appropriate way of sharing national wealth in resource-rich developing countries, and governments as diverse as those of Alaska, Bolivia and Iran have had encouraging experiences with such schemes (Hertog, 2014b; Sandbu, 2006; Segal, 2011). There is also an extensive literature about the potential advantages of unconditional cash grants over conventional welfare mechanisms in advanced, capitalist countries (for an overview see Van Parijs, 2000).[5]

There are numerous general arguments for cash grants, and these arguments apply with at least equal force to the Arab world's poorer countries: compared to existing subsidy systems that privilege insiders and rich households they are more equitable (Sandbu, 2006), distort consumption decisions less, and are more transparent (Moss, 2010). Compared to means-tested support systems, they are easier to administer, generate smaller overheads, and are less prone to stigmatisation and errors of exclusion (Segal, 2011). In the Arab world, the

5 For a global policy initiative on basic incomes, see the Basic Income Earth Network website: http://www.basicincome.org/about-bien/.

administrative capacity for means testing is particularly limited, as tax systems generating household income data are weak.

Cash grants could keep at least part of the state's resource revenues out of the hands of self-interested politicians, thereby reducing corruption (Baena, Sévi and Warrack, 2012; Birdsall and Subramanian, 2004). They could impart a sense of ownership to citizens, increasing their 'buy in' into the political system (Palley, 2003), and create a more level playing field between state and citizens (Gelb and Grasmann, 2010; Gillies, 2010).

By providing a secure revenue stream to citizens, cash grants could at least on the margin incentivise private investment, entrepreneurship and the development of local markets, including financial markets (Gelb and Grasmann, 2010; Palley, 2003; Sandbu, 2006). Authors of the cash grants literature have adduced considerable evidence that private agents are adept at investing cash windfalls well (Birdsall and Subramanian, 2004; Gelb and Majerowicz, 2012; Sandbu, 2006) and at smoothing their consumption over time (Hsieh, 2003).

While taxation capacity in the Arab world is low, basic administrative capacity is fairly high in most countries. A cash grant system could be set up quickly, as it only requires basic information about citizenship and age. Individuals without bank accounts could be reached through the use of special cash cards. As we have seen, trust in the state is particularly low in the region, making simple and hard-to-manipulate systems like a universal cash grant particularly attractive politically. The unconditional nature of grants would maximise political buy-in. Options for means testing along the lines of Latin American style conditional cash grants could be considered later on.

4.3 *Consequences for Labour Markets*

A cash grant system could help to reorient citizens towards gainful private employment in at least two ways. First, it should be accompanied by public sector employment reform that would make government hiring a more remote prospect. Citizens would hence not be incentivised to wait for easy, often unrewarding government jobs in order to secure their share of the country's wealth, but would be free to pursue their own preferences, including on the private labour market. Citizens would also be more likely to seek education relevant to the private sector, helping them to contribute to the creation of economic value. Fewer human resources would be 'parked' in unproductive, surplus government positions, and the public sector itself could reorient its staffing and HR policies away from politically determined patronage and towards needs-based, productivity-oriented strategies.

This effect would be less powerful in poorer Arab countries where public sector employment is already a fairly unlikely scenario for most new labour market entrants (although their preferences and educational behaviour indicate a continued orientation towards the public sector). There is, however, a second potential design feature through which giving cash grants could provide a universally strong incentive for private employment: excluding incumbent public servants above certain income levels—who, after all, already receive an implicit subsidy as they typically earn more than equivalent private sector employees—from receiving the grants.[6] In this way, the effective earnings gap between private and public employment would be narrowed or closed—without any net loss to existing government employees.

This citizens' income would then function in a manner somewhat analogous to an unconditional wage subsidy for private employment:[7] citizens could achieve acceptable total income levels even if they held less-well-paid private jobs, as their citizen's income would top up their wages without penalty.

An unconditional cash grant would have an 'income effect' that would potentially disincentivise work effort on the margin. Any negative effect however would be less strong than under conventional means-tested support mechanisms: unconditional grants would avoid the substitution (or 'tax') effects of unemployment assistance or insurance and other forms of conditional income support, where benefits are lost as work is found and/or wages increase (Widerquist and Lewis, 2009).[8]

A cash grant scheme could help politically justify the gradual re-engineering of the Arab world's bloated public sectors. It is quite likely that future generations would prefer a safe cash grant over the highly uncertain prospect of gaining a surplus government job at some point. This quid pro quo would allow governments to recruit on the basis of administrative needs rather than imperatives of patronage. The resulting improvements in administrative efficiency could contribute significantly to citizens' quality of life, and to the local business climate.

4.4 *Consequences for Income Distribution*

Given the regressive nature of current distribution arrangements, the cash grant alternative would reduce economic inequality. The impact could be

6 Public sector salary schemes could be adjusted to make sure that the lower earners in the government sector would not be disadvantaged vis-à-vis private employees.

7 Not strictly analogous, as wage subsidies are only paid when an individual is in paid employment.

8 Targeted subsidies for low-wage workers (like the Earned Income Tax Credit in the US) would have similar, if weaker, disincentive effects relative to the citizen's income, reducing work effort and incentives to upgrade one's skills.

substantial: Iranian energy price reforms of recent years were coupled with the introduction of a universal household cash grant. As a result, the country's Gini coefficient is estimated to have dropped to 0.37 in 2011 from 0.41 in 2010 (Sdralevich et al., 2014, 52). This is about two-thirds of a standard deviation in the international distribution of country Gini values. Similarly, World Bank simulations have estimated that poverty in Egypt would be cut by one-third if energy subsidies were reduced by 50 per cent and the savings used to finance a universal cash grant (Sdralevich et al., 2014, 57). The more even income distribution achieved through cash grants would probably also boost domestic demand, as poorer households, who would disproportionately benefit, have a higher propensity to consume.

4.5 *Consequences for Energy Consumption*

If grants were financed through energy reforms, this would positively impact domestic energy markets: higher energy prices would help reduce energy consumption both through immediate price effects and by providing longer-term incentives to choose more energy-efficient technology and lifestyles. Drawing on panel data from 66 countries, Charap, Ribeiro da Silva, and Rodriguez (2013) estimate a long-term price elasticity of energy consumption of 0.3 to 0.5. This indicates a considerable potential for energy savings: assuming that a typical Arab country's energy prices could be doubled, consumption would decrease by between 19 and 29 per cent given these elasticities. More realistic energy prices would also reduce the energy dependence of industry, end the often politicised rationing of cheap industrial energy, and provide incentives for investing in more modern production processes.

Despite maldistribution, levels of inequality in the Arab world are moderate compared to most other developing regions; basic infrastructure, state capacity and public services could be improved but again compare reasonably well to the bulk of the Global South. The region would hence have much development potential if economic distortions were reduced and distributional spending leveraged so as to empower rather than segment and immobilise populations.

4.6 *Potential Magnitudes*

How much spare cash would there be for a universal cash grant? I provide below some upper-boundary estimates based on 2011 IMF energy subsidy estimates—the last year for which we have data that is consistent across countries.

Figure 5.10 shows the size of annual cash grants that could be provided to all nationals above 15 years of age if subsidies were eliminated (i.e. energy prices increased to international levels).

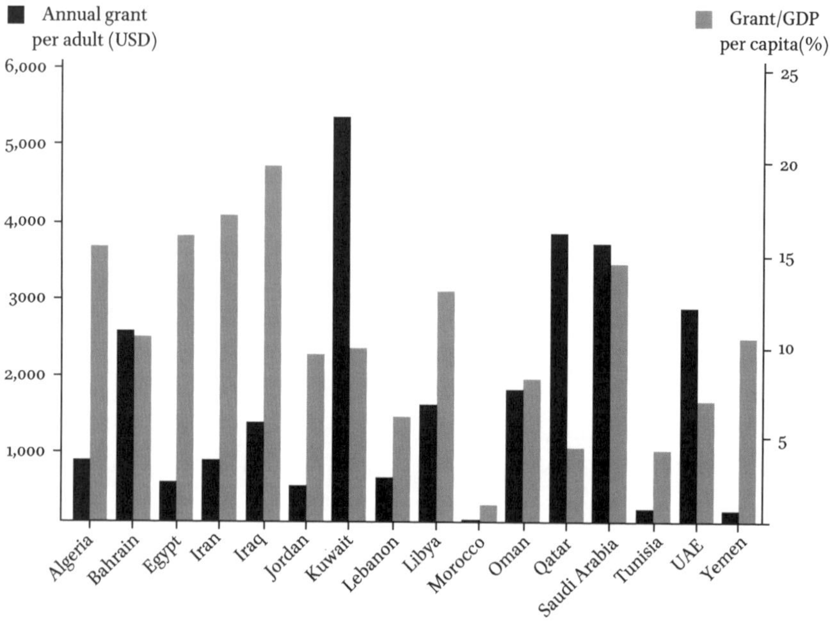

FIGURE 5.10 *Size of per capita annual cash grants that could be financed through energy subsidy reforms*
SOURCE: AUTHOR, BASED ON WORLD DEVELOPMENT INDICATORS (WORLD BANK) AND IMF DATA.
Note: GCC cases here include non-nationals. For more detailed estimates for high-rent countries see Hertog (2014b).

Actual cash grants would in all likelihood have to be lower: the current energy subsidy regime has become fiscally unsustainable and at least some of the savings made thanks to its reform would likely have to be used to reduce government deficits. Lower current energy prices mean, moreover, that the subsidies themselves have somewhat declined since 2011. Finally, any cash grant scheme would incur some administrative costs.

But even if only half of the above amounts could be realised, this would make a substantial difference to the livelihoods of poorer households in most Arab countries—especially Egypt and Yemen, where the grants amount to 10 per cent or more of GDP per capita.

4.7 *Political Feasibility of a Transition*

The political economy rationale for moving from the current distributional regime to cash grants is straightforward: Due to the stark inequality of the current system, the net winners from a more equitable system are quite likely to be a majority—certainly compared to a business-as-usual scenario, which will lead to deeper fiscal deficits and either unilateral subsidy reductions without compensation or further deteriorations in public services.

Recent World Bank research into MENA social security systems adds to our confidence in the feasibility of a cash grant system: respondents in Egypt, Jordan, Lebanon, and Tunisia all reported—in 2012—a strong preference for cash support over in-kind social benefits, and for unconditional over conditional support schemes (Levin, Silva, and Morgandi, 2012, 35f.). Low confidence in public institutions in the Arab world arguably makes citizens warier of targeted, more complex programmes, hence putting a premium on simple, inclusive distribution policies. Finally, the IMF reports that energy pricing reforms involving compensatory measures have been successful in 100 per cent of cases, while only 17 per cent of subsidy reforms without compensatory transfers succeeded (Sdralevich et al., 2014, 42).

4.8 *Political Economy Implications*

The above mentioned distributional reforms could go a long way towards increasing social security, making private employment more attractive, and weaning private industry off costly state support. The existing system of distribution is regressive (in terms of energy subsidies) and has created a rigid and unfair insider–outsider system (in terms of access to public employment). Replacing this regime with a cash grant system would provide a foundation for a new social contract based on shared access to universal channels of government support and to an integrated, more dynamic labour market.

To the extent that cash grants would boost formal private employment, the new system could also improve trust and organic linkages between citizen and business—elements that have been tenuous under the old regime. In the long run, this could contribute to the emergence of a real bourgeoisie that enjoys substantial autonomy from the state, pulls its weight in the national economy, and enjoys social legitimacy.

Distributional reform would only be one major step towards a new social contract and should be accompanied by further reforms of labour markets—for example, making formal private employment rules more flexible to reduce the size of the informal sector—and, in the medium term, by the introduction of more advanced social safety mechanisms. Labour market liberalisation itself would, however, be easier to justify politically if accompanied by a basic income guarantee, an ingredient of compensation that was lacking in many past reform efforts. The first order challenge is hence to re-engineer the distortionary and unfair distributional regime of the old Arab order, and to do so soon.

5 Conclusion

This contribution has provided an overview of the distributional regime on which the political economy of much of the Arab world has been based since the age of Arab nationalism. Even if in most countries this system 'peaked' decades ago, the legacies of subsidisation, public sector over-employment, and labour market segmentation remain strong and are likely to characterise Arab political economies for many years to come—if only in circumscribing the reform options available to Arab governments. Understanding them is hence a prerequisite for any meaningful debate on the subject of reform.

In its second half, this contribution has developed a proposal for comprehensive distributional reform: converting existing mechanisms of uneven patronage into a universal system of unconditional cash grants. The discussion has been very preliminary and there is need for much further thinking and research, including on implementation strategies, the precise mechanism for setting the amount of grants, whether and how underage dependents should be accommodated in the system, the way in which savings from public sector reform can be accounted for in this process, and how universal cash grants can be combined with or converted into a differentiated modern social security system etc.

If nothing else, I hope that the contribution will help to generate a broader debate about comprehensive reform of distributional systems in the Arab world, the various parts of which are interlocked yet seldom discussed together. Any wider-ranging solution will have to take into account political feasibility and the need for immediate compensation.

The old social pact is decaying. The region needs to move fast to replace it with a more sustainable system before existing distributional structures are whittled away entirely and governments lose their room to manoeuvre in creating anything new. Maldistribution creates social inequality and distorts economies, but it also provides an opportunity for reallocating resources in a fairer, less distortionary way. This opportunity will not last forever.

References

Adams, A, and R. Winthrop (2015) 'The Role of Education in the Arab World Revolutions'. (Washington, D.C.: The Brookings Institution) http://www.brookings.edu/research/opinions/2011/06/10-arab-world-education-winthrop(accessedonApril25).

Assaad, R. and C. Krafft (2014) *Youth Transitions in Egypt: School, Work, and Family Formation in an Era of Changing Opportunities*, Working Paper (Doha: Silatech) http://www.silatech.com/docs/default-source/working-papers/youth-transitions-in-egypt.pdf?sfvrsn=4 (accessed on 23 March 2016).

Baena, C., B. Sévi and A. Warrack (2012) 'Funds from Non-Renewable Energy Resources: Policy Lessons from Alaska and Alberta' *Energy Policy* 51 (December), pp. 569–577, DOI: 10.1016/j.enpol.2012.08.076.

Birdsall, N. and A. Subramanian (2004) 'Saving Iraq From Its Oil' *Foreign Affairs*, July 1, http://www.foreignaffairs.com/articles/59923/nancy-birdsall-and-arvind-subramanian/saving-iraq-from-its-oil (accessed on 23 March 2016).

Bodor, A. (2010) 'The Role of Public Sector Employment in Labor Market Outcomes'. presented at the WB-ILO MENA LM Policy Course, Washington D.C., October 25.

Charap, J., A. Ribeiro da Silva and P. Rodriguez (2013) *Energy Subsidies and Energy Consumption—A Cross-Country Analysis*, 13/112 Working Papers (Washington, D.C.: International Monetary Fund) http://www.imf.org/external/pubs/cat/longres.aspx?sk=40002.0 (accessed on 23 March 2016).

Devarajan, S., Mottaghi, L.,Iqbal, F., Mundaca, G., Laursen, M., Vagliasindi, M., Commander, S., Chaal-Dabi, I. (2014) *MENA economic monitor: corrosive subsidies*. MENA Economic Monitor (Washington, D.C.: World Bank Group) http://documents.worldbank.org/curated/en/2014/10/20272046/mena-economic-monitor-corrosive-subsidies (accessed on 24 March 2016).

Dougherty, Ch. (2014) *The Labour Market for Youth in Egypt: Evidence from the 2012 School to Work Transition Survey*, Working Paper 14–2 (Doha: Silatech) http://www.silatech.com/docs/default-source/working-papers/labour-market-for-youth-in-egypt.pdf?sfvrsn=4 (accessed on 23 March 2016).

El-Gammal, Y. (2013) 'Can the Arab Awakening Change an Entrenched Culture of Nepotism?' Text. *Voices and Views: Middle East and North Africa*, April 29, http://blogs.worldbank.org/arabvoices/can-arab-awakening-change-entrenched-culture-nepotism (accessed on 23 March 2016).

Gelb, A. and S. Grasmann (2010) *How Should Oil Exporters Spend Their Rents?* SSRN Scholarly Paper ID 1660570, Rochester, (New York: Social Science Research Network). http://papers.ssrn.com/abstract=1660570 (accessed on 23 March 2016).

Gelb, A. and S. Majerowicz (2012) *Oil for Uganda—or Ugandans? Can Cash Transfers Prevent the Resource Curse?* (Washington, D.C.: Center for Global Development) http://www.cgdev.org/publication/oil-uganda-%E2%80%93-or-ugandans-can-cash-transfers-prevent-resource-curse-working-paper-261 (accessed on 23 March 2016).

Gillies, A. (2010) *Giving Money Away? The Politics of Direct Distribution in Resource Rich States*, SSRN Scholarly Paper ID 1824444, Rochester, (New York: Social Science Research Network) http://papers.ssrn.com/abstract=1824444 (accessed on 23 March 2016).

Henry, C.M. and R. Springborg (2010) *Globalization and the Politics of Development in the Middle East*, 2nd ed, The Contemporary Middle East 1. Cambridge [England]; (New York: Cambridge University Press).

Hertog, S. (2011) 'The Perils of Economic Populism in the Mideast', *Bloomberg.com*, July 25, http://www.bloomberg.com/news/articles/2011-07-07/perils-of-economic-populism-in-the-mideast-commentary-by-steffen-hertog (accessed on 23 March 2016).

Hertog, S. (2014a) *Arab Gulf States: An Assessment of Nationalization Policies*, GLMM; Research Paper; 2014/1; Migration Policy Centre (Firenze (I): European University Institute), http://hdl.handle.net/1814/32156 (accessed on 23 March 2016).

Hertog, S. (2014b) *Rent Distribution, Labour Markets and Development in High-Rent Countries*, London.

Heydemann, S. (1999) *Authoritarianism in Syria: Institutions and Social Conflict, 1946–1970.*, Ithaca, (New York; London: Cornell University Press).

Hsieh, C. (2003) 'Do Consumers React to Anticipated Income Changes? Evidence from the Alaska Permanent Fund' *American Economic Review* 93 (1): 397–405, http://www.jstor.org/stable/3132183.

IMF (International Monetary Fund) (2011) *Regional Economic Outlook: Middle East and Central Asia*, World Economic and Financial Surveys (Washington, D.C.: International Monetary Fund), https://www.imf.org/external/pubs/ft/reo/2011/mcd/eng/pdf/mreo0411.pdf (accessed on 24 March 2016).

IMF (International Monetary Fund) (2013a) *Case Studies on Energy Subsidy Reform: Lessons and Implications*, 07/71 (Washington, D.C.: International Monetary Fund), http://www.greenfiscalpolicy.org/wp-content/uploads/2013/08/Case-Studies-on-Energy-Subsidy-Reform.-Lessons-and-Implications.pdf (accessed on 24 March 2016).

IMF (International Monetary Fund) (2013b) *Energy Subsidy Reform: Lessons and Implications* (Washington, D.C.: International Monetary Fund), http://www.imf.org/external/np/pp/eng/2013/012813.pdf (accessed on 24 March 2016).

Kerr, M.H. (1965) *The Arab Cold War, 1958–1964; a Study of Ideology in Politics*, Chatham House Essays 10 (London, New York: Oxford University Press).

Levin, V., J. Silva and M. Morgandi (2012) *Inclusion and Resilience : The Way Forward for Social Safety Nets in the Middle East and North Africa—Overview*. 72975. The World Bank. http://documents.worldbank.org/curated/en/2012/09/16965002/inclusion-resilience-way-forward-social-safety-nets-middle-east-north-africa-overview (accessed on 24 March 2016).

Luciani, G. (2012) 'Domestic Pricing of Energy and Industrial Competitiveness' In *Resources Blessed: Diversification and the Gulf Development Model*, edited by Giacomo Luciani, 95–113 (Berlin: Gerlach Press).

Moss, T.J. (2010) *Oil to Cash: Fighting the Resource Curse Through Cash Transfers*, SSRN Scholarly Paper ID 1824605, Rochester, (New York: Social Science Research Network). http://papers.ssrn.com/abstract=1824605 (accessed on 24 March 2016).

Palley, T. (2003) *Combating the Natural Resource Curse with Citizen Revenue Distribution Funds: Oil and the Case of Iraq*, FPIF Special Report (Washington, D.C.: Institute for Policy Studies), http://www.thomaspalley.com/docs/articles/economic_development/natural_resources_curse.pdf (accessed on 24 March 2016).

Reuters (2015) 'Egypt's Sisi Scores Early Success with Smart Cards for Bread Subsidies'. *Reuters*, January 12 http://www.reuters.com/article/2015/01/12/us-egypt-bread-idUSKBN0KL14520150112 (accessed on 24 March 2016).

Richards, A. and J. Waterbury (2007) *A Political Economy of the Middle East: Third Edition*. Third Edition (Boulder, Colorado: Westview Press).

Salehi-Isfahani, D. (2012) 'Education, Jobs, and Equity in the Middle East and North Africa'. *Comparative Economic Studies*, 54 (4): 843–861, DOI: 10.1057/ces.2012.41.

Sandbu, M.E. (2006) 'Natural Wealth Accounts: A Proposal for Alleviating the Natural Resource Curse'. *World Development* 34 (7): 1153–1170, DOI: 10.1016/j.worlddev.2005.11.014.

Sdralevich, C., R. Sab, Y. Zouhar and G. Albertin (2014) *Subsidy Reform in the Middle East and North Africa* (Washington, D.C.: International Monetary Fund) http://www.imf.org/external/pubs/ft/dp/2014/1403mcd.pdf (accessed on 24 March 2016).

Segal, P, (2011) 'Resource Rents, Redistribution, and Halving Global Poverty: The Resource Dividend'. *World Development* 39 (4): 475–489, DOI: 16/j.worlddev.2010.08.013.

Van Parijs, P. (2000) 'Basic Income: A Simple and Powerful Idea for the 21st Century'. Congress of the Basic Income European Network, Berlin, November.

Widerquist, K. and M.A. Lewis (2009) 'The Basic Income Guarantee and the Goals of Equality, Efficiency, and Environmentalism'. http://works.bepress.com/widerquist/17 (accessed on 24 March 2016).

World Bank (2008) *The Road Not Traveled: Education Reform in the Middle East and North Africa* (Washington, D.C.: World Bank) http://siteresources.worldbank.org/INTMENA/Resources/EDU_Flagship_Full_ENG.pdf (accessed on 24 March 2016).

World Bank (2009) *From Privilege to Competition: Unlocking Private-Led Growth in the Middle East and North Africa*. World Bank Publications, (Washington, D.C.: World Bank) http://siteresources.worldbank.org/INTMENA/Resources/Privilege_complete_final.pdf (accessed on 24 March 2016).

Yousef, T.M. (2004) 'Development, Growth and Policy Reform in the Middle East and North Africa since 1950'. *Journal of Economic Perspectives* 18 (3): 91–115. DOI: 10.1257/0895330042162322.

CHAPTER 6

Arab States as Shareholders: Origins and Consequences

Alissa Amico

Abstract

In the Arab world, the role of the state in the social contract has been addressed from various angles: as a provider of employment, as a supplier of goods and services, as a guarantor of security and political stability and more generally as an enabler of economic growth. State-owned enterprises (SOEs), which contribute significantly to all of the above objectives, have not been considered in economic policy making, despite the fact that they are integral to the economic history and competitiveness of most countries in the region. Tracing the history of state ownership from the nation-building process to the present time, this article argues that the scope of state capitalism in most Arab countries is not retreating and that the mechanisms of state control have become increasingly diverse. Across the region, the performance of state enterprises has been highly variable: while some operate with private governance models, those that operate as an extension of the public sector still underperform despite being subsidised. Recent experience demonstrates that in countries that have recently undergone political changes, political appetite or popular support for SOE reform is lacking and the prospects for the transfer of positive experiences of SOE management in the region are so far limited.

1 Introduction: Emergence of Arab States as Capitalists

The rise of state capitalism has emerged as a topic of growing global public and academic attention, fuelled by the virtual death of the 'Washington Consensus', the rise of economies such as Russia, China, and India, and—finally—the growth of sovereign wealth funds not only as national actors but also as major cross-border investors. While the means and mechanisms of state involvement in the economic sphere are varied, governments have emerged as owners of commercial assets across a range of sectors, challenging liberal economic ideologies that dispute the efficiency of states as economic actors. Far from playing second fiddle to private enterprise, some SOEs have become behemoths of

DOI 10.1163/9789004336452_007

economic power, with 28 of the 100 largest firms globally counting the state as a significant shareholder (The Economist, 2014).

A recent survey of 34 industrialised countries, mostly OECD members, revealed that their governments collectively own 2,111 companies, valued at USD 2 trillion and employing approximately 6 million people (OECD, 2014a).[1] State ownership in developing economies is even higher: whereas in the OECD area firms majority-controlled by governments are estimated to contribute 3 per cent of total market capitalisation, they represent an estimated 13 per cent of the value of listed equity in emerging economies. The scope of state ownership in the Arab world is higher than in most other developed and emerging markets, whether judged by government participation in capital markets, state ownership of unlisted firms, or other metrics.

Although data on unlisted MENA SOEs is unavailable, our calculations suggest that, currently, 62 per cent of market capitalisation of Arab stock exchanges relates to firms in which sovereign shareholders have 'blockholdings' (10 per cent and above). In fact, of the 600 largest listed firms, accounting for 97 per cent of the region's market capitalisation, close to 40 per cent have a sizeable number of their shares held by the state (Amico and Ozcelik, 2015). Government ownership is even more prevalent in larger firms, with governments having a considerable stake in 89 of the 100 largest listed firms in the region. While these figures are telling, they exclude the majority of state-owned enterprises, especially in strategic sectors such as petrochemicals, network industries and utilities, as they remain unlisted.

Arab governments are significant owners of both listed and unlisted commercial companies, not only in strategic sectors such as hydrocarbons, mining and minerals, and aviation but also in other, less strategic sectors. And yet, the role of the state as a capitalist in the region, as opposed to as a policymaker, has not been subject to considerable analysis. This represents a curious omission and one that is only partially accidental. Governments in the region do not publish consolidated information on their shareholdings, partly due to the fragmentation of state ownership and the difficulty of collecting data, partly due to the inherent opaqueness of state ownership in some countries.[2]

As a result, the mechanisms and the performance of state capitalism in the Arab world have eluded analysis, with the few existing studies focusing

1 For the purposes of the survey, state ownership was defined as 10 per cent and above.

2 Only Morocco and to a lesser extent Tunisia publish data on the portfolio of state shareholdings and no Arab country publishes information on the performance of SOEs.

on privatisation experiences and their impact (cf. Omran, 2009; Haider, 2008; Haider and Dawley, 2008;). After decades of economic dogma that sought to reduce the role of the state in the economy, considering all SOEs as inefficient and corrupt, the tide has turned and the emergence of successful state-backed firms, notably in the Gulf countries, has prompted a reconsideration of Washington Consensus policies. The global financial crisis has further highlighted the cost of private sector failure, prompting governments to become 'unwilling capitalists' as a consequence of their rescue of faltering firms.

The revolutions and subsequent political transitions experienced in some Arab countries provide a useful political economy backdrop against which the performance of state capitalism can be evaluated. In particular, it appears pertinent to investigate how transitions to democratic governance models, as witnessed in Tunisia, will affect the nature and extent of state ownership. Recent events provide a rich context for examining state ownership in the region considering that SOEs are a long-term fixture of MENA economies, many of them having been established to support nation building in postcolonial or independence periods.

In North Africa, the end of colonisation prompted governments to establish local institutions and companies to deliver basic services. In the Gulf, the roots of a number of the largest SOEs can be traced to the process of the forming of the states themselves, and such enterprises continue to simultaneously perform a range of regulatory, commercial and social functions. For instance, the National Bank of Abu Dhabi—today one of the ten largest Arab banks and top ten listed firms in the region—was established in 1968 to finance domestic infrastructure and also to perform central banking functions.

The emergence of governments as major shareholders followed a somewhat different trajectory in other parts of the Arab world, where it was generally delinked from the process of the formation of the state, instead being motivated by the rise of political ideologies that favoured greater state interventionism, inspired by the Soviet developmental model. This was particularly the case in Syria, Algeria and Egypt, where swaths of economic activity were brought under state control during the nationalisation process in the 1950s to 1970s.

Nationalisation of strategic assets was also a part of the story of the emergence of SOEs in the region, especially those in the hydrocarbon field or other strategic sectors. For instance, Saudi Aramco, originally established in 1933 as a result of an oil concession granted by the Saudi government to the affiliate of Standard Oil of California (today's Chevron), was nationalised in 1980.

Likewise, the Kuwait Petroleum Corporation was fully nationalised in 1975, when the government acquired the remaining 40 per cent stake from British Petroleum and American Gulf Oil.

Only in parts of the Levant, notably in Lebanon and the Palestinian Authority, has the state never emerged as a significant shareholder. Even so, in Lebanon where the government owns less than 30 SOEs their impact on the state budget is estimated to be significant. Transfers to Electricité du Liban, the national electricity company, account for 20 per cent of the budget—the second largest item after debt servicing (Hasbani, 2011). Even with such considerable subsidies, the company is unable to provide uninterrupted services to most of the country and its name has become synonymous with public sector failure in Lebanon.

Despite these similarities, the evolution of SOE sectors in the region has differed in important respects. In countries that followed a statist developmental model (Egypt, Iraq, Syria and Yemen), SOEs were established in a broader range of industries. In Lebanon and Jordan, their establishment was arguably more selective. In the Gulf countries, their emergence was more gradual, only initially resulting from nationalisations and in recent years closely related to national industrialisation and competitiveness strategies.[3]

2 Structure of State Shareholdings

The initial interest of Arab states in establishing and maintaining SOEs was supported by a number of well-known academic arguments, notably those advanced by post-World War II developmental economists such as Alexander Gerschenkron who argued that the state needed to take a leading role in capital accumulation and infrastructure development in order to 'catch up' with advanced countries. At the time, local private sector actors were perceived as weak and short-term oriented, interested in catering to consumer demand rather than in long-term investment and national competitiveness.

More recent arguments put forth advocating state interventionism in the economy include private sector coordination failures, fear of the emergence of private monopolies, and 'externalities' in production that may benefit the

3 For instance, the Executive Councils of Dubai and Abu Dhabi and the Emirates Competitiveness Council consider and integrate SOEs in their broad strategic orientations.

whole economy but in which private sector actors may invest less than is socially optimal. In recent years, the systemic risks associated with 'too big to fail' private sector firms have also entered the equation as a motivation for government ownership.

Most of these rationales for state ownership found their echo in the Arab world when governments decided to establish SOEs, and arguably continue to resonate today, although the structure and challenges of SOE sector reform differ by country, as highlighted in Table 6.1. Significant differences can be noted in terms of the number and size of SOEs in countries of the region and of the mechanisms of control used by governments. In Morocco, the Ministry of Finance reports that it owns 241 SOEs in addition to 44 companies in which the Treasury has a direct interest, some of which are newly created (Semmar, 2012). The Tunisian government holds a portfolio of approximately 200 SOEs, in addition to smaller stakes in 480 firms nationalised following the revolution in 2011. In Egypt, the Ministry of Investment holds a portfolio of approximately 150 SOEs in sectors as diverse as insurance and cotton production in addition to over 660 joint ventures between public and private firms as well as an undisclosed number of strategic firms held by sectoral ministries or the military (Bremer, 2012).

The sectoral orientation of SOEs is similar in each of the sub-regions comprising the Middle East and North Africa (the Mashreq, the Maghreb, and the Gulf). The range of sectors in which state companies are present owes its variety both to earlier development approaches and to the recent use of SOEs and Sovereign Wealth Funds (SWFs) as instruments of economic diversification and industrial competitiveness, especially in the Gulf countries. As a result, SOEs are mostly concentrated in the minerals and hydrocarbon sectors, service sectors (e.g. utilities, capital-intensive modes of transport, banking, and telecoms) and industrial sectors (e.g. heavy industry operations such as steel and cement) (OECD, 2013).

The extent of state ownership in listed companies—the only available metric of state ownership in the region—indicates high and growing levels of government participation in the economy. Sovereign investment vehicles—historically important players in local capital markets—are reported to have been increasing their participation in capital markets both for commercial reasons and, occasionally, to 'support' market valuations in times of crisis (e.g. in Saudi Arabia in 2006). For instance, the stake of the Public Investment Fund in Tadawul-listed companies had increased by 26 per cent in August 2014 year-to-year, exceeding 20 per cent of the overall market capitalisation.

TABLE 6.1 *Classification of MENA SOE sectors*

Countries	Characteristics of state ownership	Reform priorities
Iraq, Yemen, Libya	Numerous unincorporated enterprises; SOEs major recipients of state subsidies; the state seen as an employer of last resort; underinvestment in SOEs	Corporatisation and valuation of SOE assets; creating mechanisms for reducing redundant employment in the SOE sector; reviewing the SOE legal framework; attracting investment in SOEs
Algeria, Egypt, Syria, Tunisia	Large SOE sectors owing to the socialist legacy; banking sector historically dominated by SOEs; high non-performing loans in state-owned banks as a result of lending to other SOEs; the state seen as an employer of last resort	Rethinking the role of the state in specific sectors (e.g. textiles, agro industries); reorganisation of the state-ownership function; reducing political interference in SOE boards; streamlining legal frameworks applicable to SOEs
Lebanon, Jordan, Morocco	Rationalised by privatisation during the 1980s and 1990s; the state present in selected sectors and is generally not seen as an employer of last resort; SOEs are not highly present in the financial sector but remain active in network industries	Reviewing state ownership in loss-making enterprises; better co-ordination of the state's ownership function; improving the skills and independence of SOE boards; reducing political interference in boards
Bahrain, Kuwait, Oman, Qatar, Saudi Arabia, United Arab Emirates (UAE)	Hydrocarbon SOEs unlisted; minority stakes in non-strategic SOEs listed in part to develop capital markets; new SOEs being established in recent years; Sovereign Wealth Funds (SWFs) and holding companies increasingly exercise ownership	Improving SOE transparency; preparing listings of equity stakes or debt issuance by some SOEs; consolidating SOE ownership under professional management; reproducing successful ownership experiences

SOURCE: ADAPTED FROM AMICO, 2012.

3 Ownership and Regulation of MENA SOEs

Unlike OECD countries, many of which have introduced ownership or coordination entities to oversee state shareholdings, the political patronage, and hence the oversight of state shareholdings in the region, remains dispersed. Only Morocco, and to a lesser extent Tunisia and Iraq, have seen some consolidation of oversight in the hands of one or two government entities. Other countries, such as Bahrain and Saudi Arabia, have also witnessed a degree of consolidation of SOEs under national sovereign investment funds. For instance, the Ministry of Finance of Bahrain transferred government ownership in a range of large SOEs, such as Aluminium Bahrain and Gulf Air, to Bahrain Mumtalakat Holding Company in an effort to restructure the companies and limit subsidisation.

Despite recent efforts towards consolidation, ownership fragmentation of SOEs in the region is far from accidental. Sectoral ministries and ministers have often been unwilling to relinquish control of SOEs that have proven to be politically useful tools—regardless of their financial performance—and have allowed them not only to control key assets but also to create employment, decide on the provision of essential services, and ultimately intervene in the day-to-day operations of these companies. SOEs have therefore emerged not only as remnants of nationalisation policies but also, effectively, as mechanisms via which political actors control strategic assets.

In this ownership configuration and in the absence of clarity between ownership and regulatory functions, the role of sectoral regulators has emerged as an important one, with the possible exception of SOEs operating in monopoly sectors. Yet, apart from a few sectors—such as telecommunications and transport—sectoral regulators remain relatively rare, which effectively exacerbates the conflicts of interest faced by those ministries that own the SOEs in question. In addition, some sectoral regulators lack the necessary independence, precluding them from effectively exercising their functions. For instance, the Lebanese Telecommunications Regulatory Agency remains dependent on the Minister of Telecommunications and is not in a position to act as an independent regulator since it regulates services directly provided by the ministry.[4]

4 Ogero, the state-owned fixed-line operator, is managed directly by the Ministry of Telecommunications, which is the same body that issues contracts to it. At the same time, the creation of a joint stock company, Liban Telecom, that would effectively corporatise services currently provided directly by the ministry and that could be eventually privatised, was previewed but has not materialised.

Some regulatory authorities provide services while simultaneously being responsible for sectoral regulation. These include the Dubai Roads and Transports Authority (RTA), which is responsible for the construction and operation of the Dubai metro, and also operates the state-owned taxi service, and inter-city transport and bus services. This creates potential conflicts of interest, especially if state-owned incumbents are to be subjected to competition. Conversely, where independent sectoral regulators have been established (e.g. the Telecom Regulatory Authority in Bahrain or the Supreme Council for Information and Communications Technology in Qatar), their presence has allowed for the emergence of more robust competition between state incumbents and private sector competitors (OECD, 2013).

The emergence of competition frameworks to address potentially competition-distorting aspects of state capitalism is a priority for private sector development and hence for employment creation in the region. Yet the field of competition law in the MENA region has been slow to develop.[5] Few competition authorities in the region can pursue cases against SOEs, which in a number of countries are not included or explicitly excluded from the remit of competition legislation. In the United Arab Emirates (UAE) for instance, SOEs are explicitly exempt from the Competition Law, and in Egypt and Oman a narrower set of exemptions for SOEs are in place.[6] Even in countries where SOEs are subject to competition law, competition authorities are usually only empowered to prevent price gauging and cartel formation and deal with market access issues.

While the impact of competition authorities on the integrity of state ownership has been mixed, the establishment of anti-corruption watchdogs and the empowerment of state audit courts have played a positive role. The allegations of the misuse of public assets and of crony privatisations, and—more generally—calls for greater public sector transparency in the wake of recent revolutions, have resulted in more active scrutiny of state shareholdings by these entities. This focus on SOE integrity is indeed not surprising and is not limited to the Arab world: a recent global survey of 427 enforcement actions

5 Jordan was the first Arab country to adopt competition legislation (in 2002) and Oman the last to issue a Competition Law (in 2014).

6 In Egypt, public utilities managed by the state are not subject to the Competition Law, while private utilities may apply to the Egyptian Competition Authority for a total or partial exemption. In Oman, a similar exemption is in place: the Competition Law does not apply to public utilities wholly owned or managed by the state.

related to the bribery of foreign public officials found that employees of SOEs were the largest target recipient of bribes and that 57 per cent of all bribes were related to procurement transactions (OECD, 2014c).

State audit bodies in most countries in the region are empowered to review the financial and non-financial performance of companies where state ownership exceeds 25 per cent; though few state auditors are authorised to examine all state shareholdings and all types of corruption and potential abuse of public goods. Unlike most of its peers, the state audit court in Morocco (the *Cour des Comptes*) publicly discloses details of investigations into inefficient and corrupt practises in SOEs and is in the process of conducting a thematic audit of SOEs: a first in the Arab world. One of its recent reports heavily criticised one of the large real estate SOEs, Al Omrane, which in addition to its purely commercial functions is responsible for building social housing under the Cities Without Slums programme.[7]

In Tunisia, the Tunisian Anti-Corruption Commission, created immediately following the revolution, has uncovered cases of crony privatisations and rigged procurement in SOEs, including in large companies such as Tunisie Télécom.[8] In addition, expropriation measures were taken against assets unlawfully acquired by the former regime and a special Confiscation Commission was created to address this. In Egypt, in various rulings in 2011 and 2012, the courts ruled that the privatisation of formerly public companies was illegal, requiring the acquirers to return shares at the original sale price and to restore employment contracts. A number of other cases are still pending.

In the Gulf countries, governments have recently demonstrated an interest in 'cleaning up' SOEs, establishing new oversight entities and allowing corruption charges to be brought and prosecuted. In one of the most publicly followed cases in the region, the CEO of Oman Oil was sentenced in 2014 to 23 years in prison on charges related to bribery in public tender. The same year, the managing director of Galfar Engineering stepped down after being charged with giving bribes to Petroleum Development Oman in exchange for contracts. The former CEO of Aluminium Bahrain was recently sentenced in a London

7 The audit reports state that the company only built 31 per cent of planned social housing units and that only 11 per cent of its KPIs were achieved considering that built units were not allocated to defined beneficiaries of the programme.

8 Tunisie Télécom was found to have accorded a number of large advertising contracts, never approved by its board, to a private company for a total amount of 48 million Tunisian dinars, without following either the public procurement procedures or the internal approval processes.

court for accepting bribes in return for securing contracts worth in excess of USD 3 billion.

The renewed focus on the governance of SOEs owes much on the one hand to post-revolutionary expectations and low trust in governments, and on the other to poor performance of SOEs as a result of inadequate governance and management structures. While private listed companies have over the past decade been subjected to specific governance requirements in the form of corporate governance codes and regulations, all but a few state-owned firms have escaped such restrictions: only Egypt and Morocco have developed governance guidelines specifically targeted at SOEs.[9]

On the other hand, all MENA countries except for Iraq have a corporate governance code or guidelines for listed companies, and a number have also developed specific regulations for banks and insurance companies. This is important since corporate governance guidelines applicable to listed firms are not extended to state-owned firms unless those firms have listed equity, and in some countries—such as the UAE—even listed SOEs are exempt from the application of the corporate governance code.

Furthermore, governance requirements stipulated in company laws only apply to those companies incorporated under these laws, which excludes most strategic companies as they are incorporated as statutory corporations. This has resulted in governance structures in SOEs that are, on average, less transparent when compared with listed companies and with their peers globally. To bridge this 'regulatory gap', a number of leading SOEs, including Du, the second largest telecom provider in the UAE and Ma'aden, the largest Saudi mining company, have developed internal governance protocols including guidelines for board members and charters for board committees. Some SOE holding companies and sovereign wealth funds with responsibility for SOE ownership have developed guidelines for board members they nominate (e.g. Mumtalakat in Bahrain).

While some, primarily Gulf-based, SOEs have recognised the value of professionalising their boards and management, this has been far from a universal phenomenon in the region (OECD, 2015). In Tunisia for instance, SOE board members and management are not given the authority to set and implement corporate strategy and refer to the government for all operational decisions. In Iraq and Syria, where SOE reform is at earlier stages—overshadowed by the complexities of ongoing conflicts—addressing 'bread and butter' issues of

9 Tunisia and Oman are currently in the process of developing such guidelines. Globally, recent analysis by the OECD identified 33 corporate governance codes or guidelines specifically aimed at SOEs.

corporatisation and the valuation of SOE assets is an even higher priority than the professionalisation of boards and the competitiveness of SOEs.

4 The Role of the State in Capital Markets

Over the past decade, as privatisation has become unpopular in the region, governments have divested few of their stakes in SOEs, while at the same time increasing their ownership in a range of public listed firms. Privatisation activity in the region has ground to a halt, victim of allegations of crony capitalism, especially in Tunisia and Egypt—once the top 'privatisers' in the region,[10] and of the unwillingness of governments to further privatise companies in which stakes were already divested over the past 20 years.

Whereas, globally, a few countries—such as Norway and Spain—are contemplating comprehensive privatisation programmes, few countries in the region including Saudi Arabia, Egypt and Oman seriously consider this as a policy option. In recent years, privatisation activity in the region has been ad hoc and relatively insignificant with the possible exception of the listing of the National Commercial Bank in Saudi Arabia, the second largest Initial Public Offering (IPO) globally in 2014. However, even this transaction saw the allocation of 40 per cent of shares to the Public Pension Agency, a Saudi state-owned pension fund.

Other sovereign institutional investors in Saudi Arabia, including notably the Public Investment Fund and the General Organisation for Social Insurance, are increasing their investment stakes in Tadawul in advance of its planned opening to foreign investors. This reflects the growing participation of sovereign pension funds, insurance companies and banks in MENA capital markets, facilitated by their 'preferred access' to privatisation tranches as part of the subscription process.

An analysis of the 600 largest firms listed on the region's exchanges, accounting for 97 per cent of total market capitalisation, demonstrates that sovereign investors are the largest investor category in all MENA markets with the exception of Lebanon and Tunisia (see Figure 6.1), ahead of family offices. Unsurprisingly, the largest sovereign investment in capital markets occurs in the Gulf countries, where such investors are estimated to control 75 per cent of

10 According to the World Bank's Privatisation Database, Egypt was the largest privatiser in the region from 2000 to 2008 with USD 11.6 billion in privatisation revenues, followed by Morocco with USD 7.9 billion and Tunisia with USD 3.6 billion.

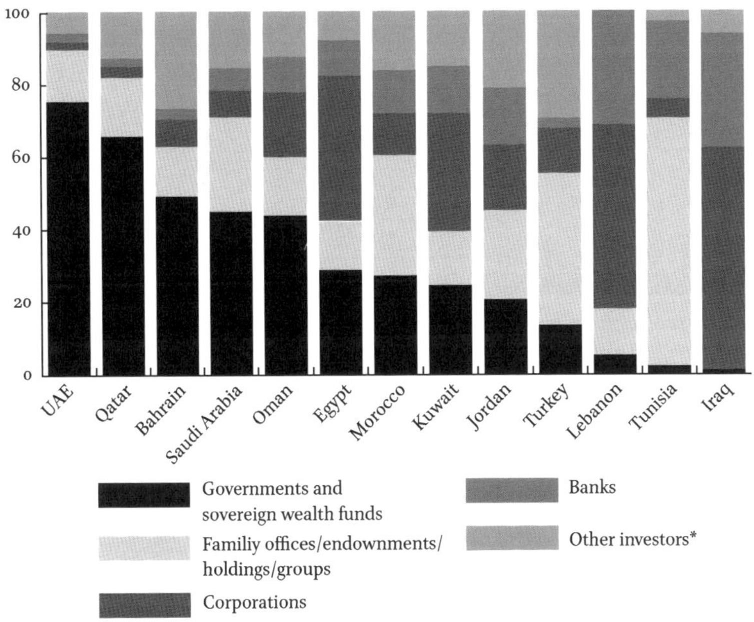

FIGURE 6.1 *Value held by institutional investors (as a percentage of market capitalisation by country)*
* Alternative investors; asset managers; insurance companies; investments/mutual funds; pension funds.
SOURCE: DATA DERIVED FROM THOMSON REUTERS, COMPILED BY ZEYNEP OZCELIK.

listed companies in the UAE and 65 per cent in Qatar (in terms of their market capitalisation).

As a result, 34 of the top 100 largest listed companies in the region are majority state-owned and a further 55 have significant but not controlling state blockholdings. Overall, 40 per cent of the 600 largest listed firms in the region have the state as a shareholder (Amico and Ozcelik, 2015). These figures are substantially higher than equivalent estimates in other emerging markets, with a few exceptions such as China.

A positive feature of this situation is that sovereign institutional investors in the region tend to act as long-term passive shareholders in MENA equity markets, which are known for their volatility driven by retail investors. However, to the extent that private institutional investor ownership in listed SOEs is poised to increase following the opening of the Saudi market and the upgrade of the UAE and Qatar to emerging market status in 2014, companies with a mix of government and private investors might find it challenging to reconcile their interests.

Unlike sovereign investors, which might take into account social or political considerations, foreign pension funds for instance would act as purely financial investors, likely implementing similar engagement tactics as those they have used in their home markets. Although the MENA region has seen virtually no shareholder dissent in recent years, some signs of this tension in state-controlled companies are beginning to emerge. At Emaar Properties, a UAE-based real estate developer, shareholders have recently questioned the involvement of the chairman and other directors in competing firms and their cross-directorships in these (The Arabian Post, 2015). However, investor dissent might be muted by the fact that the returns on investment provided by state-controlled firms are generally superior to the market average.[11]

5 Conclusion

While it is now widely accepted that private sector-led growth is necessary if structural unemployment in the region is to be addressed, state-led development remains a pervasive characteristic of the Arab world, supported by both sovereign financial and industrial actors: SWFs and SOEs. The ideologies that underpinned the privatisation momentum of the 1980 and the 1990s are no longer seen as relevant to the current socio-economic realities of the region by the general public and by policymakers across the political spectrum. This owes to the fact that privatisations in a number of countries were tainted by corruption and that today mistrust of the private sector looms large.

One manifestation of this is that many Arab governments continue to act as the largest employers of nationals, even as fiscal constraints in oil-importing and exporting countries place significant pressure on public spending. While public sector employment of nationals is a long-standing tradition in the Gulf, growing SOE employment in other countries of the region—including Tunisia, where it is estimated to have doubled from pre-revolution figures—indicates that transitioning these firms to the private sector will require politically unpopular reforms.

At the same time, question marks surround the private sector's capacity to act as a locomotive of economic growth in the Arab world. Many large, family-owned firms in the region, established post-independence, are currently going

11 A recent Morgan Stanley report found that SOEs in the Middle East, but also in other regions, generate superior returns compared to benchmark indices (Morgan Stanley, 2012).

through succession changes and their sustainability is being tested. With 65 per cent of all firms in the Middle East valued in excess of USD 1 billion being family controlled (The Economist, 2015), it is anticipated that these transitions will have a significant impact. Few new firms are being created to grow the private corporate sector as the rate of new firm creation in the region is one of the lowest globally, better only than that of Sub-Saharan Africa.

State-owned firms are thus implicitly being accepted as an integral part of Arab economies going forward; as much in the Gulf where experiments with state-led growth have been generally positive as in other countries, such as Egypt and Tunisia, where a few SOEs are largely not profitable or able to substantially contribute to established social objectives.

On the one hand, the MENA region's reliance on SOEs is a consequence of a number of 'inspiring' experiments with state capitalism in the Gulf countries, notably in Saudi Arabia and the UAE. In other countries in the region, the survival of state capitalism is linked to the difficulty of finding an alternative, private sector-led development model as experimentations with private–public partnerships and privatisations have fallen short of expectations. Recent global events have further exacerbated mistrust of the private sector, the most recent financial crisis having underscored the risks of having 'too big to fail' private companies and revealed the costs of rescuing them. On other hand, the 2008 crisis in Dubai demonstrated that SOEs can be rescued and restructured, with contained long-term economic impact.

As a result, for the foreseeable future, reliance on state-owned companies as pioneers of national infrastructure projects and as actors with diverse developmental mandates (e.g. construction of social housing, infrastructure development, employment creation) is bound to continue regardless of fiscal pressures. Post-revolutionary expectations that governments can play the role of fair arbiters of wealth distribution will arguably facilitate government use of SOEs as an active development tool.

Examples of the developmental and social activities of SOEs vary but are visible across the region. For instance, Saudi Aramco, characterised as 'an island of efficiency' within the local administration, has consistently been given mandates related to developing firms in its value chain and occasionally projects beyond its sectorial expertise (e.g. the construction of stadiums). In the UAE, SOEs such as Emaar, Jumeirah Group and the Emirates Airline have been collectively used as a lever for the development of the tourism and hospitality sectors. Unlike Saudi Arabia, the UAE's success in fostering performing SOEs is underpinned not by granting independence to the management and boards of individual companies, but instead by linking these SOEs together in competitiveness strategies and through informal networks such as those created by cross directorships.

Regardless of the 'SOE model' applied, even critics of state interventionism would find it challenging to deny the success of some state capitalism experiments in the region, though they would argue that reliance on SOEs comes at a cost to private sector growth, notably as a result of the lack of a level-playing field. Indeed, few sectors where SOEs are present—such as banking and telecommunications—have been opened to competition, precluding analysis of how state-controlled firms could fare against their private competitors. Even the telecommunications sector—which in most countries has been a success story of SOE incumbents competing against private firms—has not been fully liberalised.[12]

In addition to the efficiency losses potentially incurred by not subjecting SOEs to competitive dynamics, the cost of the subsidies or privileged treatment provided to SOEs—while not taken into account in the official statistics—remains sizeable in most countries. For example, in Tunisia where state-owned banks have extended loans on preferential terms to industrial SOEs, non-performing loans are estimated to be in excess of 15 per cent, much higher than in private sector banks (OECD, 2015; Alpha MENA, 2014). Even implicit subsidies can have other negative implications: allegations that Gulf States subsidise their national airlines have resulted in a major commercial dispute with their American and Canadian competitors.

In the long term, attaining competitive neutrality is an important policy objective in the MENA region; not only to improve economic efficiency and the fairness of competition between SOEs and private companies, but also for the future development of the private sector. Insofar as key SOEs operate in sectors with relatively high barriers to entry, they face few competitive pressures. While private sector competition does not exist in all the sectors in which SOEs operate, relatively intense competition in some sectors has emerged among state-owned incumbents.[13]

While this intra-SOE competition generates rents for governments and allows the redistribution of rents to social projects, it also generates considerable risks through the high exposure of domestic financial institutions to SOE debt. While the concern that state-led capitalism might cripple private enterprise

12 To stimulate competition without forgoing state rents, some countries have instead fostered competition between two state-owned incumbents (e.g. Du and Etisalat in the UAE).

13 Competition among state-controlled firms has emerged as a distinctive feature of the 'Gulf brand' of state capitalism, in which state-sponsored media, airlines and banks compete quite intensively.

remains valid, an equally important challenge for the sustainability of state capitalism—as highlighted by the 2009 crisis in Dubai—is adequate risk management at the level of the state to ensure, notably, that risks taken on by SOEs do not negatively affect the financial sector and overall fiscal stability.

However, given the high cost of bailing out failed private enterprises in the most recent financial crisis, and given public scepticism of private monopolies in the Arab world, the continued reliance on SOEs is perceived to be acceptable. In the Gulf, where SOEs possess 'privatised' management insofar as their governance organs feature representatives of the private sector—reflecting the historical alliances between the state and merchant families—their performance by and large does not give reason to militate for their privatisation. A few loss-making firms ought to be restructured in countries such as Kuwait and Bahrain, taking into account successful SOE experiments nationally and in other Gulf Cooperation Council (GCC) countries.

Where SOEs operate as an extension of the public sector, without the necessary autonomy being afforded to their executives and boards, poor performance has been their common characteristic, both in post-revolutionary countries (e.g. Libya and Tunisia) and in other republics (e.g. Iraq and Algeria). Somewhat paradoxically and for reasons explained above, the weak performance of SOEs in these countries has not yet stimulated any demands for SOE reform apart from calls to reduce corruption and nepotism. This suggests that, at least for the near future, SOEs will be accepted as a fixture of the new social contract in the region.

For entirely different reasons, neither the Gulf monarchies nor the regimes that have emerged as a result of recent revolutions perceive the need to dramatically alter the terms of their involvement in MENA economies. Indeed, privatisation was not on the agenda of regional governments until 2016, when the fiscal situation of some GCC countries started to deteriorate due to falling oil prices. Elsewhere in the region, the reduction of state ownership anticipated by some observers of the Arab Spring failed to materialise as populations of such countries as Egypt and Tunisia grew disenchanted with previous experiments.

References

AlphaMENA (2014) *Tunisian Banks: Sectoral Overview* (place: AlphaMENA, private database accessed on 21 June 2014).

Amico, A. (2012) 'Priorities for Improving Governance and Performance of State-Owned Companies in the Middle East and North Africa', in Amico, A. (ed.) *Towards*

New Arrangements for State Ownership in the Middle East and North Africa (Paris: OECD Publishing), pp. 13–52.

Amico, A. and Z. Ozcelik (2015) *The Role of Institutional Investors in Developing MENA Capital Markets*, unpublished manuscript.

Bremer, J. (2012) 'Transparency of Egypt's Public-Private Joint Ventures', in Amico, A. (ed.) *Towards New Arrangements For State Ownership in the Middle East and North Africa* (Paris: OECD Publishing), pp. 117–150.

Haider, J.I. (2008) 'Infrastructure Privatisation: A Multinational Review of Five Initiatives in the Middle East and North Africa Region', *International Journal of Arab Culture, Management and Sustainable Development*, 1 (1), pp. 82–122.

Haider, J.I. and D. Dawley (2008) 'Privatisation and Financial Performance: Can Value be Created by Privatising State Owned Enterprises in the Middle East and North Africa Region?' *Journal of Business Valuation and Economic Analysis*, 3(1), pp. 1–20.

Hasbani, K.U. (2011) *Electricity Sector Reform in Lebanon, Political Consensus in Waiting*, CDDRL Working Paper No. 124 (Stanford: CDDRL).

Morgan Stanley (2012) *EEMA and Latam Equity Strategy: State Controlled Companies—Where to Invest Now*, Morgan Stanley research Europe, 24 May.

OECD (2013) *State-Owned Enterprises in the Middle East and North Africa: Engines of Development and Competitiveness?* (Paris: OECD Publishing), DOI: http://dx.doi.org/10.1787/9789264202979-en.

OECD (2014a) *The Size and Sectoral Distribution of SOEs in OECD and Partner Countries* (Paris: OECD Publishing), DOI: http://dx.doi.org/10.1787/9789264215610-en.

OECD (2014c) *OECD Foreign Bribery Report: An Analysis of the Crime of Bribery of Foreign Public Officials* (Paris: OECD Publishing), DOI: http://dx.doi.org/10.1787/9789264226616-en.

OECD (2015) *Tunisia: A Reform Agenda to Support Competitiveness and Inclusive Growth* (Paris: OECD Publishing), https://www.oecd.org/countries/tunisia/Tunisia-a-reform-agenda-to-support-competitiveness-and-inclusive-growth.pdf (accessed on 30 March 2016).

Omran, M. (2009) *Post-privatisation corporate governance and firm performance: the Role of Private Ownership Concentration, Identity and Board Composition*, Economic Research Forum Working Paper No. 495 (Giza Egypt: Economic Research Forum).

Semmar, A. (2012) 'Corporate Governance of State-Owned Enterprises in Morocco: Evolution and Perspectives', in Amico, A. (ed.) *Towards New Arrangements for State Ownership in the Middle East and North Africa* (Paris: OECD Publishing), pp. 151–170.

The Arabian Post (2015) 'Alabbar in Shareholder Dissent Row', *The Arabian Post*, 3 April, https://thearabianpost.com/TAP/2015/04/alabbar-in-shareholder-dissent-row.html (accessed on 29 March 2016).

The Economist (2014) 'Government-controlled firms, State capitalism in the dock', *The Economist,* 22 November, http://www.economist.com/news/business/21633831-performance-state-owned-enterprises-has-been-shockingly-bad-state-capitalism-dock (accessed on 30 March 2016).

The Economist (2015). 'Family Firms: To Have and to Hold', 18 April, http://www.economist.com/news/special-report/21648171-far-declining-family-firms-will-remain-important-feature-global-capitalism (accessed on 30 May 2016).

CHAPTER 7

Can Finance and Credit Enable Economic Growth and Democracy?

Bassem Snaije

Abstract

Can economic growth and democracy be fuelled by finance and credit? This chapter examines mechanisms that have positive effects on democratic transition in the Middle East and North Africa (MENA) region, such as credit growth and the development of capital markets-based credit, based on a bond market and a Sukuk market, its sharia-compliant equivalent. The contribution analyses the general role of credit as a network of legally binding contracts of trust between economic actors, including the state, in any given country. By comparing the role and size of credit in the Organisation for Economic Co-operation and Development (OECD) countries and the MENA region, the author argues that, in general, the growth of credit's role in MENA countries and, in particular, the development of debt capital markets in the region, strengthen public participation in the economic activity of the region. The spread of contractual obligations requires more transparent and accessible accounting and financial reporting, and a wider network of legally binding obligations. These powerful mechanisms therefore facilitate democratic transitions in MENA countries, even in autocratic regimes.

1 Introduction

A democratic system provides 'trust between the largest number of people who do not know each other' (Leca, 2014). It is in this context that finance and credit play the important, or even central, role of providing monetary means towards industrial or commercial opportunities fuelling economic growth. In this chapter, we will examine how the financial sector, and particularly credit activity in the Arab world, can contribute to transitions to more democratic processes through fostering economic growth, and trust based on rules and institutions rather than on previous acquaintance. We will compare the place and role of credit in the Organisation for Economic Co-operation and Development (OECD) countries and in the Middle East and North Africa (MENA)

DOI 10.1163/9789004336452_008

and discuss how it could promote or impede transitions to more democratic processes and economic growth in the Arab world.

2 Capital Markets, Governance, and the Economy

The capital markets of the major OECD nations are fuelled by credit in its various forms. The banking industry and capital markets have created an economic environment, mainly through the use of debt, that is an essential component of economic activity and a determinant of the monetary policies of central banks. Credit inventories mirror the nature of economic activity, and new credit that becomes available reflects developing trends in economic activities. The financial sector, and more specifically credit (rather than equity investment), can therefore be considered the cement that binds together all the components of a given economy: producers, consumers, regulators and government agencies alike.

Financial contracts, and specifically credit availability and development, represent the *agreements of trust* between the parties involved in producing and consuming finance and credit. This network of *agreements of trust* enables the highest number of economic agents to participate in economic activity and contribute to the growth of the gross domestic product (GDP). The wider the network of trust is, the more inclusive the economy and the higher the potential for the development of a country's GDP.

Using these fundamental equations, the central role that credit plays is clear. But the role of credit is only possible if the inventory built on *agreements of trust* is within a given framework of rules. All parties—whether providers of credit, or agents accessing it to fuel their activity—must agree to these rules in a general consensus. The credibility and effectiveness of *agreements of trust* are thus a function of this framework, which is in fact a *democratic framework* in as much as it is not controlled from the top down, but responds to multiple, independent, decentralized decision-making.

The governance of advanced credit systems is composed principally of the following elements:

- *An independent judicial system*—Independent courts with fully developed commercial and bankruptcy laws.
- *Licenses and Permits*—In order to produce, distribute and manage credit, banks and financial institutions should operate within a set of regulations that impose conditions for the volume and price of credit, and that

determine which corporations, entities or individuals can access it. Banks and financial institutions must be licensed within the context of governance to which all parties subscribe.
- *Regulatory bodies*—Independent or neutral entities (central banks, capital markets authorities, and stock market boards) should oversee the functioning of the system.
- *Information*—Composed from data representing the components of credit (prices, volumes and conditions), and from the elements of risk and the price of non-performance for each transaction. Information should include documents provided by the credit distributors describing the products and their risks to potential clients, as well as the appropriate disclaimers and reports that facilitate the understanding and management of the evolution of these products over time. Information is also a function of the governance context in which credit operates, and this context should make all economic data and accounting standards available to active participants. A democratic framework provides for central, independent information institutes (national statistics institutes) and a general set of accounting and fiscal regulations, allowing all parties contracting credit transactions to have access to the same information.

The closer a country comes to this framework, the better the conditions for credit availability and growth are. It is not by accident that countries that have developed the most advanced credit systems and frameworks have democratic institutions. It is difficult to expect that appropriate conditions for a well-developed credit system may obtain under authoritarian regimes, which inevitably rely on limitations to the rule of law, to data transparency, to independent institutions, and to freedom of enterprise.

3 The Financial Structures of OECD and MENA Economies Show Significant Differences

The most developed credit systems are found in OECD member countries, the majority of member states having economies that operate with most of the desirable conditions we have described, delivering the most creditable set of 'trust contracts' to the largest possible number of participants in their economies. In OECD countries, banks' share of the total funding of the economies of member states is on average in a range of 33 to 35 per cent (OECD, 2014); capital markets' share is between 65 and 67 per cent. Within capital markets, stock markets and equities contribute between 25 and 30 per cent, and bonds between 40 and 42 per cent of the total. This shows that credit's share of total sources of finance in OECD countries as a whole amounts to 75 per cent on average.

This places credit at the centre of the OECD's economic activities, an assessment consistent with the theoretical position that credit should have in the context of developed democratic frameworks. Two primary characteristics emerge when looking at the structure of OECD country balance sheets in the banking sector:

1. Banks fully play the role of 'transformation' or gap management by having longer-term assets and relatively shorter-term liabilities. For example, within the EU, loan-to-deposit ratios show the transformation of bank deposits, which account for 50 to 60 per cent of banks' very short-term liabilities, into assets that are longer than two years (ECB, 2014).
2. Bank balance sheets show a relatively high level of leverage towards capital availability. The *median equity-to-total-assets* ratios in the eurozone banking sector are between 6 and 8 per cent. If one uses a stricter definition of capital, such as equity over total bank liabilities, these ratios are even lower.

This indicates high leverage in the sector, which confirms the level of trust in the governance framework surrounding the inventory of credit delivered through this channel, and a high level of confidence in the mechanisms in place to guarantee the protection of rights and the execution of clauses in the multitude of contracts struck between all parties related to this credit inventory. This can be considered a confirmation of the credibility of the governance framework provided by the democratic context in OECD countries.

The structures of MENA economies paint a very different picture. In early 2000, the financing structure was composed of banks, with a total share of 80 to 85 per cent, with equity markets representing 12 to 15 per cent on average and bond markets a mere 2 to 3 per cent (IMF, 2004). These numbers changed with the rise of stock markets during the years preceding the 2008 crisis, with the share of stock markets reaching 45 per cent or more (in 2007), decreasing again to 26–27 per cent in 2008, and then stabilising around 35 per cent in recent years. The share of bonds and debt securities has increased significantly in the last decade, doubling in size and number of issues. While this is an important change, the starting point was very low. Banks' share, while decreasing over the period, remains very high at around 67–68 per cent (Kern, 2012).

The primary difference in MENA's financing structure is the dominant role bank credit plays in economic activities. Moreover, state banks account for

38–40 per cent of total available bank credit (Farazi et al., 2011). However, state banks' share has decreased in the last ten years: the above ratio is an average covering all MENA economies, and the figure varies significantly from one country to another. On average, state ownership of banks in the member countries of the Gulf Cooperation Council (GCC) has significantly decreased during the last decade, but in comparison to the OECD average it remains higher by a factor of 2 to 2.5 times. In the other MENA countries this ratio has decreased far less, and in some cases has remained very high, with state-owned banks accounting for more than 70 per cent of total bank credit.

The balance sheets of banks from the MENA region show that a majority of their loans have maturities of one year or less, which indicates a lack of transformation in these banks' financing activities.

Capital adequacy ratios (CARs) in the GCC banking sector—where the percentage of direct state ownership is the lowest—were in the range of 18 to 20 per cent in 2003. These ratios were impacted by the 2008 financial crisis, but in a limited way, leaving them closer to the level of 15 to 17 per cent. Some countries were affected more than others; in particular the UAE's banking system was hit the hardest in relative terms, with the CAR decreasing from 18 to 12 per cent. While this is a significant decrease (a 35 to 40 per cent deterioration of the ratio is a very significant impact by any standards), a 12 per cent ratio remains very high compared to ratios observed in OECD countries (Khamis, 2010).

The total inventory of credit to the private sector in MENA countries represents a mere 50 per cent of GDP, while in OECD member states as a whole this ratio reaches 150 per cent of GDP. This is an indication of the significant difference in the role of credit in MENA. Although banks seem to have an important share in the economies of the region, they do not perform with the same ratios as those observed in OECD countries, delivering on average one year maturity loans—a figure that is 2.5 times lower than in OECD countries. This is low leverage given the high capital adequacy ratios they maintain. Moreover, the relatively high number of state-owned banks should discount the banking sector's share in MENA credit activity.

Such low performance leads to exclusion. A study carried out by the World Bank Financial Access Group in 2010 (CGAP, 2010) shows that small and medium-sized companies in OECD countries receive close to 27 per cent of total loans, while the figure is only 7.6 per cent for MENA countries. The study also shows that in OECD countries the number of bank accounts per 1,000 adults is 2,300, of which 750 are loan accounts—an indicator of access to the credit pool available in the economy. This compares with only 750 accounts per 1,000 adults in MENA, of which only around 100 are loan accounts. Another study, carried out by the IMF in 2007, shows—if any additional proof were needed—that in the US approximately 90 per cent of the population has access to financial services; in Europe this figure is about 75 per cent; and in MENA countries only about 30 per cent.

All these elements show that banks in MENA are highly capitalised, meaning that their potential to deliver credit is much higher than their actual contribution. Additionally, the credit they provide is very short term. This is partly a result of limited access to risk assessment tools, the absence or poor reliability of data that would allow a robust credit scoring system, and the difficulty of accessing a set of enforceable guarantees that would allow them to project credit risk visibility towards longer average maturities for their loans.

4 Finance and Democracy in MENA

Given the financial structure of the economies in the MENA region, the role credit plays is consistent with a relatively poor democratic environment delivering a weak governance framework due to the deficit in the enabling environment. MENA countries' economies are therefore fuelled by a top-down conversation, in which banks are dominant and debt securities providing credit through capital markets offer a limited contribution and alternative to bank financing. Moreover, family groups and individuals close to ruling families or to members of the states' regimes dominate the ownership structure of private sector banks with a significant size and market share. This promotes credit access only to a reduced perimeter of participants who enjoy personal relationships with members of the ownership structure itself. Name lending, rather than credit scoring and financial solvency ratios, becomes the basis for credit access.

These examples of exclusion show how the position of credit in MENA economies creates links dependent on *agreements of trust* between people who already know each other, and are linked together in a manner that is not necessarily based on economic ventures. This can lower the publicly disclosed accountability requirements that would impose a governance framework more consistent with a democratic environment.

With credit's low share of MENA economies' financing, and the banking sector being the main source for its allocation, access to financial and economic opportunity remains a 'closed' process. The ownership of banks validates the consensus of power in place and keeps gatekeeping privileges in the hands of those close to the ruling structures in MENA. This slows down the entry of new participants into the economy unless those individuals possess substantial amounts of capital and, thus, do not need to access credit.

5 The Important Role of the Market for Debt Securities

In OECD countries as a whole, credit is the central element of economic activity as indicated by the size of the inventory over total GDP. The share of the banking sector is significant, but the share of credit generated in the capital markets is even larger.

Capital markets-based financing appears to thrive and seems consistent with significant and credible democratic processes. Debt securities sold to investors demand a different type of conversation, in which the terms of the contractual agreements, commitments and obligations of the parties involved are more balanced—investors placing their trust in a transaction no longer need to do so based purely on personal connections. Rather, a given transaction would be a business proposal, a project or a cash flow, presented to investors in a conversation in which there is no certainty of the outcome in advance and the price is not fixed by a dominant party, such as a bank, in a market where alternative means of accessing financing are scarce.

The process of financing through a debt security is, in a sense, a voting process (although one in which voting powers are unequally distributed). It implies disclosure, transparency of information at inception, the obligation for information to be available throughout the life of the transaction and a set of clauses designed to manage problems, delays, and potential default. Credible enforcement agencies are necessary to convince both investors and borrowers seeking an alternative method of financing their projects. This is very clear with respect to the market for government bonds, where a government's misbehaviour is punished by an increase in the cost of borrowing and a loss of legitimacy, even if that government does not face the test of an imminent election. It is also one reason why many governments prefer to borrow internationally rather than expose themselves to the judgment of domestic investors and credit markets.

In general, bond market growth assumes a level of financial and accounting disclosure, which is necessary for the credibility of the interest payments that the transaction promises to deliver to the subscribers. This exchange of promises backed by sufficient financial and legal documentation from the issuers, and the delivery of accounting and financial tools to the investors in order to convince them first, and encourage them to increase their investments in existing or new issues, is effectively based on many elements of democratic processes and governance frameworks. *Agreements of trust* between people with no previous connection are able to expand, mirrored by the bond transactions representing this trust. The price of these bonds at inception, and the evolution of that price through independent actions of selling or buying units of the bond issue indicate the reaction of people with no previous connection to the issuers and assess the level of trust that these people have. This is a typical example of capital market *voting* behaviour, implying independent decision-making based on required information, disclosure, transparent price fixing and access to the mechanisms of investing or divesting, buying or selling in an anonymous process.

The growth of credit through the issuance of bonds is therefore an important development; it encourages behaviour and expectations within the economic sphere, which can support the transition towards more democratic behaviour in the political realm. It allows the number of participants in economic activity to increase. The *trust* and links are no longer between previously connected parties, allowing the number of conversations and growth impulses to increase. Increasingly available and accessible credit fosters economic expansion.

6 The Market for Debt Securities in MENA

In MENA, the amount of credit available through debt securities is limited compared to the dominant share of the banking sector. However, as described above, the rate of growth in different segments of the financial sector varies. Bond issuance is accelerating significantly. Taking the example of the GCC, where capital markets are developing faster, bond issuance volumes have been increasing at a rate of 30 per cent for more than a decade, from a mere USD 9 billion total issuance in 2003 to USD 57 billion in 2012, and an accelerating trend leading to expected bond issuance levels of more than USD 80 billion in 2015.

Another important phenomenon is the growing *Sukuk* (Sharia-compliant debt equivalent securities) market. Between 1996 and 2010, a total of 276 Sukuk bonds were issued in the GCC. For the year 2011 alone, 150 *Sukuk* bonds were issued. Domestic *Sukuk* amounts reached USD 120 billion in 2014, from a level of USD 5 billion equivalent in 2001, while the international *Sukuk* market saw issues increasing from USD 1.6 billion in 2003 to USD 28 billion in 2014, and increasing interest from non-Islamic or non-GCC or MENA participants—both sovereign and corporate issuers (IIFM, 2014; Markaz, 2010).

Debt issue trends observed in both conventional bond markets and more importantly in the *Sukuk* market point to strong and accelerating momentum, attracting international borrowers and investors. While the international *Sukuk* market remains small, its development—matching the pace of domestic and global issues from GCC-based borrowers—is an important indicator of the fact that these markets are gaining depth and credibility, an important factor in the further acceleration of growth.

Access to credit made available via capital markets remains limited; but the probability of a widening of the perimeter of new participants entering credit markets is increasing in line with the growth of the debt capital market. Furthermore, the existing actors involved in credit are changing the nature of their relationships, going from trust based on pre-existing relationships to an exchange of rights and obligations via instruments that are regulated and supervised within a set of rules and pricing mechanisms, and reflecting a trading activity that makes price, and its evolution, transparent to a wider set of potential participants.

The development of capital markets-based finance is in turn helping create additional rules and regulations and pushing the improvement of the regulatory and legal environment of the credit activities delivered through these channels. While the financial crisis in 2008 significantly slowed growth for two years, it also created in certain cases a need for restored credibility and the incentive to improve the regulatory environment. The quick recovery of issuance and volumes is testimony to the strength and potential of these markets.

The development of capital markets and credit has taken place within an environment of high oil prices in the last decade, generating tremendous cash reserves and making the need for credit less essential for economic activity. In the new context of significantly lower price levels, and considering the stress that this puts on the spending budgets of many MENA countries, credit is expected to play a more central role, accelerating the growth of its share in the financing of economic activities.

As credit growth accelerates, it will progressively shape and improve a governance framework that will provide a stronger foundation for increasing reliance on capital market debt. If the currently observed trends continue, we should see the ratio of credit to MENA countries' GDP rise, approaching levels observed in OECD economies. This will encourage a more open economic playing field, where people who do not necessarily have personal connections can *trust* each other, progressively influencing the way economies function and how they are fuelled by credit.

The rising market for debt eventually encourages the uptake of behaviour that resembles voting processes in the economic and financial sphere. This fosters changes in economic structure, which can also progressively promote democratic features in the political spheres of MENA.

7 Financial Crises and the Development of Regulations

Credit's role in OECD member democracies is at the core of the functioning of their economies. This does not mean that the credit system itself functions well at all times. The evolution of the credit inventory and its rate of growth, as well as instruments developed by the financial industry, can be the cause of major economic crises.

The crisis of 2008 showed how banks and financial markets, through their excessive use of leverage and their ability to 'exclude' competitors from the information and transparency necessary for the proper functioning of the system (particularly through the development of complex financial instruments known as derivatives), became one of the main reasons for the economic collapse.

One of the measures of a political system's strength can be the manner in which it reacts to crises and produces effective corrective actions. Credit's inventory size in OECD countries reached a level that was excessive compared to the underlying GDP. In this instance, credit became a risk to democratic processes and jeopardised the political sphere in which it operated.

An oversized credit inventory, operated by banks that are 'too big to fail', can be a risk for advanced OECD member democracies. Capital requirements were imposed on these banks, aiming to provide a more transparent 'price' for leverage rather than changing the mechanism at the core of the financial system.

MENA countries, in contrast, face the opposite risks, associated with credit being too small a component in the way economic activity is financed. The trends we have described with regards to the evolution of the financial sector in MENA point to a healthy and promising level of growth. These trends vary from country to country and are most evident in GCC member states. While such positive trends are solid, credit still plays too small a part in the financing of these economies to become a main agent of change towards greater reliance on democratic processes.

Regardless, the influence of credit is growing and the financial crisis of 2008 could end up having a positive impact. In 2009, several defaults in MENA were triggered as spillovers of the collapse of global capital markets. In particular, the default of Dubai's flagship corporations significantly impacted the emirate's access to credit and capital markets. The credibility of Dubai's implicit guarantees—on which previous loans and bonds, both international and domestic, were based—has been permanently damaged. This can have positive consequences if we consider that compliance with the more transparent and commonly used tools of guarantees and accounting will need to occur. This in turn improves the conditions for credit to grow, as it strengthens the quality of contracts struck between lenders and borrowers, potentially attracting new participants to the credit market.

The defaults of Kuwait's Investment Dar and Global Investment House, the liquidity difficulties of Gulf Bank in 2009, and—in Saudi Arabia and Bahrain—the Al-Gosaibi's financial crisis (triggered by the default of the International Banking Corporation and Awal Bank, controlled by Maan Al Sanea) did not endanger the overall solvency of the system given the relatively limited size of credit in the economies of those countries. However, the restructuring of these failed institutions' debt involved more than 80 banks internationally and domestically. This will tend to force the emergence of improved standards of accounting and increased transparency. The quality of guarantees that borrowers in the Kingdom of Saudi Arabia and in Kuwait will need to provide in order to access credit or issue *Sukuks* will need to improve. The acceleration of *Sukuk* issuance throughout the region and beyond reflects the improved quality of 'trust contracts' struck, and the increase in the number of participants accessing and providing credit.

At the end of 2014, the Egyptian government issued investment certificates soliciting the savings of national investors to fund infrastructure projects and the expansion of the Suez Canal. The transaction was a success: three weeks after the certificates were issued they sold out; the government netted USD 8.5 billion. The certificates represent an important commitment as they promise a return (12 per cent) and capital protection, providing credit guarantees based on the cash flow of the commercial activity of the Suez Canal as a security for capital and interest payments.

While an autocrat is again in power in Egypt, credit in this example introduces an element of commitment from the issuer or borrower towards the investors, similar to that of an electoral process, given the accountability that the certificates impose. It is difficult for the issuer to default on these commitments without damaging its credibility or facing consequences that would weaken its hold on power. The universe of investors that has subscribed to the certificates is obviously far from representative of the whole of Egyptian society, and only a few Egyptians that had the means to subscribe to the certificates are 'voters' in this exercise. Nevertheless, the process still imposes a significant degree of accountability.

8 Conclusion

Democratic transitions benefit from expanding credit within the economy. Autocratic governments that use the benefits of credit to finance growth are also faced with new governance obligations that increase the level of accountability in their regimes. For this reason, the trend towards a growth of the share of credit in the financing of MENA economies should be encouraged, especially by new democratic regimes.

One of the priorities of new democratic regimes should be the reform of the banking system and the promotion of capital markets-based finance in order to spread 'trust contracts' within their countries, helping to trigger higher levels of growth. The development of credit within a strong regulatory context, can only strengthen new democratic regimes.

References

CGAP (Consultative Group to Assist the Poor) (2010) *Financial Access 2010: The State of Financial Inclusion Through the Crisis* (Washington D.C.: CGAP/The World Bank Group) September, https://www.cgap.org/sites/default/files/CGAP-Financial-Access-2010.pdf (accessed on 27 March 2016).

ECB (European Central Bank) (2014) *Banking Structures Report* (Frankfurt am Main: ECB), October, https://www.ecb.europa.eu/pub/pdf/other/bankingstructuresreport201410.en.pdf (accessed on 27 March 2016).

Farazi, S., E. Feyen, R. Rocha and R. de Rezende (2011) *Bank Ownership and Performance in Middle East and North Africa Regio,* World Bank Policy Research Working Paper No. 5620, April (Washington D.C.: World Bank) Available at SSRN: http://ssrn.com/abstract=1803000 (accessed on 27 March 2016).

IIFM (International Islamic Financial Market) (2014) *Sukuk Report, A Comprehensive Study of the Global Sukuk Market,* 4th ed. (Manama, Bahrain: IIFM) November, http://www.iifm.net/system/files/private/en/IIFM%20Sukuk%20Report%20%284th%20Edition%29%20A%20Comprehensive%20study%20of%20the%20Global%20Sukuk%20Market_0.pdf (accessed on 27 March 2016).

IMF (International Monetary Fund) (2004) *Global Financial Stability Report: Market Developments and Issues* (Washington D.C.: IMF), September, http://www.imf.org/External/Pubs/FT/GFSR/2004/01/index.htm (accessed on 27 March 2016).

Kern, S. (2012) *GCC financial markets: Long-term prospects for finance in the Gulf region* Deutsche Bank Research, (Frankfurt am Main : Deutsche Bank AG), November 14, https://www.dbresearch.com/PROD/DBR_INTERNET_EN-PROD/PROD0000000000296909/GCC+financial+markets%3A+Long-term+prospects+for+finance+in+the+Gulf+region.pdf (accessed on 27 March 2016).

Khamis, M. (2010) *The Impact of the Global Financial Crisis on the GCC Region: Lessons and Reform Priorities,* Presentation at the Roundtable on Effective and Efficient Financial Regulation in the MENA Region, Doha December 6–7.

Leca J. (2014) Opening speech at the conference *Whither the Arab World? Revisiting Democratic Transition Theory,* (Paris: KFAS-SciencesPo) 5–7 November.

Markaz (2010) *GCC Bonds & Sukuk Market Survey* (Kuwait: Kuwait Financial Centre Markaz), October, http://www.markaz.com (accessed on 27 March 2016).

OECD (2014) *Economic Survey Euro Area* (Paris: OECD), April, DOI: 10.1787/eco_surveys-euz-2014-en.

CHAPTER 8

Agriculture and Development in the Wake of the Arab Spring

Eckart Woertz[1]

Abstract

This paper analyses the role of agriculture in the political economy of the Middle East and North Africa (MENA). It outlines agriculture's relative contribution to development and employment, shows linkages with food security policies, and discusses possible future scenarios. Agriculture's role in the economies of MENA is limited nowadays, but its contribution to employment is still substantial. In many countries it is at the heart of the region's water crisis as it withdraws about 80 per cent of water resources. Agricultural constituencies have played an important role in sociopolitical transformations of the region. Populist regimes tried to win them over—as support base—with land reforms enacted in the 1950s and 1960s. Since the 1980s these earlier reforms have been pushed back and the sector has been liberalised under bureaucratic-authoritarian reform coalitions. In other countries, such as Saudi Arabia, extensive production subsidies have been maintained. The MENA region is the largest cereal importer in the world and its governments regard this dependency as a strategic liability. However, the quest for self-sufficiency has proven to be elusive in the light of natural constraints and population growth. The major challenge in MENA is not macro food security or lack of calories, but deficiencies of micronutrients such as vitamins and iron and a lack of accessible food for the poor. Hence, inclusive growth, rural livelihood strategies, and political participation will be crucial for food security in MENA.

1 Introduction

Worldwide, agriculture has seen a relentless decline in its gross domestic product (GDP) contribution and employment capacities compared to industry and services. The Middle East and North Africa (MENA) is no exception. Agriculture's share of GDP hovers in the single digits in most countries. Its developmental and political importance is often overlooked. However, the

1 A Marie Curie Grant from the European Commission funded this research. Some parts of this article were first published in a report for the Union for the Mediterranean, Barcelona (http://ufmsecretariat.org/).

figures for its contribution to employment are higher and it withdraws the vast majority—around 80 per cent—of scarce water resources. Agricultural constituencies have played an important role in sociopolitical transformations of the region. Populist regimes tried to win them over—as a support base—with land reforms that enacted in the 1950s and 1960s. Since the 1980s these earlier reforms have been pushed back and the sector has been liberalised under bureaucratic-authoritarian reform coalitions. In other countries, such as Saudi Arabia extensive production subsidies have been maintained.

The region is the largest food importer in the world, and its governments are keenly aware of the geopolitical vulnerability that comes with such dependence. Maintenance of domestic subsidy regimes is crucial for legitimacy, but difficult in light of fiscal constraints and structurally higher food prices on international markets since the global food crisis of 2008. Economic development, or lack thereof, was a contributing factor to the Arab-Spring uprising, and it is crucial for democratic transitions (e.g. Tunisia) and autocratic perseverance (e.g. the Gulf States or Egypt) alike.

Against this backdrop, this paper analyses the role of agriculture in the political economy of the region and its relative contribution to development and employment. It then shows linkages with general food security policies and discusses possible future developments.

2 The Importance of Agriculture in MENA

Agriculture is MENA's largest water consumer and still provides a substantial proportion of employment in some of the region's countries. Its contribution to economic prosperity is much smaller. In most countries agriculture's value added as percentage of GDP is in single digit territory. In Libya, the Gulf countries and Israel it is at 2 per cent or below. In some countries, such as Egypt, Iran, Syria and Morocco, the rural population is a relatively large proportion of the total, at 31–56 per cent; but even in these countries agriculture's contribution to employment and value added is limited, as Table 8.1 shows. In Sudan and Yemen, where a majority of the population still live in rural areas, agriculture's contribution to employment and value added also trails behind. This points to low productivity and hidden unemployment in the countryside. In a substantially urbanised country like Turkey, for example, 30 per cent of the labour force still work in agriculture, but generate only 8.5 per cent of the value added.

Agriculture is by far the largest water user in the region, withdrawing roughly 80 per cent—with Syria (90 per cent) and Israel (60 per cent) as outliers. Agriculture's water use is consumptive; following evapotranspiration through the plants that are grown it cannot be recycled like residential water supplies

TABLE 8.1 *Share of agriculture (%)—rural population, labour force, value added*

	Rural population (% of total population) 2013	Labour force in agriculture (% of total labour force) 2013	Agriculture, value added (% of GDP)
Morocco	42.24	23.47	14.6 (2012)
Algeria	25.32	20.09	9.3 (2012)
Tunisia	33.27	19.59	8.7 (2013)
Libya	21.94	2.53	1.9 (2008)
Egypt	56.19	23.22	14.5 (2013)
Israel	7.99	1.53	1.6 (2013)
West Bank and Gaza	25.22	7.06	6.9 (2011)
Jordan	16.79	5.60	3.4 (2013)
Syria	43.15	18.74	17.9 (2007)
Lebanon	12.53	1.47	7.2 (2013)
Turkey	26.60	30.40	8.5 (2013)
Kuwait	1.72	1.01	0.5 (2003)
Qatar	0.92	0.64	n.a.
Iran	30.65	20.42	10.2 (2007)
Iraq	33.61	4.65	n.a.
Bahrain	11.19	0.61	0.9 (1995)
Saudi Arabia	17.29	4.17	2.2 (2012)
Oman	26.05	27.56	1.9 (2004)
UAE	15.05	2.73	0.7 (2012)
Yemen	66.52	35.74	10.1 (2006)
South Sudan	70.07	48.64	n.a.
Sudan	70.07	48.61	27.7 (2012)
Mauritania	57.99	49.65	17.0 (2012)

SOURCE: FAOSTAT, 2014; WORLD BANK, 2014; UNITED NATIONS, 2014.

or used twice like the cooling water of power plants. Hence, agriculture's share of *consumptive* water use is even higher, hovering around 92 per cent (Allan et al., 2015; Allan, 2011; Allan, 2001; Dawoud, 2007).

Past agricultural expansion has been ecologically and economically questionable because of its reliance on limited water resources and costly producer subsidies. Water tables in the region have been sinking at an alarming rate. In 2008 Saudi Arabia started to phase out its subsidised wheat programme (until

2016) as aquifers containing non-renewable fossil water have been depleted. In a next step it will need to cut back its production of alfalfa, which is used as feed for livestock and is even more water intensive than wheat. In the future, Saudi Arabia plans to direct scarce water resources to more value-added crops like fruit and vegetables grown in greenhouses. Yet a reduction in the water-hungry flood irrigation of date palms is difficult because of their importance for hobby farms and weekend retreats.

Syria is another example of agricultural expansion that has been ecologically unsustainable. Unlike many other MENA countries, Syria did not neglect agriculture in the wake of the oil boom. For strategic reasons it had a keen interest in self-sufficiency. With the help of land reform and agricultural subsidies it cultivated a political support base in the countryside (Hinnebusch, 2011). The system was geared towards large-scale flood irrigation for water-intensive crops like cotton and wheat. The irrigated area doubled between 1985 and 2000. Like in neighbouring Iraq, much of this irrigation relied on pumped groundwater, not on surface water (Voss et al., 2013). By the mid-1990s Syria had become self-sufficient in wheat and barley. With a short, drought-induced interruption in 1999/2000 it remained so until 2008. However, aquifers were over-pumped and agricultural production was expanded in fragile steppe ecosystems. Competing agencies of the segmented, bureaucratic Syrian state cultivated an opaque culture of secrecy around water issues and were unable to introduce more efficient water management practices (de Chatel, 2014).

Agricultural production in MENA countries cannot, then, be substantially increased due to natural constraints. At best it can be stabilised at current levels with improved water management and rain-fed farming. In some cases a greater focus on more value-added crops like fruit and vegetables is indicated; this will require different technologies, infrastructure and distribution networks. Reliance on food imports is here to stay and will likely increase with population growth and more varied diets. This raises crucial questions about the reliability of global markets in supplying such food imports. Agriculture in MENA is undergoing a process of reorientation against the backdrop of past development policies, lasting socio-economic importance, and natural constraints.

3 Historical Evolution of Land, Food, and Agricultural Policies

'Peasants defy categorization' is the title of an introduction by John Waterbury to a book about peasants in the Arab world (Kazemi and Waterbury, 1991). Peasants made up the majority of the MENA population until not too long ago. As recently as 1980 the share of the rural population was above 50 per cent in many MENA countries (World Bank, 2014). MENA peasants are a heterogeneous population ranging from sharecroppers[2] through mid-sized farmers to large landowners. Their participation in political unrest has often articulated itself in the form of ethnic-cum-peasant protests rather than as class-based conflict. Yet the agricultural question has loomed large in MENA history and there is no escaping that it still plays a role today.

In global, comparative terms, parts of MENA—such as Egypt and Iraq—had one of the most unequal distributions of land ownership in the first half of the twentieth century. This was the result of the region's integration into a quasi-colonial export trade of agricultural commodities, including cotton, sugar, opium and silk. In the course of time, the land tenure system witnessed a transformation from Ottoman tax farming to the establishment of private land ownership and a cadastre system (Issawi, 1995; Owen, 1993).

Absentee landlords and colonialism not only embodied inequality of land ownership, they were also an impediment to the industrialisation that could have provided alternative avenues for economic development in the absence of land reform. Only Egypt saw attempts at import-substituting industrialisation in the 1920s by the urban bourgeoisie, under the aegis of Bank Misr (Davis, 1983).

These sociopolitical conflict constellations led to revolutions and land reform in the Arab world after World War II, especially in Egypt, Syria and Iraq (Waterbury, 1983; Hinnebusch, 1989; Batatu, 1978). It was mostly an upper-middle segment of the peasantry that benefited from such reforms, being able to increase its holdings and market access. The landless and poor peasants saw only limited gains, while the power of large landlords of the *ancien régime* was curtailed. Building a political support base in the countryside trumped economic motivations such as developing the agricultural sector as a source of inputs and demand for the nascent import-substituting industrialisation drive. Non-distribution of nationalised land and lack of extension services after reform proved to be an issue, particularly in Iraq.

The advent of the oil boom and related Dutch-Disease phenomena further affected the efficient management of the agricultural sector. At the same time, the capacity of cities to absorb rural migration flows proved limited. The infant industries of the import-substituting industrialisation strategies did not, in some MENA countries, grow up. They only shifted import dependency from manufactured to intermediate goods and contributed to a deterioration of the balance of payments. Informal sector employment increased as the formal sector and the bureaucratic apparatuses failed to provide enough job opportunities. New arrivals often retained their rural lifestyles as part of their livelihood strategies, exemplified by the raising of goats and poultry in backyards and

2 Tenant farmers who give a part of each crop as rent.

on rooftops. Alaa al Aswany describes this incomplete urbanisation and the ruralisation of cities in his novel *The Yacoubian Building*, in which he portrays a poor rooftop community of rural migrants in Cairo who lead seemingly separated lives from the more fortunate dwellers below, while the earlier, bourgeois tenants have moved to the suburbs.

MENA countries expanded food and energy subsidies in the wake of the oil boom of the 1970s. In the case of Egypt, a particularly prominent example, the government regulated cotton, wheat, rice, sugar cane, beans and winter onions via an often paradoxical mix of production taxation and consumer subsidies. In contrast, it protected livestock production by tariffs and bureaucratic import hurdles until 1987. Only the markets for fruit and vegetables remained free of government interference. This encouraged a shift of acreage into horticulture and fodder production, including clover (*birsim*).

In the 1980s the Egyptian state began to dismantle these policies. Fiscal pressures were one reason for this, but the government was also alarmed about a widening food gap and declining self-sufficiency. Liberalisation policies were pushed further in the 1990s. Low oil prices and reduced opportunities for the acquisition of strategic rents after the end of the Cold War strained public finances. The overextended security states of MENA that relied on institutionalized networks of coercion on a limited economic base implemented neo-liberal reform agendas that cut government expenditure and support schemes. By 1995 only cotton and sugar cane remained under government regulation in Egypt. On the consumption side the peak for food subsidies occurred in 1980 when they covered 20 commodities and accounted for 15 per cent of government spending. By 1997 this figure had declined to 6 per cent. Subsidies now only covered four commodities: coarse 'baladi' bread, coarse 'baladi' flour, edible oil, and sugar (Richards and Waterbury, 2008; Adams Jr., 2003).

Israel and Turkey are particular cases in MENA. Both reduced consumer subsidies early on, but still retain considerable producer subsidies. Turkey used to have a far-reaching programme of agricultural producer subsidies that entailed price supports, input subsidies and marketing monopolies. These have been pushed back with policies that have favoured privatisation and the removal of trade barriers. Turkey is the seventh largest agricultural economy in the world. It is one of the few countries in MENA that is a significant agricultural exporter and it has considerable self-sufficiency in cereals. It is the world's largest producer of hazelnuts, apricots, figs, cherries, quinces, raisins and poppy seeds. It is also the second largest producer of melons, watermelons, strawberries and leeks and the third largest of lentils, apples, cucumbers, green beans, green peppers, chestnuts and pistachios (USDA, 2014c). Similarly, Morocco, Tunisia and Egypt are significant exporters of fruit and vegetables—to the European Union—while importing the majority of their staple foods (López et al., 2013).

Reform pressures on Egypt and Syria have been particularly pronounced. Both countries have faced declining oil production and became net importers of oil and petroleum products by the first decade of the new millennium. Reform measures have deeply affected rural populations. Syria embarked on an aggressive liberalisation drive in the 1990s that aimed at cutting domestic spending and mobilising international private capital (Hinnebusch, 2012). These policies accelerated by 2000, benefits accrued to accomplices, urban clients of the business community and military–security networks, while rural areas were neglected (Haddad, 2012). Small-scale farmers suffered from the withdrawal of agricultural support schemes, and—as a result—were highly vulnerable to the epic drought that wreaked havoc in Syria between 2006 and 2010. The resulting food insecurity and migration movements to cities in the west of Syria caused severe stress to the socio-economic fabric. The Syrian uprising of 2011 has been blamed on climate change in crude Malthusian terms; yet, for a fuller understanding, one needs to consider that—prior to the drought—increasing social polarisation took place, and that the regime's reaction to it was inadequate (de Chatel, 2014; Woertz, 2014).

Structural adjustment policies also affected agriculture in Egypt and contributed to increased inequality. Law 96 was fully implemented in 1997 and pushed back the land reforms of the Nasser era (Bush, 2002; Bush, 2014). The Egyptian Minister of Agriculture, Yousef Wali, was a driving force for the policy of economic liberalisation under Mubarak and a large landowner himself. The process of rolling back land reform was fraught with influence trading. Wali was stripped of his official positions following corruption charges in 2004—a remarkable feat in a regime that was not known for its excellence in governance. Thus these examples from Syria and Egypt illustrate how MENA food security has been affected by social inequalities, rural neglect, and exposure to volatile global markets for food imports.

4 The State of Food Security in MENA

Food self-sufficiency is not food security, although the two are often wrongly equated in MENA. Hardly any country in the world is not reliant on other countries for at least some food items, while net export capacities are concentrated in a few countries (FAO, 2012; MacDonald, 2013). Such food imports can provide security, but also constitute vulnerability. Food importing countries like Singapore and Kuwait can be perfectly food secure if they have the foreign exchange to pay for food imports and world food markets are not disrupted by export restrictions or political crises. The lower the share of food imports as a share of total exports and net remittances, the more food secure a country is on a macro level (see Table 8.2). Yet this does not preclude the existence of food insecurity in vulnerable households on a micro level.

Food security can be measured on different levels: globally, nationally, and locally. Furthermore, different approaches to measurement exist. The categories of the *Global Hunger Index* (*GHI*) of the International Food Policy Research Institute (IFPRI), Concern Worldwide, and Welthungerhilfe mainly indicate calorie deficiency (percentage of the undernourished among the general

TABLE 8.2 *Status of food security (FS) in MENA countries*

	Macro FS: food imports/(total exports + net remittances) (%)	Micro FS: prevalence of stunted children (% of total)	Overall FS risk	Score in global food security index, 2013	Proportion of undernourished/ total population (%), 2012–14
Morocco	8.2	21.6	Serious	49.4	<5
Algeria	7.3	15.6	Serious	45.2	< 5
Tunisia	6.5	9	Moderate	58	< 5
Libya	3.4	21	Moderate	N/A	N/A
Egypt	8.7	30.7	Serious	51.7	< 5
West Bank and Gaza	31.9	11.8	Serious	N/A	N/A
Jordan	13.9	8.3	Serious	52.3	< 5
Syria	9.7	28.6	Serious	36.7	N/A
Lebanon	16.5	15	Serious	N/A	< 5
Turkey	2	13.9	Moderate	62.9	< 5
Iraq	0	27.5	Serious	N/A	23.5
Iran	2.4	16.6	Moderate	N/A	< 5
Saudi Arabia	4	9.1	Low	65.7	< 5
Kuwait	2.4	3.8	Low	N/A	< 5
Bahrain	2.9	9	Low	N/A	N/A
Qatar	2	4	Low	N/A	N/A
UAE	3.4	N/A	Low	N/A	< 5
Oman	6.2	9.6	Low	N/A	N/A
Yemen	15.4	59.6	Ex. Alarming	29.6	25.7
Sudan	8.4	37.9	Alarming	25.2	24.3 (2009–11)
Mauretania	20.6	24.2	Alarming	N/A	6.5

SOURCE: BREISINGER ET AL., 2012; EIU, 2013; FAO ET AL., 2014.

population, prevalence of the underweight, and mortality among children younger than five). Here the MENA region does not score badly on average, with low food security risk. Only Syria (moderate), Iraq and Mauritania (serious) and Yemen and Sudan (alarming) have more serious food security risks and issues with calorie deficiencies, according to the *GHI* (IFPRI et al., 2014). This is also reflected in the low proportion of undernourished people in most MENA countries as per the *State of Food Insecurity* report, issued by the Food and Agriculture Organization (FAO), the International Fund for Agricultural Development (IFAD), and the World Food Programme (WFP) (see Table 8.2).

Yet food security has an important micro-nutritional dimension. One can have enough calories, even too many of them, and yet be food insecure. In all, 30 per cent of the Egyptian population are obese, many of them poor, and all the while they face food insecurity due to a lack of micronutrients such as iron and vitamins. Besides poverty, uninformed dietary choices and increased consumption of junk food are contributing to a growing intake of calorie rich food. A lack of micronutrients affects pregnant women and children in particular. This can have a lasting impact. Nutritional deficiency in the womb and during the first 1,000 days after birth can lead to stunting. It can affect the cognitive abilities and educational achievements of children for the rest of their lives. When poor people cannot afford a balanced and varied diet they have to resort to basic, calorie-rich food, either permanently or as a temporary stopgap solution in the case of sudden price spikes. Hence, the cost of food price volatility and inflation are only insufficiently measured by their short-term impact on financial indicators and nutrition. By compromising the physical and mental abilities of children for life, both factors can have severe long-term developmental effects.

To address these shortcomings, the *Beyond the Arab Awakening* report issued by Washington-based IFPRI uses stunting (insufficient height for age) as an indicator of food insecurity on the micro level, and captures micro-nutritional shortcomings and other important development aspects such as clean drinking water and access to health care better than the *GHI* (Breisinger et al., 2012). The findings of the report are less positive for MENA countries. While only 5 to 15 per cent of children under five in the Arab world are underweight, between 15 and 25 per cent are too short for their age (Woertz, 2013b, 17).

On a macro level many MENA countries face challenges, as they spend more than 5 per cent of their export earnings and net remittances on food imports. Only Libya, Turkey, Iran and the oil-exporting Gulf countries spend less. For Jordan and Lebanon the figure is above 10 per cent. Despite these constraints on a macro level, Jordan has managed to achieve one of the best levels of food security among MENA countries on a micro level. Libya, on the other hand, had one of the worst levels of micro-level food security even before its current internal turmoil began. And this occurred despite a very comfortable position on a macro level. The West Bank and Gaza face the worst food security situation on a macro level, as 31.9 per cent of their export earnings and remittances are spent on food imports; but they are relatively food secure on a micro level compared to other MENA countries.

Micro-nutritional deficiencies and high occurrences of stunting lead mainly to the classification of MENA countries' food security risk as 'serious' in the IFPRI report. Only the Gulf countries have a 'low' risk, and Turkey, Tunisia and Libya a 'moderate' one. At the other end of the spectrum the food security risk in Sudan and Mauritania is deemed 'alarming', and in Yemen even 'extremely alarming'.

Like Egypt, Syria has a very high proportion of stunted children. The IFPRI report was written before the outbreak of fully fledged civil war in the country. Even at that time, Syria's food security risk was regarded as 'serious'. By now, it has presumably moved beyond being 'serious' and might have become 'alarming' or even 'extremely alarming'. Food security has massively deteriorated and the Assad regime has used food embargoes to starve rebel-held areas into submission. This is also reflected in a relatively low ranking in the Global Food Safety Initiative (GFSI) and in *Maplecroft's Food Security Risk Index*, both of which comprise a broad-based average of indicators (EIU, 2013; Maplecroft, 2013). Similar food security deterioration might apply to Libya. In sum, MENA countries do relatively well in terms of calorie provision and indices that measure undernourishment. They do less well when broader issues—such as nutritional value, stability of supply, food accessibility and food safety—are taken into consideration.

5 Domestic Food Prices and the Politics of Subsidies

Global food prices are different from local food prices, which are moderated by subsidies and local costs of food processing and distribution. The latter partly depend on the quality of logistics infrastructure and on domestic fuel costs and might show different price dynamics than those of agricultural raw materials. In developed countries like the US people spend a relatively low proportion of their overall budget on food, and packaged foods constitute a large proportion of spending on food items (see Figure 8.1). Hence, inflation with regard to crops only affects a fraction of overall spending on food, and the impact on overall consumer price inflation is more limited than in developing countries where people spend a larger share of their income on food and rely less on processed and packaged foods.

People in many MENA countries, including Egypt, Algeria and Morocco, spend more than a third of their disposable income on food. This is close to the figures for developing countries like Kenya, and considerably above other

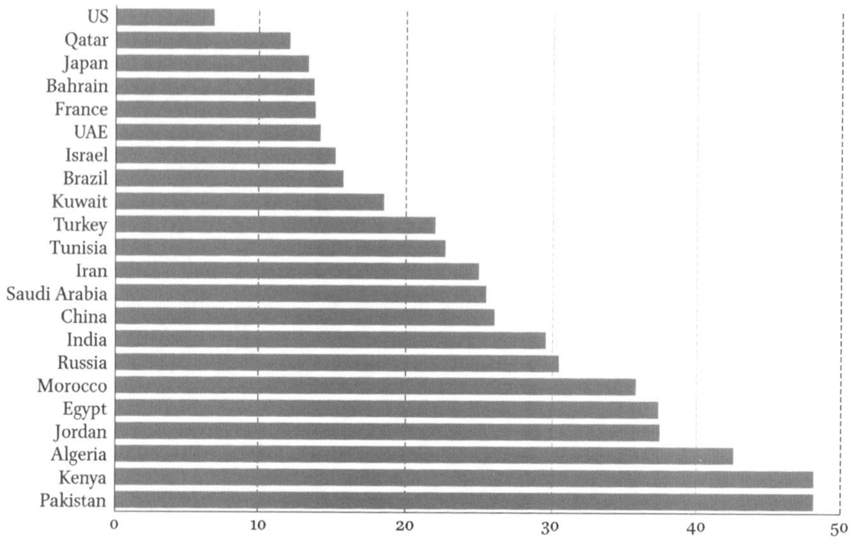

FIGURE 8.1 *Percentage of income spent on food, 2013*
SOURCE: USDA, 2014A.

middle-income countries such as China or Russia. Hence, these MENA countries are particularly vulnerable to food price inflation. Only the smaller Gulf countries with their higher incomes have allocation profiles that resemble those of developed countries, with food accounting for less than 20 per cent of overall household spending (see Figure 8.1).

Food, and fuel subsidies for food distribution networks, can cushion the impact of global food price shocks for local consumers and place the burden of adjustment on the shoulders of respective governments. Subsidy regimes have absorbed some of the global price hikes for consumers in MENA countries, but there has been pass-through of global food price rises by a factor of 0.2–0.4, in line with a global average of 0.3. With the exception of the United Arab Emirates (UAE) and Yemen, food prices in MENA countries are also downward-sticky—meaning that they adjust on the way up, but do not fall back to the same extent when price corrections occur on global markets (Ianchovichina et al., 2012).

Food prices in MENA countries outpaced overall inflation rates from late 2005 to mid-2008. Overall consumer price inflation rose from 3.4 per cent in July 2007 to 10 per cent in July 2008, driven to a large extent by food price inflation, which jumped from 5.8 per cent to 14.8 per cent over this 12-month period (Albers and Peeters, 2011, 10). It has been argued that such food price rises were a contributing factor to the Arab-Spring protests. Jane Harrigan points out that this impact did not occur as a quasi-mechanical transmission, but should be seen in the broader context of socio-economic deterioration and a lack of political freedoms, both of which were in place prior to the protests. The impact was also uneven: while there was a significant correlation between food prices and unrest in the poorer MENA states, this was not the case in the oil-rich Gulf monarchies, and food prices did not play a role in the Libyan protest that led to the fall of the Gaddafi regime (Harrigan, 2014b). Domestic price increases in MENA have been considerably below international averages. Rather than causing outright depravation they led to a reorientation of household budgets towards basic food needs. Thus they compromised purchasing power for non-food items, which contributed to widespread grievances about stagnating or declining living standards that have been associated with economic liberalisation, corruption, and inequalities of wealth and opportunities (Cammett et al., 2015; Verme et al., 2014).

Food and fuel subsidies in MENA countries as a proportion of GDP vary, especially in the case of fuels. In 2008 at the time of the global food crisis, they stood at around 2 per cent for food in many MENA countries and—for fuel—reached more than 6 and 12 per cent, respectively, in Egypt and Syria. Fuel subsidies have usually been considerably higher than food subsides: only Tunisia and Jordan spend more on food subsidies (Albers and Peeters, 2011). These expenditures on subsidies have been a substantial fiscal burden. In the cases of Morocco and Egypt, that burden accounted for 20 and 31 per cent, respectively, of total budgetary expenditure. This has raised questions about the sustainability of such spending. International organisations such as the World Bank and the International Monetary Fund (IMF) have called for indiscriminate food and energy subsidies to be replaced with targeted aid for the poor.

General subsidies applied to basic food items are self-targeting, as poor people spend a larger share of their disposable income on these items. They are less distorting than subsidies on energy, which disproportionately benefit the middle and upper classes with their higher ownership ratios of cars and energy-using appliances (air conditioning, washing machines, etc.). For this reason, and because they are much higher, energy subsidies are more likely candidates for further subsidy reforms than are food subsidies. Kuwait and Egypt both cut fuel subsidies in 2014, but maintained food subsidies, although Egypt introduced a smart-card system to better target bread subsidies. Food subsidies have great significance with regard to political legitimacy. This could be seen during the Arab Spring when Egyptian protesters strapped loaves of bread to their heads. It is unthinkable that they would have done the same with gallons of gasoline. Food clearly commands a greater emotional appeal and—because of their self-targeting nature—the abolition of subsidies on staple foods would disproportionately hurt the poor. Moving to targeted financial aid is easier said than done, as it requires considerable monitoring capacity. Financial aid can also be subject to considerable erosion via inflation, as the recent experience of Iran with subsidy reform has shown (the Guardian, 2014).

6 Macro Food Security, Import Dependence and Self-sufficiency Agendas

Even if food security in MENA countries should not be confused with self-sufficiency and depends to a large extent on broader economic development and food imports, it does not mean that domestic agriculture does not play a role. It provides for a significant proportion of food consumption and helps create livelihoods for a still substantial part of the population, even though its contribution to value added in GDP terms lags behind and the water consumption it requires is unsustainable in many cases (Babar and Mirgani, 2014).

Table 8.3 shows how much of their own food Arab countries produce on average. Import dependence is most pronounced for cereals, sugar, and fats and oils, which are strategically crucial. Dairy products are also imported to a large degree, while meat, fish and eggs show higher self-sufficiency ratios. Some countries, such as Syria, Lebanon, Egypt, Morocco and Tunisia, even have export capacities for fruit and vegetables. Self-sufficiency ratios are lowest in the Gulf countries, Libya, Jordan, Lebanon, and the West Bank and Gaza.

Low self-sufficiency ratios are a concern in MENA countries, as they are a strategic vulnerability in times of geopolitical crisis. In the past, food imports have been threatened. During World War I a naval blockade of the Ottoman Empire by the Entente Forces caused starvation in Greater Syria, although MENA as a whole had been self-sufficient before the war. During World War II food imports were disrupted because of combat operations and lower shipping capacities; famines in the region were only averted by domestic production and the rationing and distribution system of the Allied Middle East Supply Center (MESC) in Cairo. More recently the US contemplated food embargoes in the 1970s in retaliation for the Arab oil boycott and the Iranian hostage crisis. In the 1990s Iraq saw its food imports and oil exports cut off by a unilateral UN embargo (Woertz, 2013b).

Apart from clientelism and the politics of rent distribution, strategic concerns about macro food security have motivated programmes that have sought to increase domestic self-sufficiency, for example in Syria in the 1990s and Saudi Arabia in the 1970s and 1980s. Even Jordan, with its limited natural assets and low self-sufficiency ratio, maintains production incentives for cereals (Harrigan, 2014a). Egypt increased its self-sufficiency ratio with regards to wheat from

TABLE 8.3 *Self-sufficiency ratios (% of consumption) in Arab countries by food product category, 2011*

	Arab region average	Egypt	Jordan	West Bank and Gaza	Syria	Lebanon
Cereals, total	51	57	4	10	58	11
Wheat and flour	50	47	2	11	78	17
Corn	38	46	3	25	14	2
Rice	66	99	0	0	0	0
Barley	34	91	6	7	86	22
Potatoes	100	113	81	100	110	107
Pulses	60	43	7	8	111	25
Vegetables	102	105	177	126	158	91
Fruit	97	112	78	115	109	150
Sugar	30	70	0	0	10	2
Fats and oils	32	24	21	87	56	18
Meat, total	81	87	70	78	99	84
Red meat	87	79	30	71	96	47
Poultry	73	96	85	82	105	99
Fish	103	104	3	30	20	24
Eggs	93	101	107	92	128	107
Milk and dairy products	71	84	46	94	107	33

SOURCE: AOAD, 2012.

21 per cent in 1986 to 46 per cent in 1998, mainly by abandoning wheat taxation and introducing improved seed varieties (Kherallah et al., 2003). By 2011, self-sufficiency had reached 60 per cent and Egypt announced a plan to reach complete self-sufficiency. Yet this aim has not yielded tangible results thus far and may prove impossible given resource constraints. Growing reliance on food imports is not going away. As it cannot be avoided it has to be managed.

7 World Market Dependence and Trade-based Food Security

Given population growth, limited agricultural potential and changing diets, MENA economies will continue to rely heavily on food imports. Sourcing these imports has become more expensive since the food price spikes of 2007/08 and 2011. There have been subsequent corrections, but—overall—food prices are currently at structurally higher levels than their long-term averages of the preceding two decades. Various supply- and demand-side factors support these more elevated price levels, among them slowing productivity growth, environmental backlash and climate change on the supply side, and population growth, changing diets in emerging markets, and biofuels on the demand side (OECD-FAO, 2014).

Wheat and rice account for about 40 per cent of caloric intake globally and MENA is the largest importer of cereals in the world. At 92 million tons, its net imports are higher than the 66 million tons of East Asia, which has a much larger population. The most important net exporter countries for such food trade are North America and the former Soviet Union states, followed by Oceania/Australia, Europe, South Asia, and South America (see Figure 8.2).

Net food imports constitute more than half the caloric intake in Arab countries; only in Syria was the share lower (before full-blown eruption of civil war) (FAO, 2012). A few strategically important net exporters satisfy this demand—namely Canada, the USA, Brazil, Argentina, France, Ukraine, Kazakhstan, Russia, Thailand, Vietnam, Australia and New Zealand. Over the last decade 70 per cent of global cereal exports were provided by only eight countries that comprised a mere 11 per cent of the global population. This global food trade is expected to rise in many countries—among them, the MENA countries—until 2050, given prevalent trends of population growth, demand patterns, and agricultural productivity and production (MacDonald, 2013).

All this food trade constitutes 'virtual water' that can be imported by MENA countries (Allan, 2001; Allan, 2011). The term *virtual water* describes the water that is needed to produce a particular commodity. Agriculture is by far the largest 'blue water' consumer worldwide. Globally it accounts for 70 per cent of blue water withdrawal; in MENA countries the figure is even higher, around

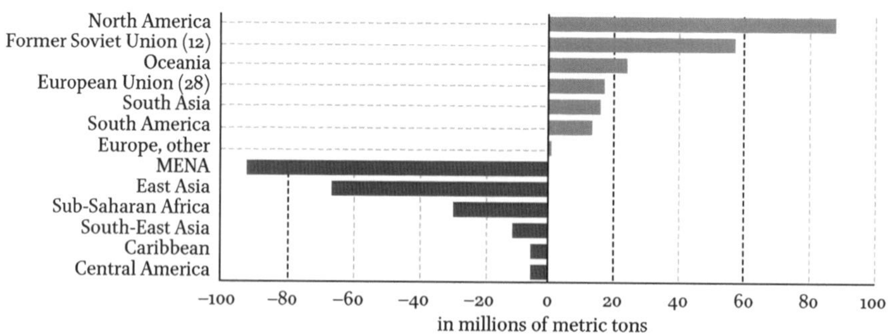

FIGURE 8.2 *Global net trade in cereals 2013–2014 (millions of metric tons)*
SOURCE: USDA, 2014B.

80 per cent. As water used in agriculture evaporates and cannot be reused or recycled, the sector's global share of blue water use even reaches 92 per cent if *consumptive* water use is considered (Allan et al., 2015). More important still, around 70 per cent of global crops are not produced by irrigation agriculture that uses blue water, but by rain-fed agriculture. The latter uses 'green water' that is contained in the soil. Such green or soil water cannot be metered, bottled or shipped by pipeline. Thus it does not figure in the global statistics regarding total renewable water reserves, which only comprise surface and groundwater. Yet green water is extremely important for global food security and for the import needs of MENA countries. By importing rain-fed cereals from Brazil, Canada or Australia, MENA countries are effectively importing the rainfalls of these locations, and can benefit from them.

Between 70 and 90 per cent of the global trade in staple food commodities is carried out by just a few food-trading houses; mainly the 'ABCDs': Archer Daniels Midland (ADM), Bunge, Cargill, and Dreyfus, plus Glencore as a fifth company (Sojamo et al., 2012). The trade in crops and derived products constitutes 76 per cent of global virtual water trade and 68 per cent of this figure comes from green water. Blue and 'grey' (waste) water contribute only 13 per cent and 19 per cent, respectively (Mekonnen and Hoekstra, 2011, 20). Currently global virtual water net exports are focussed on North America (40 per cent), Australia and New Zealand (40 per cent) and South America (20 per cent). Given available water reserves, Australia's share will likely decrease while that of Brazil is expected to rise (Allan, 2011).

Oil-rich Gulf countries have announced land investments abroad in the wake of the global food crisis, often in food-insecure countries like Sudan, Ethiopia and Pakistan. Contrary to widespread media perceptions there has been a huge implementation gap and none of these investments have provided any meaningful contribution to the region's food imports thus far. Much more important is the growing interest of MENA countries in strategic storage, food trade logistics and trade initiatives. Like Asian food importers, MENA countries are poised to engage with the global food system more extensively and more proactively (Woertz, 2013a; Keulertz and Woertz, 2015b). At the same time domestic agriculture and rural constituencies continue to play an important role in political development considerations.

8 Challenges of Agriculture, Food Security, and Development in MENA

Arable land and water resources in particular are scarce in MENA countries and form an impediment to any expansion of agriculture. In some countries agricultural production has actually had to be reduced in order to ensure water security (Alterman and Dziuban, 2010). Agricultural productivity gains might be achieved in some cases, but countries like Egypt already have some of the highest wheat productivity rates in the world. In such cases there are no meaningful yield gaps to be closed (Fischer et al., 2005).

Rather than increasing agricultural production, the focus should be on more efficient water management in order to stabilise that production. Other measures that could lead to more sustainable agriculture in MENA countries include improved extension services, fighting desertification, climate change adaptation, better distribution networks and market access, waste reduction along the value chain, broader rural development programmes, and new approaches to the governance of collective range land (CIHEAM, 2008 and 2009). The EU tries to support such reforms with its European Neighbourhood Programme for Agriculture and Rural Development (ENPARD), which runs from 2014 to 2020.

Other issues include market access to the European Union and the system of EU producer subsidies that grants considerable advantages to European farmers. One goal of the Barcelona Process or 'Euro-Mediterranean Partnership' is the establishment of a Euro-Mediterranean Free Trade Area. Manufactured goods of Partnership member countries from the southern Mediterranean shore currently enjoy duty-free access to the EU and there is preferential treatment for exports of about 80 per cent of agricultural products. Yet quantitative restrictions for some items remain and EU food safety standards can be a difficult hurdle for MENA producers to negotiate. The EU has become more competitive and runs an increasing agricultural trade surplus with MENA as a whole. Its agricultural exports almost doubled between 2006 and 2011 from EUR 4.9 to EUR 9.6 billion, while its imports from MENA only increased slightly from EUR 3.1 to EUR 3.5 billion. Turkey and Morocco are the only MENA countries that run an agricultural trade surplus with the EU, but their levels have been decreasing. Further trade liberalisation would entail winners and losers on both sides. EU producers of fruit and vegetables are concerned about competition from the south; MENA producers have similar fears with regards to cereal and livestock products from the north. Compensation payments could make such changes more palatable, but family farms are likely to face pressures and MENA governments are concerned about macro food security being compromised as a result of declining domestic cereal production (López et al., 2013).

Climate change and increased climate variability will likely exacerbate existing scarcities of water. The first changes are already visible in the eastern Mediterranean, which has witnessed an increased occurrence of drought

(NOAA, 2011; Breisinger et al., 2011). This calls for adaptation measures from MENA countries and for their increased participation in global mitigation efforts (Luomi, 2012).

MENA governments have shown an inclination to look for supply side solutions to address water scarcity. Large-scale projects like dams, desalination, inter-basin water transfers, and tapping fossil groundwater aquifers have been the most prominent of these. One reason for this approach is that the provision of water and other public services carries great weight in terms of political legitimacy in these states, especially those that are under authoritarian rule. Directly or indirectly financed by rents from resource extraction, they try to buy the consent of a general public that is excluded from political participation. Subsidies applied to water, food and energy are part and parcel of this social contract, alongside public sector jobs and health care services. In the future, MENA governments will need to modify their focus on technical fixes and supply-side solutions and address the demand-side issues of wasteful consumption, which is encouraged by untargeted subsidies. Such an approach would require a greater integration of civil society into the processes of political decision-making (Sowers et al., 2011).

While attention of politicians and experts has focused on blue water and improved irrigation efficiency, dry land farming has been neglected. Yet blue water resources are over-utilised in MENA, whereas green water resources and dry land farming offer considerable potential to improve productivity and livelihoods (Chatterton and Chatterton, 1996; Doukkali and Lejars, 2015).

The water–energy–food nexus is eminently political and not just a technocratic construct. Concessionary finance from Gulf funds could provide an impetus, in capital-scarce MENA countries, for its improved management, particularly as climate funds, domestic capital markets, national development funds, and traditional concessionary finance from international organisations such as the World Bank are limited and entail specific trade-offs (Keulertz and Woertz, 2015a).

The political economy of food and agriculture was also highlighted by developments in the wake of the Arab Spring. Neo-liberal adjustment polices implemented by bureaucratic-authoritarian reform coalitions favoured urban clients and the economic interests of military–security networks. They disenfranchised rural constituencies and rolled back land reforms that had been enacted during the populist mobilisations of the 1950s and 1960s. The resulting impoverishment and rural flight was a contributory factor to the unrest, which started in disadvantaged rural towns in the case of Tunisia and Syria and not in the major urban agglomerations. The inability of regimes to implement more efficient water management policies while cutting back support services for farmers also made the latter vulnerable to natural hazards such as the drought that ravaged Syria and some neighbouring countries from 2006 to 2011 (de Chatel, 2014).

The rural population and food producers who have no access to other sources of income than those generated by agriculture are often the most affected by food insecurity in MENA (Zurayk, 2011; Hamadeh et al., 2014). The economic empowerment of rural populations and their eased transition and integration into urban sectors is a major challenge. It carries implications for political stability and entails trade-offs between rural producers and urban consumers. It is unclear whether a more democratic polity in the Arab world could muster the capacity to moderate these conflicts better and implement necessary policies. Frustration with the neo-liberal clientelism of the recent past and unrealistic idealisations of the dissolved populism of yesteryear are both widespread. Meanwhile MENA seems to oscillate between unreformed authoritarian backlash and chaotic decline.

Beyond agriculture per se, inclusive economic development that keeps (imported) food affordable and accessible to MENA countries' citizens is arguably the most important long-term measure for ensuring food security. MENA countries could have fared better in this regard. With the exception of Israel and Turkey their manufacturing bases are small. Their service sectors do not have the same degree of sophistication as present in India, which is outward-oriented and geared towards provision of higher-value-added services. The tourism sectors of MENA countries have been badly hit by the ongoing wave of conflict. Innovation is hampered and barriers to entry are high. It is difficult for small and medium-sized enterprises (SMEs) to secure financing. The financial sector in MENA is dominated by bank lending (63 per cent), followed by stock markets (29 per cent). Bond markets are underdeveloped (7 per cent) (IMF, 2014). Bank financing leans heavily towards large companies that are owned either by influential business families or the state. SMEs that lack the necessary connections find access to funding difficult (World Bank, 2006).

Rent seeking and reliance on direct or indirect resource rents via remittances are both widespread. Military expenditure in MENA is among the highest in the world and constitutes a drain on scarce resources. In terms of GDP it stands at 4.9 per cent as compared to the global average of 2.4 per cent. It is particularly high in the Gulf States, and in Jordan, Yemen, and Syria (Harrigan, 2014b). Resource allocation has also been fraught with cronyism. Inequalities have increased globally over recent decades, harming social equitability and growth perspectives (Piketty, 2014). MENA countries are no exception to this trend. Ordinary households have hardly participated in economic development.

A focus on economic growth alone is insufficient, as the example of Egypt shows. Child malnutrition spiked in the country between 2003 and 2008, right at a time when GDP per capita continued to rise and the country implemented a reform agenda that was regarded favourably by international donor institutions (Breisinger et al., 2012). In 2008, in its Ease of Doing Business Index (EDBI), the World Bank referred to Egypt as the world's leading reformer. By 2010, the country had been among the top ten reformers cited in the EDBI for four years in a row (Springborg, 2012).

Yet appealing real GDP growth rates of 5–7 per cent did not trickle down to the general population. The simple averages of GDP per capita figures are misleading, as benefits only accrued to a minority. Real incomes declined for most Egyptian households throughout the first decade of the new millennium. Surprisingly, at the same time income inequality—as measured by the Gini coefficient—decreased slightly, from levels that were already relatively low compared to other developing countries with similar income per capita levels on a purchasing power basis.[3] The World Bank explains this conundrum by the fact that most of the GDP growth went to private enterprises that retained or exported it; the rest of the population was worse off, despite formally decreasing income inequality (Verme et al., 2014).

It should also be kept in mind that data sources in Egypt are insufficient for reliably estimating those top incomes that have increased dramatically over the past decade. Furthermore, income inequality on a regional level is extremely high in the MENA region because of disparities between oil exporting and non-oil exporting countries (Alvaredo and Piketty, 2014). Against the backdrop of these increasing wealth inequalities and the lack of democratic institutions to address grievances, households perceived their decline in welfare terms to be even more significant than it actually already was—a combustible mix that arguably played a role in the downfall of the Mubarak regime (Harrigan, 2014b). Currently, Egypt relies on politically motivated transfer payments from the Gulf countries to pay a substantial part of its foreign bills—hardly a sustainable scenario. The elusive search for inclusive growth and the provision of social safety nets will be a crucial challenge for MENA food security.

9 Conclusion

Micro-nutritional deficiencies are the most pressing food security issue in the Arab world. They are more important than the lack of self-sufficiency or lack

3 Gini coefficients in the Arab world range between 33 and 40. With 34 in 2009, Egypt was at the lower end of that range, comparable to many countries in Western Europe and below the US (40). Most countries with similar GDP per capita (PPP), such as Guatemala (57), China (47) or Georgia (39), were above that level.

of calories, although these are often wrongly portrayed as the most salient of food security challenges. The food import dependence of MENA is here to stay and will likely grow. Inclusive economic growth is the single most important measure for safeguarding food accessibility for vulnerable people; whether that food is imported or comes from domestic production. MENA governments have fared badly in this regard during the era of economic liberalisation that began in the 1990s.

Food producers without supplementary sources of income are among the most food insecure people in MENA. In a region with already low democratic participation, their lack of access to political decision-making is pronounced. More sustainable land management policies and alternative sources of income outside agriculture would be needed to improve their livelihoods. Better extension services and distribution networks and access to credit and markets are an urgent imperative in MENA. Agricultural development will also need to move away from an overt focus on water-intensive crops like cotton and wheat towards more value-added crops like fruit and vegetables. The promulgation of water-saving technologies like drip irrigation can provide important benefits, but these technologies will not be a 'silver bullet' if efficiency gains are used to increase production and hence water consumption. Compared to irrigated agriculture, sustainable, dry-land farming has only received limited attention in MENA; but it offers considerable potential. Given the still substantial rural populations in some MENA countries and the limited absorption capacities of cities, rural livelihoods clearly have a role to play in development plans and in processes of political participation.

References

Adams R.H. Jr. (2003) 'The Political Economy and Distributional Impact of the Egyptian Food Subsidy System'. *In:* Lofgren, H. (ed.) *Food, Agriculture, and Economic Policy in the Middle East and North Africa* 1st edition ed. (Amsterdam; New York: JAI).

Albers, R. and M. Peeters (2011) *Food and Energy Prices, Government Subsidies and Fiscal Balances in Southern Mediterranean Countries*, Economic Papers (Brussels: European Commission, Economic and Financial Affairs Directorate-General), http://ec.europa.eu/economy_finance/publications/economic_paper/2011/pdf/ecp437_en.pdf (accessed on 17 March 2016).

Allan, T. (2001) *The Middle East Water Question: Hydropolitics and the Global Economy* (London; New York: I.B. Tauris).

Allan, T. (2011) *Virtual Water: Tackling the Threat to Our Planet's Most Precious Resource* (London: I.B. Tauris).

Allan, T., M. Keulertz and E. Woertz (2015) 'The Water–Food–Energy Nexus: An Introduction to Nexus Concepts and Some Conceptual and Operational Problems', *International Journal of Water Resources Development*, 301–311, DOI: 10.1080/07900627.2015.1029118.

Alterman, J.B. and M. Dziuban (2010) *Clear Gold. Water as a Strategic Resource in the Middle East* (Washington D.C.: Center for Strategic and International Studies (CSIS)).

Alvaredo, F. and T. Piketty (2014) *Measuring Top Incomes and Inequality in the Middle East: Data Limitations and Illustration with the Case of Egypt*, Working Paper Series (Cairo: Economic Research Forum), http://piketty.pse.ens.fr/files/AlvaredoPiketty2014ERF.pdf (accessed on 17 March 2016).

AOAD (Arab Organization for Agricultural Development) (2012) *Arab Agricultural Statistics Yearbook* (Khartoum), http://www.aoad.org/Agricultural_Statistical_Book_Vol32.pdf (accessed on 17 March 2016).

Babar, Z. and S. Mirgani (eds.) (2014) *Food Security in the Middle East*, (London: Hurst).

Batatu, H. (1978) *The Old Social Classes and the Revolutionary Movements of Iraq: A Study of Iraq's Old Landed and Commercial Classes and of Its Communists, Ba'thists, and Free Officers*, (Princeton, N.J.: Princeton University Press).

Breisinger, C., O. Ecker, P. Al-Riffai and B. Yu (2012) *Beyond the Arab Awakening. Policies and Investments for Poverty Reduction and Food Security*, Food Policy Report (Washington D.C.: International Food Policy Research Institute (IFPRI)).

Breisinger, C., T. Zhu, P.A. Riffai, G. Nelson, R. Robertson, J. Funes and D. Verner (2011) *Global and Local Economic Impacts of Climate Change in Syria and Options for Adaptation*, IFPRI Discussion Paper 01091, June (Washington D.C.: IFPRI).

Bush, R. (2002) 'Land Reform and Counter-Revolution'. *In:* Bush, R. (ed.) *Counter-Revolution in Egypt's Countryside: Land and Farmers in the Era of Economic Reform.* (London, New York: Zed Books).

Bush, R. (2014) 'Food Security in Egypt'. *In:* Babar, Z. and Mirgani, S. (eds.) *Food Security in the Middle East.* (London: Hurst).

Cammett, M., I. Diwan, A. Richards and J. Waterbury (2015) *A Political Economy of the Middle East*, (Boulder: Westview Press).

Chatterton, L. and B. Chatterton (1996) *Sustainable Dryland Farming: Combining Farmer Innovation and Medic Pasture in a Mediterranean Climate*, (Cambridge England; New York, NY, USA: Cambridge University Press).

CIHEAM (International Centre for Advanced Agronomic Studies) (2008) *Mediterra 2008: The Future of Agriculture and Food in Mediterranean Countries*, (Paris).

CIHEAM (International Centre for Advanced Agronomic Studies) (2009) *Mediterra 2009: Rethinking Rural Development in the Mediterranean*, (Paris).

Davis, E. (1983) *Challenging Colonialism: Bank Miṣr and Egyptian Industrialization, 1920–1941*, (Princeton, N.J.: Princeton University Press).

Dawoud, M.A. (2007) *Water Scarcity in the GCC Countries: Challenges and Opportunities*, Research Papers (Dubai: Gulf Research Center).

De Chatel, F. (2014). 'The Role of Drought and Climate Change in the Syrian Uprising: Untangling the Triggers of the Revolution', *Middle Eastern Studies*, 50, 521–535.

Doukkali, R. and C. Lejars (2015). 'Energy Cost of Irrigation Policy in Morocco: A Sam Assessment', *International Journal of Water Resources Development.*

EIU (The Economist Intelligence Unit) (2013) Global Food Security Index 2013 (London: EIU) http://knoema.com/GFSIEIU2013R1/global-food-security-index-2013 (accessed on 18 February 2015).

FAO (2012) *Role of Imports and Net-Trade (Exports-Imports) in Total Food Consumption.* Rome. http://www.fao.org/fileadmin/templates/ess/documents/food_security_statistics/Net_Trade_Calories_en.xls, (accessed 15 June 2012).

FAO, IFAD and WFP (2014) *The State of Food Insecurity in the World 2014: Strengthening the Enabling Environment for Food Security and Nutrition*, http://www.fao.org/3/a-i4030e.pdf, (Rome: FAO, IFAD, WFP).

FAOSTAT (2014) *FAOSTAT Country Profiles.* Rome: FAO. (accessed 30 September 2014), http://faostat.fao.org/site/666/default.aspx (accessed on 17 March 2016).

Fischer, G., M. Shah, F. Tubiello and H. Van Velhuizen (2005). 'Socio-Economic and Climate Change Impacts on Agriculture: An Integrated Assessment, 1990–2080', *Philosophical Transactions of the Royal Society B: Biological Sciences*, 360, 2067–2083.

Haddad, B. (2012) *Business Networks in Syria: The Political Economy of Authoritarian Resilience*, (Stanford, California: Stanford University Press).

Hamadeh, S., S. Tohmé Tawk and M. Abi Said (2014) 'Urban Agriculture and Food Security in the Middle Eastern Context: A Case Study from Lebanon and Jordan'. *In:* Babar, Z. and Mirgani, S. (eds.) *Food Security in the Middle East.* (London: Hurst).

Harrigan, J. (2014a) 'An Economic Analysis of National Food Soverignty Policies in the Middle East: The Case of Lebanon and Jordan'. *In:* Babar, Z. and Mirgani, S. (eds.) *Food Security in the Middle East.* (London: Hurst).

Harrigan, J. (2014b) *The Political Economy of Arab Food Sovereignty*, (Basingstoke; New York: Palgrave Macmillan).

Hinnebusch, R. (1989) *Peasant and Bureaucracy in Ba'thist Syria: The Political Economy of Rural Development*, (Boulder: Westview Press).

Hinnebusch, R. (2011) *Agriculture and Reform in Syria*, (Fife, Scotland; Boulder, CO: University of St Andrews Centre for Syrian Studies; Lynne Rienner Publishers).

Hinnebusch, R. (2012). 'Syria: From "Authoritarian Upgrading" to Revolution?', *International Affairs*, 88, 95–113, DOI: 10.1111/j.1468-2346.2012.01059.x.

Ianchovichina, E., J. Loening and C. Wood (2012) *How Vulnerable Are Arab Countries to Global Food Price Shocks?*, (Washington D.C.: World Bank).

IFPRI (International Food Policy Research Institute), Concern Worldwide & Welthungerhilfe (2014) *Global Hunger Index 2014: The Challenge of Hidden Hunger* (Bonn;

Washington D.C.; Dublin), http://www.ifpri.org/sites/default/files/ghi/2014/index.html (accessed on 17 March 2016).

IMF (International Monetary Fund) (2014) *Global Financial Stability Review* (Washington D.C.).

Issawi, C.P. (1995) *The Middle East Economy: Decline and Recovery: Selected Essays,* (Princeton, N.J.: Markus Wiener Publishers).

Kazemi, F. and J. Waterbury (1991) *Peasants and Politics in the Modern Middle East,* (Miami Gainesville, Fla.: Florida International University Press ;Distributed by University Presses of Florida).

Keulertz, M. and E. Woertz (2015a). 'Financial Challenges of the Nexus: Pathways for Investment in Water, Energy and Agriculture in the Arab World', *International Journal of Water Resources Development*, 1–14, DOI: 10.1080/07900627.2015.1019043.

Keulertz, M. and E. Woertz (2015b). 'States as Actors in International Agro-Investments', *International Development Policy,* 6, DOI: 10.4000/poldev.2023.

Kherallah, M., N. Minot and P. Gruhn (2003) 'Adjustment of Wheat Production to Market Reform in Egypt'. *In:* Lofgren, H. (ed.) *Food, Agriculture, and Economic Policy in the Middle East and North Africa.* (Amsterdam, New York: JAI).

López, R.C., J.-M. García-Álvarez-Coque and T.G. Azcárate (2013) *Eu-Mediterranean Relations in the Field of Agriculture: The Example of Morocco and Turkey,* Policy Paper (Paris: Notre Europe-Jaques Delors Institute), http://www.eng.notre-europe.eu/media/mediterraneanagriculture-lopezgarciagarcia-ne-jdi-apr13.pdf?pdf=ok (accessed on 17 March 2016).

Luomi, M. (2012) *The Gulf Monarchies and Climate Change: Abu Dhabi and Qatar in an Era of Natural Unsustainability,* (London: Hurst & Company).

Macdonald, G.K. (2013). 'Eating on an Interconnected Planet', *Environmental Research Letters,* 8, 021002.

Maplecroft (2013) *Maplecroft's Food Security Risk Index 2013* (Bath, UK), http://maplecroft.com/about/news/food_security_risk_index_2013.html, (accessed on 18 February 2015).

Mekonnen, M. and A. Hoekstra (2011) *National Water Footprint Accounts: The Green, Blue and Grey Water Footprint of Production and Consumption,* Value of Water (Delft: UNESCO-IHE Institute of Water Education) http://www.waterfootprint.org/Reports/Report50-NationalWaterFootprints-Vol1.pdf.(accessed on 17 March 2016).

National Oceanic and Atmospheric Administration (NOAA) (2011) *NOAA Study: Human-Caused Climate Change a Major Factor in More Frequent Mediterranean Droughts* (Wahsington D.C.: NOAA) http://www.noaanews.noaa.gov/stories2011/20111027_drought.html (accessed 8 January 2014).

OECD-FAO (2014) *Agricultural Outlook 2014–2023* (Paris: OECD Publishing) DOI: 10.1787/agr_outlook-2014-en.

Owen, R. (1993) *The Middle East in the World Economy, 1800–1914,* (London; New York: I.B. Tauris).

Piketty, T. (2014) *Capital in the Twenty-First Century,* (Cambridge, Mass.: Belknap Press of Harvard Univeristy Press).

Richards, A. and J. Waterbury (2008) *A Political Economy of the Middle East,* (Boulder, Colo.: Westview Press).

Sojamo, S., M. Keulertz, J. Warner and J.A. Allan (2012) 'Virtual Water Hegemony: The Role of Agribusiness in Global Water Governance', *Water International,* 37, 169–182, DOI: 10.1080/02508060.2012.662734.

Sowers, J., A. Vengosh and E. Weinthal (2011). 'Climate Change, Water Resources, and the Politics of Adaptation in the Middle East and North Africa', *Climatic Change,* 104, 599–627, DOI: 10.1007/s10584-010-9835-4.

Springborg, R. (2012) 'Egypt: Attempting to Improve "Quality of Administration" without Increasing "Public Accountability"'. *In:* Kadhim, A. (ed.) *Governance in the Middle East and North Africa: A Handbook* (London; New York: Routledge).

The Guardian (2014) 'Iranians Brace for Price Hikes as Government Rolls Back on Subsidies'. *The Guardian,* 28 April, http://www.theguardian.com/world/iran-blog/2014/apr/28/iranians-price-hikes-government-subsidies (accessed on 19 February 2015).

United Nations (2014) *United Nations Indicators,* https://data.un.org/ (accessed on 17 March 2016).

USDA (2014a) *Food Expenditures by Families and Individuals as a Share of Disposable Personal Income* (Washington D.C.: USDA) http://www.ers.usda.gov/data-products/food-expenditures.aspx (accessed on 19 February 2015).

USDA (2014b) *Foreign Agricultural Service Database. Production, Supply and Distribution (PSD).* (Washington D.C.: USDA) http://www.fas.usda.gov/psdonline/psdQuery.aspx (accessed on 23 May 2014).

USDA (2014c) *Turkey: 2014 Food Processig Ingredients Report,* GAIN Report TR4053 (Washington D.C.: USDA) http://gain.fas.usda.gov/Recent GAIN Publications/Food Processing Ingredients_Ankara_Turkey_12-5-2014.pdf (accessed on 17 March 2016).

Verme, P., B. Milanovic, S. Al-Shawarby, S. El Tawila, M. Gadallah and E.a.A. El-Majeed (2014) *Inside Inequality in the Arab Republic of Egypt. Facts and Perceptions across People, Time, and Space* (Washington D.C.: World Bank).

Voss, K.A., J.S. Famiglietti, M. Lo, C. De Linage, M. Rodell and S.C. Swenson (2013). 'Groundwater Depletion in the Middle East from Grace with Implications for Transboundary Water Management in the Tigris-Euphrates-Western Iran Region', *Water Resources Research,* 49, 904–914.

Waterbury, J. (1983) *The Egypt of Nasser and Sadat: The Political Economy of Two Regime,* (Princeton, N.J.: Princeton University Press).

Woertz, E. (2013a) 'The Governance of Gulf Agro-Investments', *Globalizations,* 10, 87–104, DOI: 10.1080/14747731.2013.760932.

Woertz, E. (2013b) *Oil for Food. The Global Food Crisis and the Middle East* (Oxford; New York: Oxford University Press).

Woertz, E. (2014). 'Environment, Food Security and Conflict Narratives in the Middle East', *Global Environment*, 17, 490–516, DOI: 10.3197/ge.2014.070209.

World Bank (2006) Middle East and North Africa. *Economic Developments and Prospects 2006: Financial Markets in a New Age of Oil* (Washington D.C.: World Bank).http://siteresources.worldbank.org/INTMENA/Resources/MainReport.pdf (accessed on 17 March 2016).

World Bank (2014) *World Bank Indicators* (Washington D.C.: World Bank) http://data.worldbank.org/indicator/NV.AGR.TOTL.ZS/countries?display=default, (accessed on 30 September 2014).

Zurayk, R. (2011) *Food, Farming and Freedom. Sowing the Arab Spring,* (Charlottesville, Virginia: Just World Books).

CHAPTER 9

Mass Migration and Uprisings in Arab Countries: An Analytical Framework

Philippe Fargues

Abstract

Is there a relationship between political movements and population movements in the Arab world? More specifically, are the uprisings that spread throughout Arab countries starting at the end of 2010 linked in any way with the international migration of their citizens? This paper first reviews the common determinants of revolt and emigration and addresses the question of how the two phenomena are partly rooted in the deep demographic changes Arab populations are currently going through. The paper then reviews the migratory outcomes of revolt both in terms of voluntary and forced migration. It finally explores diasporas' impact on homeland politics, or—more precisely—the role played by national expatriates in the revolts unfolding in their homelands, in particular through political remittances.

1 Introduction

Is there any relationship between political movements and population movements in the Arab world? More specifically, are the uprisings that, from the end of 2010, spread through Arab countries, linked in any way with the international migration of their citizens?

It should be noted, here from the outset, that the links between revolt and migration, if they exist, can neither be unidirectional nor necessary. Indeed, while major uprisings happened in countries with strong emigration traditions (Tunisia, Egypt, Syria, Yemen...), others took place in countries where immigration outweighs emigration (Libya and Bahrain). Moreover, some countries that are major migrant senders did not experience any large-scale uprisings (Jordan, Lebanon, Morocco, Algeria...) and the same applies to countries that are major receivers (the GCC states apart from Bahrain).

The two phenomena can, however, be linked in many ways (Figure 9.1). Indirect links may be found by which popular revolts and mass migration can be shown to share certain determinants. Direct links also exist in both directions. Indeed, revolts have generated massive flows of, mostly forced,

FIGURE 9.1 *Framework of interaction between emigration and revolt*
SOURCE: AUTHOR

migration and more must be expected; and migration is, likewise, capable of affecting revolts.

The first section of this chapter will review the common determinants of emigration and revolt and show that both exit and voice respond to the deep demographic changes Arab populations are currently experiencing. The second section will describe the migratory outcomes of revolt both in terms of voluntary and forced migration. The third section will explore the impact of diasporas on homeland politics, and more precisely the role played by national expatriates with regard to the revolts unfolding in their homelands.

2 Exit or Voice Trade-off

Photographs taken in large Arab cities suggest that two crowds, demonstrators gathering for mass protests and visa applicants lining up at foreign consulates, have at least one thing in common: both are comprised predominantly of young men. Would then some of the factors that pull young men on to the streets for demonstrations be the same as those that push them into international migration? Certainly—as we shall see—'relative deprivation' has been used to explain revolt and migration and the two phenomena are tied to a single model of 'exit or voice'. After reviewing this evidence, we will advance the claim that demographic change is a key factor linking revolt and migration.

Relative deprivation is the feeling experienced by people who discover that their lot is not as good as that of their peers. Comparing themselves to their 'reference group', they have the sentiment that they are deprived of a material or a symbolic object they believe they have a right to have, or they expect more than they can actually achieve (Merton, 1938). Transposed from the individual to the social level of groups and social classes, relative deprivation becomes a driver of collective violence (Gurr, 1970). Revolution is most likely to take place when 'men become angered because they acquire new or intensified expectations which cannot be satisfied by means at their disposal' (Gurr, 1973, 365). And certainly much of what has happened in Arab countries since the end of 2010 can be understood as discontent generated by 'the perceived gap between expectations and capability' (Gurr, 1973, 365).

Not only can relative deprivation trigger collective violence, it can also motivate individuals' international migration. People who judge that they do not, at home, receive rewards commensurate with their capacities may consider leaving their own country to find a country where they think these rewards *are* available. Emigration is influenced by 'how individuals evaluate what they have (satisfaction) and what they do not have (deprivation) [...] the decision by households to send migrants to foreign labour markets is influenced by their initial perceived relative deprivation within the reference group' (Stark and Taylor, 1989, 3–4). Typically, transnational networks spanning origin and destination countries are, at the same time, the reference group that make migration desirable, and the source of information on distant labour markets and the social capital that make it possible.

Both revolt and migration respond to the same sentiment of relative deprivation and take place when frustration rises and resignation ceases to be an option. They are a perfect illustration of Hirschman's model of exit or voice as opposed to loyalty (Hirschman, 1970). A relevant question in the present case will be to ask whether revolt and migration are substitutes or possible complements, whether there is a trade-off by which people who exit lose their voice, or whether they keep 'voicing' but through other channels and in another fashion; put in other terms—do emigrants remain political actors in their homelands?

What creates relative deprivation in contemporary Arab societies leading to exit or voice among the young? Many reasons residing in the social and political systems of Arab countries have been put forward in the lavish literature on the Arab Spring. In what follows, we confine ourselves to recalling what has been developed elsewhere. Demographic change is a key contextual—or 'predisposing', to borrow from epidemiology—factor that created fertile ground for both migration and revolt. More precisely, we argue that a lack of opportunities combined with a demographic bulge among the young accounts for many migratory and political processes at play in the Arab world today (Fargues, 2012).

In a nutshell, our argument is based on the fact that the decline of birth rates in Arab populations came late (with a few exceptions, it did not occur significantly before the mid-1980s) but steady (more so in the Maghreb than in the Mashreq). In the early 2010s, the largest generations ever born in these countries were aged between 20 and 35, a phenomenon commonly described as a 'youth bulge' (Figure 9.2). In the case of Arab populations, not only is

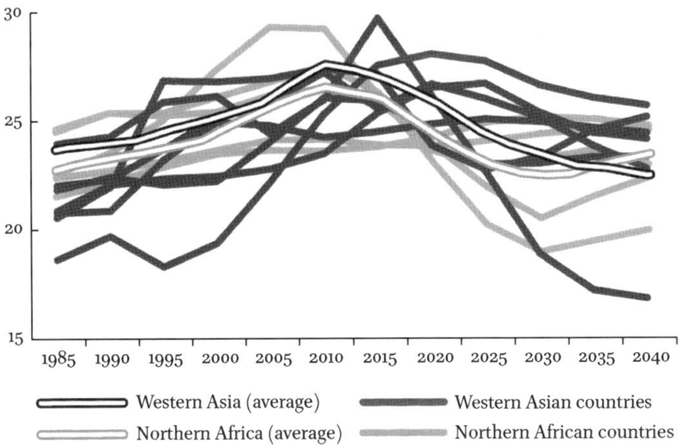

FIGURE 9.2 *The youth bulge in Arab countries*
Note: Western Asian countries include Iraq, Jordan, Lebanon, Libya, Palestine, Syria, Yemen. Northern African countries include Algeria, Egypt, Mauritania, Morocco, Sudan, Tunisia.
SOURCE: AUTHOR'S CALCULATION FROM UNITED NATIONS, POPULATION DIVISION, *WORLD POPULATION PROSPECTS: THE 2012 REVISION* HTTP://ESA.UN.ORG/WPP/UNPP/PANEL_INDICATORS.HTM.

intra-group competition more acute than ever before, it is also exacerbated by a radical change in the status of young adults.

Indeed, with now low birth rates and dominant patterns of late marriage, family responsibilities—that until recently were the common lot of young Arab adults—have been lifted: at 30, a typical citizen of an Arab country is not yet married and has no children. We have described this phenomenon elsewhere as the birth of the individual (Fargues, 2000). Such a change is particularly meaningful in societies comprised of families and clans with an immemorial tradition of negating the individual. It provides unprecedented personal freedom of movement and opens the way to mobility and risk-taking.

Moreover, the demographic transition has been paralleled by a steady increase in the level of education, with the gross enrolment ratio at tertiary level reaching 33 per cent after 2010, a level typical of upper-middle-income countries (World Bank, 2015). Rising education levels naturally translate to rising expectations. But due to governance failures (among other factors) young Arab adults' expectations are cruelly frustrated, making them a generation kept in waiting (Dhillon et al., 2009). Economically, expectations are barred by unemployment, underemployment and low rewards for those skills that characterise local labour markets. On the eve of the Arab revolts, the rate of unemployment amongst Arab youth was close to 30 per cent—that is, more than twice the world average of 14 per cent (UNDP, 2009; Handoussa, 2010). Unemployment,

TABLE 9.1 *Migrants originating from Arab Mediterranean countries, by region of residence, ca 2012.*

Country of origin[a]	Total population	Migrants by region of destination				Migrants % population	Migrants in the EU %
		European Union	Arab states	Rest of the world	Total		
Mauritania	3,796,141	28,807	24,000	169,500	222,307	5.9%	13%
Morocco	32,521,143	3,056,109	214,438	101,432	3,371,979	10.4%	91%
Algeria	38,481,705	877,398	11,209	73,243	961,850	2.5%	91%
Tunisia	10,874,915	911,400	154,900	31,900	1,098,200	10.1%	83%
Libya	6,154,623	66,344	9,824	24,397	100,565	1.6%	66%
Egypt[b]	80,721,874	224,122	4,783,800	404,945	5,412,867	6.7%	4%
Lebanon	4,647,079	148,717	162,663	290,900	602,280	13.0%	25%
Syria[c]	21,889,682	247,880	2,191,313	1,823,305	4,262,498	19.5%	6%
Jordan	7,009,444	33,066	218,149	88,540	339,755	4.8%	10%
Palestine[d]	4,218,771	14,627	844,063	13,234	871,924	20.7%	2%
Total	210,315,377	5,608,470	8,614,359	3,021,396	17,244,225	8.2%	33%

SOURCES: FOR THE EU—EUROSTAT, EXCEPT FOR MOROCCANS (CONSULAR RECORDS); ARAB STATES AND OTHER REGIONS—ESTIMATES PROVIDED BY ORIGIN COUNTRIES.

[a] Origin defined as country of birth (preferred) or country of nationality (second best).

[b] Egyptian temporary migrants in the Gulf States (2,283,800) and Libya (2,000,000 as estimated by the Egyptian government—the number of Egyptian migrants still in Libya in early 2015 is believed to have been less than 100,000).

[c] Syrian residents by region + refugees (in the Arab states and Turkey) and new asylum seekers (EU) from March 2011 until March 2015.

[d] Palestinian UNWRA refugees in Jordan (1,979,580) who have Jordanian citizenship are not included.

which until the 1980s was limited and confined to illiterate segments of the population, has now become the lot of a large proportion of young, educated people and university graduates. Politically, young Arab adults' expectations are negated by authoritarian regimes.

Frustration calls for a response. In the non-democratic, repressive context of Arab countries, exit came before voice. Emigration from Arab countries (except from the large oil and gas exporters of the Gulf and Libya) has been intense over the last two to three decades. Stocks of current emigrants represent 8.7 per cent of the aggregate population of Arab Mediterranean states (table 9.1), which is almost three times the world average. Comparable levels must be expected for non-Mediterranean Arab states (Yemen, Sudan...) for which reliable data are not available.

Just as importantly, the desire to emigrate is now peaking. In Tunisia, the country where the Arab revolts started in 2010, a large, national, representative survey of young people (15–29 years old), repeated at three points in time, revealed an unexpectedly high (and increasing) wish to emigrate: in 1996, 22 per cent of the young people interviewed expressed such a desire; in 2000 the figure was 45 per cent, and in 2005, 76 per cent (Fourati, 2008). These 'desires' are not a predictor of actual mobility (after all, a wish does not necessarily become reality), but they *do* constitute a revelation of remarkable discontent among the young.

3 Migratory Outcomes of Revolt

Revolts have already brought about considerable movements of mostly forced migration, but also some fresh outbreaks of voluntary, economic migration.

There have been two cases of mass displacements: Libya and Syria. They differ greatly in terms of nature and magnitude. The Libyan revolution that overturned the Gaddafi dictatorship in 2011 displaced more than 1.1 million persons, including 422,000 Libyans seeking temporary refuge abroad and 706,000 migrant workers, who left the country; 43 per cent of these reached Tunisia and 32 per cent Egypt (IOM, 2012). While it is believed that most Libyan refugees returned to Libya once the regime had been overthrown, not much is known about the migrant workers who left the country in 2011. Many will have either returned to Libya or have been replaced by new migrants, in particular from Tunisia and Egypt. At the time of writing, the numbers of migrant workers in Libya and of refugees waiting to be smuggled to Europe are unknown. One can assume that, with the collapse of the Libyan government and the development of rival militias, the exploitation, abuse, detention and killings orchestrated by the Islamic State in Iraq and the Levant (ISIL) will encourage departures from Libya among newly arrived migrants (Grange and Flynn, 2015; Government of the Netherlands, 2014).

In Syria, the protests that soon turned into civil conflict triggered an implacable spiral of repression and protest. At the time of writing (April 2015) 7–10 million people have been forcibly removed from their homes, including more than 4 million refugees and perhaps a larger number of internally displaced persons (UNHCR, 2015). To these Syrian refugees, one must add all the non-Syrians (Iraqis and Palestinians) who were refugees in Syria and who fled to become second order refugees in other countries, in particular Lebanon.

At the time of writing large numbers in need of protection continue to pour out of Syria.

The bulk of Syria's refugees are sheltered among four of its five neighbours: Lebanon (1.2 million), Turkey (1.8 million), Jordan (630,000) and Iraq (220,000). Israel, which is at war with Syria, has kept its borders closed. Not only do massive waves of refugees exert unbearable pressure on the economy of the host nation, they also bring with them the risk of political destabilisation. This is particularly the case in Lebanon where Syrian refugees, almost all belonging to the Sunni branch of Islam, risk setting alight dormant tensions between Lebanese religious communities. In a country where history has shown that refugees may wait a lifetime and still never return home, there is a fear that not all the refugees will return to Syria when the conflict ends. The fragile equilibrium between communities would then be threatened.

Other Syrian refugees have reached more distant destinations in the Arab world (135,000 in Egypt) and in the European Union (ca 220,000). Many of those who eventually reached Europe were unable to get a visa to travel regularly and safely to their destination. Instead, they undertook a long journey through Jordan, Egypt and then Libya from where they were smuggled across the Mediterranean at the risk of their lives. Among the 250,000 migrants smuggled by sea to Italy from January 2012 until April 2015, more than 55,000 were Syrians (Fargues and Di Bartolomeo, 2015).

Less spectacular than mass flight induced by war and civil conflict is the modest increase in labour migration that has been observed in the wake of revolts, in particular from Tunisia. In the first half of 2011 an upsurge of irregular migration to Italy was recorded, with some 25,000 unauthorised migrants from Tunisia reaching Italy and Malta by sea. This sudden, short-lived movement can be explained by a conjunction of facts: Tunisian border police operations broke down during the revolution and—as control over departures was relaxed—a large pool of would-be migrants were stranded, waiting for an opportunity to leave the country; and migratory pressure increased as Tunisia had to accommodate hundreds of thousands of migrant workers fleeing Libya, including many Tunisians (Boubakri, 2013).

One might expect that revolts will affect migration in the medium term, but it is not clear how. There might be an increase in the emigration of citizens or the return of expatriates, depending upon the achievements of governments put in place after the revolts. At the time of writing, it seems likely that emigration will continue for some time. Indeed, revolts may have so far created more incentives than deterrents to emigration.

A survey conducted amongst young Egyptians in 2013 (during the short presidency of the Muslim Brotherhood's Mohamed Morsi) helps to identify

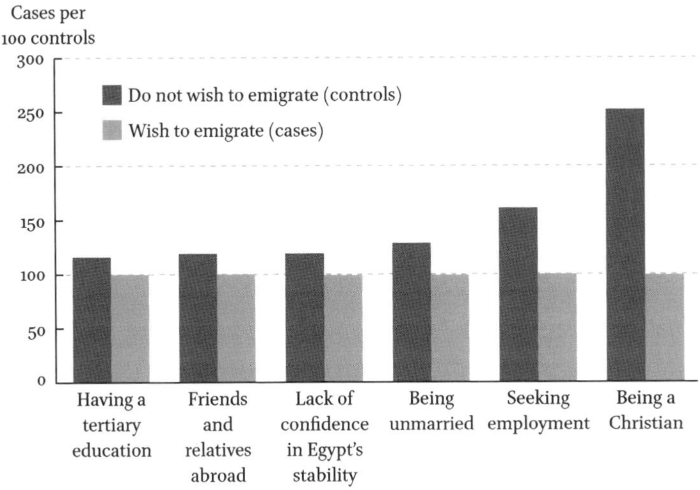

FIGURE 9.3 *Drivers of the intention to emigrate among young Egyptians in 2013*
SOURCE: AMER AND FARGUES, 2014.

the main drivers of the intention to emigrate, as shown in Figure 9.3 (Amer and Fargues, 2014; see also Pitea and Abdel Mohsen, 2011). A case-control was adopted and characteristics that were found to be significantly more frequent among cases (those who wished to emigrate) than controls (those who did not wish to emigrate) were considered drivers of emigration. A number of drivers are not directly linked to the revolution, including having a university education, being unmarried, seeking (better) employment and being exposed to others' migration through friends or relatives living abroad. Other drivers are more susceptible to be linked to the post-revolutionary situation, in particular religion and the lack of confidence in Egypt's stability. Being a Christian was found to be a key driver of the intention to emigrate. Are Egyptian Christians more inclined than Muslims to emigrate because they share more of the features of those young people who wish to emigrate, such as a higher education or friends and relatives abroad? Or is it that Christians feel more insecure at home than do Muslims? The survey does not help to disentangle the two.

4 Diaspora Impact on Homeland Politics

As the same factors explain both emigration and revolt could it be that emigrants, or some of them, played a direct role in revolts and the process of political change that followed? Put in other terms, was exit, sometimes, transformed into voice? This could happen through different channels: the return of migrants or exiles to take part in the revolution, their participation in elections in their homeland, or their contribution to disseminating ideas that, in turn, affect political developments, often referred to as political remittances.

4.1 *Return of Exiles*

From the outset it must be said that the revolts in Arab countries were conducted from within by local people and owe very little to the direct involvement of diasporas. It is true that several high-profile figures of the Arab Spring have a history of migration or exile. This is the case in Tunisia. There, the winner of the first post-revolution presidential election, Moncef Marzouki, and the leader of the Islamist party Ennahda, which won the 2011 parliamentary elections, Rached Ghannouchi, both returned from a long exile in Europe just days after former President Ben Ali was ousted.

In Egypt several popular figures of the Revolution were at the time established abroad. Take Mohamed Elbaradei, the former Director General of the International Atomic Energy Agency and overt opponent to President Mubarak; or Wael Ghonim, the internet activist, whose Facebook page—run from Dubai—provided, in real time, key information on developments during the Midan Tahrir demonstrations in Cairo. In the case of Syria, the main opposition institution, the Syrian National Council, was created abroad (in Istanbul in 2011) by exiles of the Muslim Brotherhood and other political movements.

In the other countries of the Arab Spring—in particular Libya, Yemen and Bahrain—no eminent figure of the uprisings seems to have come from the diaspora and such figures' experience abroad was at best a few years spent overseas as students or civil servants.

4.2 *External Voting*

The emigration from Arab countries started more than a hundred years ago and gained momentum in the last quarter of the twentieth century, resulting in the formation of Arab diasporas in Europe, the Americas, Africa and Oceania. For decades, Arab states paid little or no attention to those who had left the country and to their descendants. In post-independence years several states even showed distrust towards communities they suspected as serving as hotbeds of plotters and political opponents.

In roughly the late 1980s and early 1990s, Arab states relinquished state-centred, planned economies for market economies and adopted International Monetary Fund inspired policies of 'structural adjustment': at this point diasporas started to be regarded in a different way. While governments continued to see destination countries (the West as well as the Gulf) as havens for their opponents, they had become sufficiently strong not to feel threatened by their émigrés and exiles. On the contrary, they began to see these émigrés as a potential resource for the nation: first as a source of income; then, of cultural pride; and finally, of political support.

Specific institutions were established by each Arab state with a mandate to fostering transnational links with their diasporas. These institutions were concerned with economic links in the first instance. Draining money from Arab expatriates (workers' remittances sent to families left behind, entrepreneurs' investments in the national economy, etc.), making use of their skills and tapping their business networks could make a substantial contribution to development efforts in origin countries. Cultural links came later. Reviving a sense of belonging to the homeland among migrants and especially their sons and daughters born in the diaspora was cultural diplomacy. But perhaps more importantly, it could sustain such individuals' motivation to remit and invest money in the homeland.

Eventually, political links were sought. Arrangements enabling expatriate nationals to exercise their voting rights from abroad were made by a number of Arab states, including Algeria, Morocco and Tunisia (Collyer, 2014; Jaulin, 2014). Morocco went a step further with its constitution of 2011, granting eligibility rights in the kingdom to expatriate nationals. Another significant step towards the political integration of the descendants of migrants has been the recognition of dual citizenship by a number of countries and the granting of the right to transmit nationality to children born of a native woman and a foreign father (Tunisia, 1963; Egypt, 2004; Algeria, 2005; and Morocco, 2007).

4.3 *Political Remittances*

In a variety of locations, from the neighbourhood to the workplace, migrants mix with natives. They are, often unconsciously, exposed to the ideas and models of their host societies, which are new to them. With the passing of time, they adopt some of these values and models, which they unwittingly transfer to their home society. Direct communication with relatives and friends established abroad, as well as mass communication through media paying special interest to countries where the diaspora lives, will—therefore—expose non-migrants in origin countries to ideas and models typical of societies that they have never lived in. This mechanism, described as 'social remittances' (Levitt, 2001), is thought to apply to a wide range of domains, including political values (Docquier et al., 2011; Tabar, 2014).

What political values migrants convey will depend upon the political environment of their destination country. Arab migrants have two main destinations, the Gulf States and the West. The polity migrants find when they reach their destination is either more conservative than that of their country of origin, or more liberal, according to whether they go to the Gulf or to the West. Schematically, one might hypothesise that a dominant pattern of emigration to

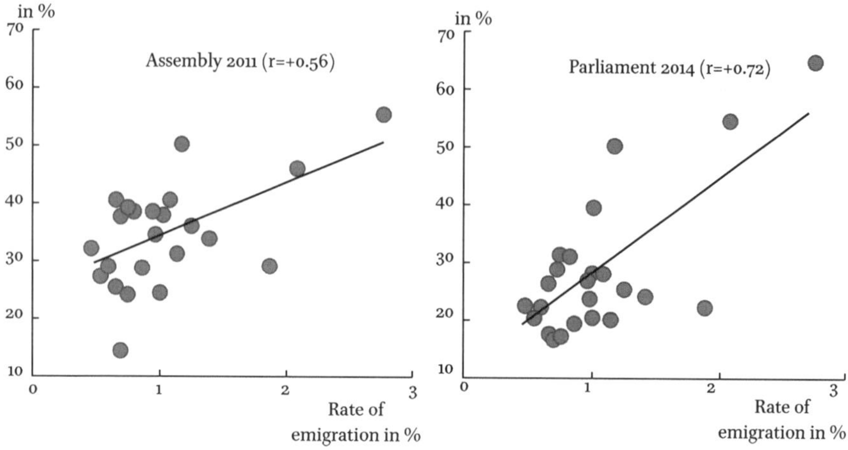

FIGURE 9.4 *Rates of emigration and voting for Ennahda in the Tunisian elections of 2011 and 2014, at governorate level*
SOURCE: AUTHOR'S CALCULATIONS.

the Gulf will translate into conservatism spreading in the origin communities of migrants; while a dominant pattern of emigration to the West will disseminate progressivism and democratic values in these same communities.

Do the contrasting post-revolution developments in Egypt and Tunisia bring any credit to this argument? In both countries popular uprisings occurred in 2011, but they ended very differently. In Tunisia, Islamist and secular parties engaged in a democratic process resulting in a peaceful changeover of political power and the adoption of a resolutely progressive constitution. In Egypt the first free election of a president soon led to an Islamist dictatorship, which did not last long and which was replaced by authoritarian rule. This new authoritarian rule is in many regards comparable to the regime overthrown in the revolution, except that the new authoritarian ruler was freely elected by an overwhelming majority.

The political remittances hypothesis sheds light on differences, not only between countries, but also within a given country. For example, in Tunisia there is Ennahda, the 'Renaissance' party influenced by the Egyptian Muslim Brotherhood, which had been banned for more than two decades under the Ben Ali dictatorship. It was reinstated in the early days of the revolution. In both the constituent assembly election of 2011 and the parliamentary election of 2014, a strong positive space-correlation is observed between the score of Ennahda and the rate of emigration, at governorate level (figure 9.4). It might be that voting for Ennahda and emigrating are responses to the same factors, from poverty to unemployment. It might also be that emigration has fostered a culture of protest in the governorates of origin of migrants. Indeed, Tunisian migrants are mostly destined for France and Italy—two countries with an established tradition of protest. Because the party had been banned by the ousted dictator, voting for Ennahda became a natural form of protest.

5 Conclusion

Expatriation and political protest are both rooted in deprivation and discontent and in the notion that life could be better, either in another place or at home under another regime. Moreover, they work in synergy, as expatriation can be the result of protest failing to achieve its goals and protest can find inspiration in ideas and models gathered abroad by migrants. So, what does the future look like? Migration and revolt have an age: both are typical of young adults. As a result of long-term demographic trends, young adults in Arab countries are now to be counted in greater numbers than ever before (the 'youth bulge'), and for the first time they are free of family constraints ('the birth of the individual'). Their availability with regards to mobility and to risk-taking will not suddenly end.

Voluntary, economic migration, or the reasons behind it, will—indeed—continue. Unless a miraculous economic upturn keeps the mass of young people at home, dreaming of a future fit for their expectations, many will keep trying their luck abroad. Where they will go is less clear. Apart from the most talented, Arab migrants are likely to find more and more hurdles barring their way to traditional destinations. The Gulf States are committed to replacing expatriates with nationals and the West is slowly exiting its worst unemployment crisis since the Great Depression of the 1930s. Exit may no longer fill the role of safety valve that it has for decades. Will, then, voice be the only choice left? The Arab awakening has not finished speaking. But, at the time of writing, one must acknowledge that revolt has produced a surge in departures.

Forced migration has gained unprecedented momentum in the Arab Middle East, which is by far the world's largest producer and receiver of refugees. Refugee movements must be expected to continue, since the restoration of peace and security—which would stop the exoduses of families fleeing war and persecution—is not in sight at the time of writing. Where they will find shelter is unclear. Jordan and Lebanon have now closed their borders to the entry of new refugees and put in place more stringent conditions that must be met if those already there are to stay. Turkey may follow, while Europe is not keen to fling open its doors to refugees. The result might be an increase in the number of internally displaced persons. It is doubtful, however, that forced migration could rekindle the dynamics of the Arab Spring, for internally displaced persons are uprooted people who lack the necessary territorial base for revolt.

References

Amer, M. and P. Fargues (2014) *Labour Market Outcomes and Egypt's Migration Potential*, EUI/RSCAS Working Papers, MPC Series No. 55, http://cadmus.eui.eu//handle/1814/17794 (accessed on 6 April 2016).

Boubakri, H. (2013) *Revolution and International Migration in Tunisia*, MPC Research Report No. 4, http://www.migrationpolicycentre.eu/docs/MPC-RR-2013-04.pdf (accessed on 6 April 2016).

Collyer, M. (2014) 'A Geography of Extra-Territorial Citizenship: Explanations of External Voting', *Migration Studies*, 2(1), pp. 55–72, DOI: 10.1093/migration/mns008.

Dhillon, N., P. Dyer and T. Yousef (2009) 'Generation in Waiting: An Overview of School to Work and Family Formation Transitions', in Dhillon, N. and T. Yousef (eds.) *Generation in Waiting: The Unfulfilled Promise of Young People in the Middle East* (Washington D.C.: Brookings Institution Press), pp. 11–35, http://www.brookings.edu/~/media/Files/Press/Books/2009/agenerationinwaiting/agenerationinwaiting_chapter.pdf (accessed on 6 April 2016).

Docquier, F., E. Lodigiani, H. Rapoport and M. Schiff (2011) *Emigration and Democracy*, IZA Discussion Paper Series No. 5496 (Bonn: Institute for the Study of Labour), http://ftp.iza.org/dp5496.pdf (accessed on 6 April 2016).

Fargues, P. (2000) *Générations Arabes. L'Alchimie du Nombre* (Paris: Fayard).

Fargues, P. (2012) 'Demography, Migration and Revolt in the South of the Mediterranean', in C. Molini and O. Roy (2012).

Fargues, P. and A. Di Bartolomeo (2015) *Drowned Europe*, Policy Brief No. 5 (FI: European University Institute), DOI: 10.2870/417003.

Fourati, H. (2008) *Consultations de la Jeunesse et Désir d'Emigrer Chez les Jeunes en Tunisie 1996–2005*, CARIM *Analytic and Synthetic Notes* No. 47 (FI: European University Institute), http://cadmus.eui.eu/handle/1814/10091 (accessed on 6 April 2016).

Government of the Netherlands, Ministry of Foreign Affairs (2014) *Libya: Militias, Tribes and Islamists* (Amsterdam: Ministry of Foreign Affairs), http://www.government.nl/documents-and-publications/reports/2014/12/20/libya-militias-tribes-and-islamists.html (accessed on 6 April 2016).

Grange, M. and M. Flynn (2015) *Immigration and Detention in Libya*, (Geneva: Global Detention Project), http://www.globaldetentionproject.org/fileadmin/docs/Libya_report.pdf (accessed on 6 April 2016).

Gurr, T.R. (1970) *Why Men Rebel* (Princeton: Princeton University Press).

Gurr, T.R. (1973) 'The Revolution, Social-Change Nexus: Some Old Theories and New Hypotheses', *Comparative Politics*, 5 (3), pp. 359–392.

Handoussa, H. (2010), *Egypt Human Development Report 2010: Youth in Egypt, Building our Future* (Cairo: United Nations Development Programme and the Institute of

National Planning), http://www.undp.org.eg/Portals/0/NHDR%202010%20english.pdf (accessed on 6 April 2016).

Hirschman, A.O. (1970) *Exit, Voice, and Loyalty. Responses to Decline in Firms, Organizations, and States* (Harvard: Harvard University Press).

International Organization for Migration (IOM) (2012) *Humanitarian Response to the Libyan Crisis*, February–December 2011 Report (Geneva: IOM), http://publications.iom.int/bookstore/free/final_mena_10_months_compressed.pdf (accessed on 6 April 2016).

Jaulin, T. (2014) 'Géographie du Vote à Distance: l'Election Tunisienne de 2011 à l'Etranger', *L'Espace Politique*, 2(23), DOI: 10.4000/espacepolitique.3099.

Levitt, P. (2001) *The Transnational Villagers* (Berkeley and Los Angeles: University of California Press).

Merlini, C. and O. Roy (eds.) (2012) *Arab Society in Revolt* (Washington D.C.: Brookings Institution Press), pp. 17–46.

Merton, R.K. (1938) 'Social Structure and Anomie', *American Sociological Review*, 3(5), pp. 672–682.

Pitea R. and R. Abdel Mohsen (2011) *Egypt after January 25: Survey of Youth Migration Intention*, (Cairo: IOM), http://www.egypt.iom.int/Doc/IOM%20%282011%29%20Egypt%20after%20January%2025%20Survey%20of%20Youth%20Migration%20Intentions.pdf (accessed on 6 April 2016).

Stark O. and E. Taylor (1989) 'Relative Deprivation and International Migration', *Demography*, 26(1), pp. 1–14.

Tabar, P. (2014) '"Political Remittances": The Case of Lebanese Expatriates Voting in National Elections', *Journal of Intercultural Studies*, 35(4), pp. 442–460.

UNDP (United Nations Development Programme) (2009) *Arab Human Development Report 2009: Challenges to Human Security in the Arab Countries* (New York: United Nations Publications), http://www.arab-hdr.org/contents/index.aspx?rid=5 (accessed on 6 April 2016).

UNHCR (United Nations High Commissioner for Refugees UNHC) (2015) *Syria Regional Refugee Response*, Inter-agency Information Sharing Portal, http://data.unhcr.org/syrianrefugees/regional.php (accessed on 6 April 2016).

World Bank (2015) *Gross enrolment ratio, tertiary, both sexes (%)*, World Development Indicators, http://data.worldbank.org/indicator/SE.TER.ENRR (accessed on 6 April 2016).

CHAPTER 10

Egypt's Economic Transition: Challenges and Prospects

Robert Springborg

Abstract

Egypt faces the Herculean task of simultaneously rebuilding its polity and economy and doing so in the absence of broad social consensus on either. State institutions underpinning both, ranging from the legislative and judicial branches to executive agencies with direct responsibility for economic management require substantial if not total overhauls. It is only the bedrock of the deep state that remains firmly in place, but that solid foundation is an inappropriate one upon which to construct a competitive and inclusive political economy. Any regime, in short, would face profound challenges in either creating a 'second republic' or re-invigorating the first, now badly discredited one. The military regime that seized power in July 2013, faces particularly intense ones not only because of the means by which it assumed power, but also because of its very nature. Military regimes are out of step with the times. One of the reasons they are is that they fail to deliver development, thereby suggesting that militaries are inherently incapable of devising and implementing successful economic models. Whether the Egyptian one might differ in this regard is the question this paper addresses. It does so by providing a brief overview of the broad political and economic challenges Egypt faces, followed by more detailed investigations of specific challenges in the areas of fiscal management, fostering a capable business elite, improving the capabilities and performance of the labor force, and generating growth in particular sectors. An effort is then made to foretell the 'Sisinomic' model likely to be crafted to meet these and other challenges, followed by an evaluation of its prospects for success.

1 Introduction

Egypt faces the Herculean task of simultaneously rebuilding its polity and economy and doing so in the absence of a broad social consensus on either. Moreover, the status quo ante has been discredited, as the 'January 25 Revolution' attested, so its economic and political models provide only limited foundations, at best, for erecting new ones. State institutions underpinning both, ranging from the legislative and judicial branches to executive agencies with direct responsibility for economic management, including taxation and regulatory bodies, were not particularly robust prior to January 2011. They have been so buffeted by events since then that in most cases they require substantial if not total overhauls, as the new constitution of 2014 signifies. Only the bedrock of the deep state remains firmly in place, but that solid foundation is an inappropriate one upon which to construct a competitive and inclusive political economy.

Any regime, in short, would face profound challenges in either creating a 'second republic' or re-invigorating the first, now badly discredited. The military regime that seized power in July 2013 faces particularly intense trials not only because of the means by which it assumed power—which has created a backlash of violent and non-violent dimensions, both of which challenge its legitimacy—but also because of its very nature. Military regimes are out of step with the times. One of the reasons for this is that, whether in Latin America, Africa or Asia, they have failed to deliver development, thereby suggesting that militaries may be inherently incapable of devising and implementing successful economic models. Whether or not the Egyptian military might be the exception to this rule is the question this chapter addresses. It will do so by providing a brief overview of the broad political and economic challenges Egypt faces, followed by more detailed investigations of specific challenges in the areas of fiscal management, fostering a capable business elite, improving the capabilities and performance of the labour force and generating growth in particular sectors. An effort will then be made to predict the 'Sisinomic' model likely to be crafted to meet these and other challenges; and this will be followed by an evaluation of its prospects for success.

2 President Al-Sisi's Impoverished Inheritance

President al-Sisi has inherited a state, a market, and relations between them that are sorely in need of overhaul. On comparative scales of state performance in managing the economy—whether the World Bank's Governance or Ease of Doing Business indices, Transparency International's Corruption Perception Index, the Bertelsmann Foundation's Transformation Index, The Economist Intelligence Unit's Business Environment Ranking or the Arab Reform Initiative's Democracy Index, the last of which contains several dimensions of state economic management—Egypt significantly underperforms regional and global comparators.[1] The much noted, brief, dramatic improvement on the Ease of

1 On the Arab Reform Initiative's Democracy Index, see Shikaki et al. (2011). For a review and assessment of Egypt's performance on various governance indices, see Springborg (2013). The

Doing Business Index in 2007–08 resulted from strategic legislative changes that were intended precisely to improve Egypt's ranking on that index but were never implemented (Springborg, 2013). Indeed, the gap between official policy and actual performance in state economic management is, according to the Arab Reform Initiative's Democracy Index, greater in Egypt than in any other Arab country included in the assessment (Shikaki et al., 2011, 28). That overcoming the legacy of poor state management of the economy will not be quick or easy is suggested by the World Bank's 2015 annual Doing Business report, published some fifteen months after General al-Sisi seized power. Egypt's ranking remained essentially unchanged over that period, ranking 112th out of 189 countries. Its lowest performance, 152nd place, was on the key indicator of 'enforcing contracts', reflecting—at best—stagnation of the vital legal/judicial system and an overall weakness of the rule of law.[2]

Mubarak's increasingly decrepit, corrupt state relied ever more heavily on rents as the years passed, particularly on those from the hydrocarbon sector, which by the global collapse of 2008 had come to provide about half of the country's total exports (Springborg, 2012). The surge of foreign direct investment (FDI), which peaked at USD 11.5 billion in 2007, was roughly equally divided between investment in the hydrocarbon sector, almost all of which was from multinational oil and gas companies, and investment related to real estate—whether in commercial or residential building or tourism—almost all of which was from Gulf Cooperation Council (GCC) states. While strictly speaking FDI is not rent, its concentration in the main rent generating sectors reflects the state's dependence upon and interest in those rents and its concomitant disinterest in steering and stimulating broader economic growth.[3] Cronyism—the

Economist Intelligence Unit's Business Environment Ranking of 2014 ranked Egypt 69th out of 82 countries, a deterioration of eight places since the 'January 25, 2011 Revolution', at which time Egypt was already in the bottom half of the 17 Middle Eastern and African countries ranked. Egypt's performance on this index, which is composed of ten separate criteria including taxes, policy with regards to free enterprise and competition, and foreign trade and exchange controls as well as measures less directly related to government, is better than on the other indexes; probably because Egypt's size creates substantial market opportunities. For a review of Egypt's scoring, see http://country.eiu.com/article.aspx?articleid=300997214&Country=Egypt&topic=Business&subtopic=Business+environment&subsubtopic=Rankings+overview.

2 For an analysis of the World Bank's 2015 Doing Business report, see Abaza (2014b).

3 That Arab FDI is more likely to be rent seeking than FDI from sources external to the region is further supported by evidence with regards to the motivations of Arab investors. According to Khalid Sekkat, 'human capital, quality of institutions, infrastructure and openness don't affect an Arab investor's decision to locate in a given Arab country while they affect non-Arab investors'. (Sekkat, 2014). FDI fell dramatically as a result of the January 25 Revolution, dropping to a net outflow of half a billion dollars in 2011 before recovering to some USD 2.8 billion

market's conjoined twin to a corrupt, rent seeking state—grew in tandem with these maladies of governance, as recent research has empirically demonstrated. Amirah El-Haddad's careful study of vertical integration in Egypt's clothing industry, for example, found that 'Those [businessmen] linked to power, prospered, whilst the businesses of others foundered against the wall of bureaucracy and red tape'. (El-Haddad, 2013, 1). Hamouda Chekir and Ishac Diwan's investigation of share prices on the Cairo exchange revealed that 'Connected firms have lost more value than others during these events [i.e. the 25 January Revolution] *on account* of their connections'. (Chekir and Diwan, 2013, 13). *Egypt's Lost Power*, a documentary on Egypt's gas industry prepared by al Jazeera, alleges that the country lost billions of dollars of potential revenue as a result of profits extracted from commercial transactions, most notably with Israel, by Mubarak's cronies, particularly those drawn from the military and intelligence services.[4]

With state–market relations driven by rent seeking, the performance of economic sectors varied according to their proximity to those rents. Tourism, for example, prospered in part because it is primarily a land-based activity. Land transactions provided substantial rents, particularly to the military, the largest single owner of land in Egypt.[5] The telecom industry flourished behind barriers to new entrants to the mobile phone market. Manufacturing industry, however, stagnated unless servicing protected local markets. As a consequence of this distorted growth the labour market became misshapen, with unemployment and education increasingly positively correlated and the already low female participation rate steadily dropping as informal steadily supplanted formal employment, accounting for more than two thirds of new jobs by the end of the Mubarak era. Although the rate of growth of the civil service slowed, it accounted for some seven million jobs by the time of the 'revolution', accounting for more than half of all female employment and 30 per cent of total employment. A 2005 survey revealed that the single most important source of family income even in rural areas was government employment, with agriculture coming second (Mayfield, 2012, 293–297).

in 2012. In the first quarter of 2015 it was almost double that of the previous quarter, rising to some USD 4.8 billion. This appears to have been the result of announcements made at the March donors' conference rather than the commencement of a sustained, dramatic rise in FDI. See the Egypt Foreign Direct Investment website at http://www.tradingeconomics.com/egypt/foreign-direct-investment.

4 This documentary can be viewed at http://www.aljazeera.com/investigations/.

5 This was already the case in Mubarak's Egypt. Under President al-Sisi the military has deepened and broadened its control of land throughout the country. For a description of the ways and means by which this has been accomplished, and for estimates of the amount of land the military has recently appropriated, see Abul-Magd (2016, forthcoming).

With little demand for highly qualified graduates, secondary and tertiary education continued to deteriorate, with even newly created private universities producing graduates as underqualified as those graduating from the old, decaying public ones (Assaad, Badawy, and Krafft, 2014). Although the birth rate declined during the first decade of the Mubarak era, it began to grow again after that as a result of female members of the 'youth bulge' reaching child bearing age and a surprising increase in fertility rates driven by increasing poverty and decreasing female participation in the labour force (Krafft and Assaad, 2014). In 2013, 2.6 million babies were born, almost 50 per cent more than a decade previously. By 2011 almost 800,000 new jobs were required annually to stabilise the unemployment rate, whereas only some half a million annually had been needed when Mubarak took power in 1981. The rate of economic growth required to produce this number of jobs, in excess of 7 per cent, was only almost achieved during one year of the Mubarak era. As the private sector failed to expand sufficiently rapidly to absorb new entrants to the labour market, the state continued to act as a labour sponge. In a related effort to deter unrest, the government spent steadily more of its budget on consumer subsidies, most notably for energy, while not increasing tax revenues sufficiently to absorb those costs, which consumed over one fifth of all government expenditures by the end of the Mubarak era. The resultant annual budget deficit bounced along at some 7–8 per cent for Mubarak's final years, thereby adding to the accumulated public debt, interest payments on which also absorbed more than one fifth of the budget. Savings and investment declined in parallel, dropping to some 12 per cent of Gross Domestic Product (GDP) by 2010, placing Egypt in the world's lowest quartile of countries on this vital measure of economic growth (World Bank, 2016).

These interconnected problems of the civilian economy, resulting from a rent seeking state nurturing its favoured clients, were exacerbated by the military's increasing interventions in that economy. Military- and officer-owned companies benefiting from a host of subsidies and preferential treatments—of which conscript labour, tax-free status and preferential treatment in government contracting were key—to say nothing of immunity from official oversight and regulation, increasingly shouldered aside civilian competitors.[6] Competition over rents between officers and cronies intensified, becoming a major cause of the military refusing to stand by Mubarak. The military was particularly sensitive to any efforts to encroach on its economic autonomy and the tax-exempt status of its enterprises. The two civilian cabinet members

---

6 For illustrative examples, see Abul-Magd (2016, forthcoming).

who were brave enough to advocate a change to the latter arrangement—Minister of Finance Yusuf Butrus Ghali and Minister of Trade and Investment Rashid Muhammad Rashid—were the only high profile ministers not related to the Mubaraks subsequently tried, convicted and then pursued abroad by the military-dominated government.[7] In sum then, President al-Sisi inherited a misshapen political economy distorted by rent seeking and the overweening role of his very own military. The challenges—resulting from this state of affairs—that he now faces include managing a deep fiscal crisis, empowering a new business elite, creating jobs and a labour force able to fill them and stimulating growth in various sectors.

3 Fiscal Problems and Solutions

Coterminous with Field Marshal al-Sisi's election as president was the announcement by Russell's Annual Index that after a three year review it was downgrading Egypt's status from emerging to 'frontier' market, a term coined in 1992 by the International Finance Corporation to refer to equity markets riskier and less developed than emerging ones (Zaazaa, 2014b). Among the reasons cited by Russell's were currency controls imposed by the central bank—a step taken to slow the rate of devaluation and preserve scarce foreign currency reserves, which at some USD 15–17 billion were not enough to cover more than three months of imports. But saving the Egyptian pound by restricting access to foreign exchange resulted in collateral damage to the market, to confidence, and to business in general; damage that intensified in 2015 in tandem with the central bank's further tightening as foreign reserves slipped further. For example, Egypt's largest steel producer, Ezz Steel, reported its first-quarter net loss had increased to USD 19.5 million from USD 2.7 million (EGP 136 million from EGP 19 million) in the same period in 2014. The company's chairman attributed the downturn to Ezz's inability to 'source sufficient foreign currency, due to a major change in the regulations of the banking sector'. He noted that, 'as a consequence we had to limit imports of raw materials and to reduce the volume of our production and sales'. (Ahram Online, 2015b). Russell's reclassification followed a series of downgrades, since 2011, of Egypt's sovereign debt by Moody's and Standard and Poor's, taking it to junk bond status. Unable to float an international bond issue for more than a year because of anticipated

7 As reported to the author by eyewitnesses, in cabinet meetings on this issue both men clashed with Minister of Defense Muhammad Husayn Tantawi.

negative market reactions, Egypt—by the summer of 2014—was facing a severe fiscal crisis. Its sovereign debt, attracting interest of up to 17 per cent, was predicted by the Minister of Finance to require a full quarter of the country's budget to service in the coming financial year, up from 22 per cent in 2013–14. The stimulus package financed by Saudi Arabia and the UAE launched a year previously in the wake of the military's takeover had consumed several billion dollars, but not resulted in more rapid economic growth. Indeed, GDP growth, estimated in early 2013 to be 3 to 3.5 per cent, dropped in the first half of 2014 to 1.2 per cent, its lowest level since the war years of the Nasser and Sadat eras. Inflation reached more than 9 per cent in April 2014, while the currency, despite central bank efforts to prop it up, had fallen 15 per cent against the dollar and euro over the previous twelve months. National savings collapsed in 2013–14 to some 7 per cent, from over 13 per cent the previous year. Unemployment, climbing steadily—according to official figures, which systematically and substantially understate it—from 8.9 per cent in 2010, reached almost 14 per cent in the first quarter of 2014. All that seemed to stand between Egypt and the fiscal calamity of runaway inflation coupled with a collapsing currency and economic stagnation were cash infusions from the Gulf. Small wonder that the Saudi and Emirati governments were both seeking to draw the International Monetary Fund (IMF) into the Egyptian rescue effort, lest they have to pay for it all themselves, with the estimated bill being in the tens of billions of dollars. Left with virtually no alternative, the new al-Sisi government moved in the summer of 2014 to reduce the government deficit by lowering subsidies and increasing taxes, moves which caused Moody's to upgrade its assessment of Egypt's outlook from negative to stable, although not to raise its low (Caa1) government bond rating.

The outlines of the stabilisation plan had long been clear. By 2015, over three-quarters of the annual budget was consumed by a combination of subsidies (27 per cent), government wages (25 per cent) and interest payments (28 per cent), with repayment of loan capital requiring a further 15 per cent. This leaves only some 5 per cent of the budget for all other expenditures, capital and recurring. If the savings and investment rate is to be driven from its present 7 per cent of GDP to the Organisation for Economic Co-operation and Development (OECD) average of around 20 per cent—with any thoughts of reaching Chinese and East Asian figures of over 40 per cent being consigned to the realm of dreams—then subsidies, wages and interest payments have to be dramatically reduced. Of these three, only subsidies and interest payments can be reduced absolutely, assuming that government workers cannot be dismissed, which would be a revolutionary step in Egypt in both the meanings of the word.[8] So, the immediate tasks at hand were to cut subsidies and reschedule loans while hopefully obtaining further debt forgiveness.

Of the two, attacking the debt burden is easier because it involves foreign support, some of which will be forthcoming. But generous as foreigners might prove to be, because Egypt's foreign debt, now approaching USD 50 billion, is only about 20 per cent of its GDP, whereas its domestic debt is more than 90 per cent of GDP, and because less than 20 per cent of the foreign debt is short term, even substantial relief of the foreign debt would not be a miracle cure. The government's domestic debt is owed overwhelmingly to public and private sector banks. Attracted by the secure, high spreads between interest for deposits and that paid on government paper, and smarting from large portfolios of non-performing loans they had unwisely extended to Mubarak cronies, these banks have for several years now essentially turned their backs on private borrowers. World Bank and other surveys reveal that the single largest obstacle faced by most Egyptian entrepreneurs is obtaining finance. In this sense, Egypt's banks are zombies, netting profits by collecting deposits on behalf of the government, but contributing almost nothing to the private sector's financial needs.

The government has the usual leverage a debtor has over a creditor and it could be tempted to use it. But since the public sector banks still account directly for about half the loans and deposits of the entire banking sector, and indirectly—as a result of cross ownership—for considerably more, the government would be taking money out of one of its pockets to put it in another, in the process rendering much of the banking sector even more irrelevant to the country's private economy. But given the magnitude of debt servicing this may be the path that is chosen, with concomitant, negative consequences for economic growth as neither the government nor the private sector would retain much access to credit. To the extent Sisinomics depends upon private sector-led growth, the benefits of achieving better fiscal balance at the expense of domestic creditors would come at a substantial cost. Assuming the government

8 As the fiscal imbalance continued to worsen, the government decreed a new civil service law in March, 2015, intended primarily to contain that sector's wage bill, which had risen to 25.2 per cent of the 2015/16 budget's expenditures from 23.9 per cent three years previously. Civil servants' fears that this decree would seriously erode their total remuneration packages, of which the greatest share for many is in the form of 'bonuses' rather than base salaries, led to a series of strikes in the summer of 2015, the most intense of which were staged by tax collectors. In response, President al-Sisi announced on 17 August that the intent of the law was to restructure the civil service, not to reduce salaries, thereby reflecting his fear that labour unrest would spread (Ali and Ahmed, 2015).

does not want to shoot itself in the foot in this way, the progress it can make on debt reduction can only be gradual, even with foreign support.

Subsidies are another matter. They are a better test of the government's political self-confidence and coherence because, unlike debt renegotiations, which do not directly and visibly impact the public or private sectors of the economy, subsidy reduction would. It thus becomes a question of which constituencies will suffer more. Because food subsidies benefit the poor proportionately more than energy subsidies, and because poverty has steadily increased since 2011, now affecting almost half the population, food subsidies can be better targeted but not substantially reduced; or at least not without a potential popular explosion that no government would want to face. Indeed, in 2014 the government moved to slightly increase the price of bread and to expand the use of smart cards for purchases of subsidised food commodities, but since food subsidies other than bread comprise a small fraction of total subsidies, their more precise targeting had relatively little overall budgetary impact.

This left cutting energy subsidies as the only major, immediate, potential source of government savings. Indeed this, more than any other economic issue divides not only the beneficiaries, but also members of the cabinet and the broader decision-making elite who represent them. Cheap electricity and gas disproportionately benefit the heaviest users, who are the wealthiest 10 per cent of the population. Within that group, owners of energy-intensive companies in the cement, steel, ceramic, fertiliser, petrochemical and related industries benefit most. While electricity prices have risen only slightly in the past decade, the price of natural gas delivered to factory gates was raised in 2014 to some USD 8 per million British thermal units (BTU), compared to a global average of USD 10; the proportionate price differential having dropped substantially since the gas-fired boom of the late Mubarak years when Egyptian industries were paying only some USD 2 per million BTU. It was indeed this cheap energy that resulted in foreign takeovers in several of these industries, most notably cement, about four-fifths of the production of which is now carried out by foreign-owned companies.[9] That fact alone, combined with the global decline in oil and gas prices from June 2014, makes it easier for the government to raise prices, as indeed it did for some grades of transport fuels in 2014. But even if there is less political resistance to price hikes now, the cabinet remains divided between advocates and opponents of electricity and gas price increases. The ministers of Finance and National Planning, for example, strongly favour price increases, whereas those representing industry and charged with attracting

9 In October 2014, Suez Cement—one of the country's largest producers—reported a 14 per cent decline in net profits for the first nine months of the year, blaming fuel shortages and the new, higher price of USD 8 per million BTU for the decline (Abaza, 2014a).

foreign investment, led by the ministers of Trade and Investment, want to hold the line against significant price rises (Zaazaa, 2014a). This choice not only implies relative rewards and costs for different Egyptian constituencies, but future industrial policy and whether it will continue to rely on cheap energy inputs or seek to shift to a broader base, in which the benefits to manufacturing of cheap labour would be key. Precisely because decisions on energy subsidies are of such political and economic significance they require coherent, confident governmental leadership, which has been lacking since the January 25 Revolution. Whether the new government formed under President al-Sisi can provide it in this key area will thus be a crucial test of its preferences, its base, and its coherence. As of early 2015 its potential reform of energy subsidies had primarily targeted transport fuels and electricity and gas for domestic consumption, leaving open the issue of long-term energy prices and potential new sources of supply, both vital for industry. In the last quarter of 2014 the government granted permission to two private sector consortia—one of which brings together Egypt's richest man, Nassif Sawiris, and his company Orascom Construction, and the Abu Dhabi Government's International Petroleum Investment Corporation—to construct two coal-fired power plants, one in South Sinai and the other on the Red Sea coast; their very location suggesting that the electricity generated would be used primarily by the cement industry.[10]

On the revenue side of the fiscal imbalance there is also substantial need for reforms that require political will. As on the expenditure side, therefore, they serve as a test of leadership. Privatisation of public sector enterprises would provide little in the way of windfalls as the jewels from that crown were plucked during the Mubarak era. Privatisation would, however, staunch the flow of public monies into them, which remains sizeable even though it has tapered off over the past three years. Clearing these public sector companies' bad debts from the books of their sister public sector banks is in any case a necessary step on the road to restoring effective financial intermediation. Worker remittances remain a substantial source of foreign exchange, if not directly of government revenue. But after rising steadily from 2010 on to reach some USD 19 billion in 2012, they fell significantly in the second half of 2013 as around 300,000 Egyptians were forced to leave Saudi Arabia as a result of its crackdown on foreign labour, while others still fled the growing conflict in Libya. Saudi Arabia alone accounts for about one half of all remittances to Egypt and if it and other GCC states step up expulsions of foreign workers, as they pledge to do, the flow of remittances to Egypt could yet be more negatively affected. Suez Canal revenues have remained relatively flat at USD 5–6 billion and are projected to increase

10 For further information on, and analysis of, Egypt's energy policy under the military government, see Springborg (2016, forthcoming).

by less than 5 per cent annually despite the USD 8.5 billion spent on the canal's upgrade, completed by the military in August, 2015. Egypt is now a net importer of fuels, and so does not profit on balance from the export of oil and gas.

Meaningful revenue increases, in sum, will not come from windfalls or from the traditional sources of government revenue. They will have to come from increased taxation. Therein lies the problem, as no one—of course—wants to bear that burden. Indeed, Egyptians have been steadily shirking it since the late 1980s when tax revenue constituted about 30 per cent of GDP, falling to 20 per cent in 2000 and now to about 15 per cent, well below the average for comparator countries. During the Mubarak era finance minister Yusuf Butrus Ghali, a strong advocate of tax reform, pushed through a new VAT tax and additional sales and real estate taxes. They were, however, never fully implemented, although the legislation and enabling administrative decrees have remained on the books. In the second half of 2014 as the economic crisis intensified the government dusted them off and reintroduced them, along with new taxes on stock market gains, on individual's and company's earnings abroad, and—on a temporary basis—a tax on annual incomes in excess of EGP 1 million. These new taxes, combined with reductions in subsidies, appeared to be intended primarily to send a message to Egypt's present and future creditors that the government was intent on reducing the fiscal imbalance, which by the end of the year was still hovering at around 12 per cent of GDP, thus imperilling Egypt's credit rating and further complicating its desperate need to raise new loans, signalled to be a new issue of a EUR 1 billion bond following the March 2015 donors' conference. The issue of whether the government was intent on real, permanent fiscal reform, or was just seeking to appease its creditors due to its present, desperate need, remained unanswered in 2015, for the promised raises in value added, real estate, and capital gains taxes were postponed yet again in the budget announced in July of that year.

In sum, Egypt's daunting fiscal problems cannot be resolved at a technocratic level. They are too deep and pressing and involve such sensitive political questions of who gets what, when and how that their effective resolution requires direct engagement by the political elite. Since President al-Sisi now towers over that elite, he will have to become personally involved in this decision-making process and identify himself publicly with policy choices if real progress is to be made. Whether he can come to understand the technical complexities and political trade-offs involved, choose decisively and well from among the options, and then sell the policies to those whom they impact will be a primary and presumably early test of his leadership. By the autumn of 2015, his prevarication, vacillation, and cancellation of policy reforms, combined with a fixation on grandiose projects, suggested that he was seeking to substitute the latter for the former, a strategy with limited long-term prospects for political or economic success.[11]

4 A New Business Elite?

Under Mubarak the business community consisted of a private sector dominated by cronies connected to the regime, independent civilian owners of large and medium-sized modernised enterprises, retired officers now running their own firms, a small but emerging 'Islamic' sector composed primarily of leaders of the Muslim Brotherhood, and literally millions of proprietors of micro, small, and traditional, medium-sized companies. That community also included a public sector in which the officer–managers of military companies were steadily growing in importance at the expense of the 'state bourgeoisie' of civilian managers of state-owned enterprises who had played much more important roles in Nasser's and even Sadat's era.[12] The Mubarak private sector has been accurately characterised as having had a 'missing middle'. Business activity, in other words, was clustered in a few large firms and a multitude of very small ones, the latter of which could not easily expand because of lack of access to capital and a discriminatory regulatory environment. The principal tensions within the business community were at its elite levels, most notably between the cronies connected to the Mubaraks and the generals, active and retired, who managed military enterprises or owned their own companies that existed primarily as contractors to the state, especially the Ministry of Defence, and agencies—such as the Suez Canal Authority—dominated by it. The de facto CEO of this sprawling 'Military Inc'. was Minister of Defence Muhammad Husayn Tantawi, of whom General al-Sisi was a favoured client. In the wake of Mubarak's overthrow, Tantawi, al-Sisi and their fellow officers, acting in concert with anti-Mubarak forces, were able first to bring the cronies to heel; then, after ousting the Brothers in July 2013, they dispossessed the Islamist capitalists.[13] Paradoxically, the July 2013 coup was made possible in part by support

11 For discussion and analysis of al-Sisi's policymaking style and fixation on grandiose, ill-thought-out projects, including those for the Suez Canal, land reclamation, housing construction and the building of a new capital, see Springborg (2015).

12 On the shifting balance between the civilian and the military public sectors, see Abul-Magd, (2016, forthcoming).

13 The government steadily extended its appropriations of the assets of those it accused of being connected to the Brotherhood. In 2015 it seized the travel agency of Egypt's most famous soccer player, Abu Treika, and the shares Safwat Thabet held in the sprawling dairy conglomerate Juhayna—a company that he had founded and directed.

from the cronies, who feared the Brothers more than they resented the officers, and so unleashed their media outlets against the former and opened their pockets to the latter. Fully in control, the military then began to selectively rehabilitate once disgraced cronies, including even the notorious Hussein Salem, architect and primary beneficiary of the costly gas deal with Israel (Zaazaa, 2014c). Presumably they were brought into the new, military-dominated fold because of the need for their capital and expertise. Other cronies who rejected overtures from the military, such as Rashid Muhammad Rashid, remained in exile, typically being subject to carrot and stick strategies intended to extract financial commitments to the government from them. New fraud charges were brought against Rashid, while those of tax evasion against Nassif Sawiris were dropped in return for his 'donation' of EGP 2.5 billion to the military's 'Long Live Egypt Fund', which was followed less than a week later by the announcement that the government had approved Sawiris' proposal to build a USD 2–3 billion coal-fired power plant on the Red Sea. One of the Mansour brothers was allowed to return to Egypt to sort out the mess surrounding his joint venture real estate development with a major Emirati firm, presumably as a result of the government's attentiveness to the Emiratis. The other brother, however, remained in his London exile, uncertain of his treatment should he return to Egypt.[14] During this turmoil, as a new business elite was being configured by the military, independent businessmen who operated medium-sized firms were left to their own devices to cope with political disorder, macroeconomic decay and infrastructural breakdown, including disruption to electricity supplies.[15] As for the business minnows in small and micro firms, a host of supply and demand problems, including interruptions to the flow of raw materials due to hard currency shortages, rendered their existence yet more precarious.

The new business elite is thus a work in progress under military tutelage. Mubarak cronies, presumably to be joined by others, are scrambling for whatever patronage officers dole out, enhancing their appeal by bringing more retired officers into their companies and forging joint ventures with officer-owned companies.[16] This fusion notably excludes most of the old state bourgeoisie based in the civilian public sector, a component of the economy treated with contempt by officers, with the notable exception of Arab Contractors, the

14 Both brothers have been listed by Forbes as being among the ten richest Africans.

15 For a review of how policy inconsistency has negatively impacted Egypt's once proud textile industry, see Esterman (2015).

16 For examples of these new 'partnerships', see Abul-Magd (2016, forthcoming).

former CEO of which—Ibrahim Mahlab, who had long-standing ties with both the presidency and the military—was chosen by President al-Sisi to serve as his first prime minister.

The tightly structured decision-making elite emerging under President al-Sisi will reinforce the importance of access to him and his confidants, simultaneously narrowing it; processes that will impact both the polity and the economy. In the cabinet reshuffle following his election as president, for example, al-Sisi ejected Foreign Minister Nabil Fahmy, who—like Finance Minister Ahmad Galal, who had been dumped in the previous reshuffle—had been too high profile and independently minded to be trusted by al-Sisi. Fahmy's successor, Sameh Shukri, had been Mubarak's long-serving head of information within the presidency, and thus someone closely connected to the military, the primary source of staffing for that department. By contrast, Fahmy was a known opponent, when ambassador in Washington, of the further expansion of military influence in the Ministry of Foreign Affairs. Several members of the first al-Sisi cabinet were also members of the board of the Arab Organization for Industrialization, the most important of the three holding companies through which the Ministry of Defence manages Military Inc. The al-Sisi presidency, in other words, is configuring a political–economic elite that depends on the military and those either with well-established ties to it or willing to assist it with their resources in return for a share of the action. Excluded from playing any active role in this emerging political–economic elite and presumably from having their concerns and desires taken into consideration, are virtually all other elements of the business community, including the few occupying the 'missing middle', the remainder of the public sector managerial elite, and the small and micro enterprise owners—this final category paradoxically being the one from which President al-Sisi himself hails. While he might have some lingering sympathies for and interests in this last, struggling component of the business community, its needs could only be met by a thorough overhaul of the bureaucracy and the financial sector, tasks that the new president is unlikely to undertake or achieve.

In sum, the emerging al-Sisi business elite will be more homogenous, smaller and more military dominated than that of his predecessor. Islamist businessmen and public sector officials will be denied significant economic roles, while the design and operation of the economy will be in the hands of the military, assisted by a limited number of recycled cronies with a few new ones likely joining the elite in the future. The independent, medium-sized businessmen who struggle in the missing middle will find their struggle harder still, as will owners of small and micro enterprises. These businesses do not appeal to officers, whose preferred model for the economy is that of major projects designed by themselves and implemented by military or crony managers/owners, frequently in joint ventures with Egyptian or foreign enterprises. They have contempt for the public sector and civilian government more generally, so they will privatise whatever state-owned enterprises they can while creating their own authority structures parallel to the civil administration. Independent businesses of any size, in any sector, will find it increasingly difficult to compete in an economy of this nature. The political elite will be similarly tightly and narrowly structured, thus denying most independent owners of capital avenues of participation, influence, or protest.

4.1 *Labour Force in Search of Jobs*

Even during the period of rapid economic growth from 2002 to 2008, when the official unemployment rate fell to a low—in the final year of the period—of 8.8 per cent, the labour market continued to manifest weakness. The proportion of informal employment provided by small and micro enterprises continued to grow, accounting for more than two-thirds of new entrants into the job market as formal public and private sector employment stagnated. Female participation in the labour market receded in tandem with the relative decline in size of the civil service, as the majority of women in formal employment are employed by the government. The youth unemployment rate continued to be at least double the overall rate. The correlation between education and unemployment intensified as the private sector was generating an insufficient number of skilled jobs, while the public sector was no longer expanding in pace with the growing supply of graduates. Official unemployment figures did not accurately reflect steadily growing underemployment, in part because the definition of employed was anyone working one hour a week or more. Increasingly, the unemployment rate reported primarily the proportion of university and higher technical school graduates who had failed to find jobs, as the less educated simply dropped off the books. Labour market weakness by the end of the Mubarak era could not be attributed in the main to the youth bulge, since by 2012 its peak lay in the 25–29 age range, and thus above the average age of entry into the job market. In 2006 the peak had been in the market-entering, 15–24 age group (Krafft and Assaad, 2014, 2).

Since the January 25 Revolution the labour market has further deteriorated. Based on the 2012 Egyptian labour market survey and other data, Ragui Assaad and Caroline Krafft conclude that even though demographic pressures have decreased, 'Overall, the labor market post-revolution is in a weaker position than in 2006'. (Assaad and Krafft, 2013a, 1). They further note that Egypt only has a temporary respite from these demographic pressures, as the 'echo' effect of the youth bulge, whereby the leading edge of that bulge come of age and these individuals, themselves, become parents, is beginning to be felt. The cohort of 0–9 year olds is much larger than that of 10–19 year olds. In all, 2.1 million children were born in 2008, whereas 2.6 million were born in 2012. This increase in births between 2010 and 2012 was 'the largest two-year increase since records began' (Rivlin, 2014, 4). In the coming decade 'there will be an unprecedented number of labor market entrants' as Egypt's population is on course to overtake those of Russia and Japan by 2050 (Krafft and Assaad, 2014, 3). A source of further concern is that a primary cause of the rebound in the fertility rate is a declining rate of employment of women of childbearing age. In 1998, 22 per cent of female high school graduates were employed, whereas in 2012 only 17 per cent were. The equivalent percentages for female university graduates were 56 per cent dropping to 41 per cent. This deterioration of female employment figures will presumably drive the fertility rate up still higher, thereby further exacerbating the challenge of job creation.

Segmentation of the labour market and its consequences have become more profound since the January 25 Revolution. The increasingly woeful conditions of the informal sector, combined with inadequate job creation in the formal private sector and successive governments' practice of cultivating support from the civil service by increasing its numbers and pay has caused job entrants to focus more and more on government employment (Assaad and Krafft, 2013b). In the 2014/15 budget, the salaries of government employees, which now consume one quarter of that budget, will increase by 13 per cent over the previous year (Esterman, 2014). During the Mubarak era an outspoken Minister of Administrative Reform stated that Egypt's civil service should not provide more than three million posts if it is to be made more efficient; now it employs in excess of 7 million people. While both the military-dominated and the Muslim Brotherhood-dominated governments formed between 2011 and 2014 curried favour with civil servants, President al-Sisi's recurring emphasis on hard work and sacrifice and the need for budgetary austerity, combined with his power now having been consolidated, suggests that the civil service will come under substantial economic pressure, as signalled by the announcement of a new civil service law in March, 2015. If this law and other measures do indeed restrict growth in the size and the overall wage bill of the civil service, this will parallel pressure already being applied to employees of state-owned enterprises, a significant percentage of whom have not been awarded promised minimum wage increases. The pressure being applied to these workers, and to those in private sector concerns, has taken a political form in the banning of strikes—a step called for by the Minister of Manpower, the Prime Minister and various other officials. It was incorporated into legislation decreed under President Adly Mansour and has been sporadically implemented beginning in 2014, most notably in Alexandria

(Charbel, 2014). Strikes in military-owned enterprises are illegal and employees who have sought to organise them have been prosecuted and imprisoned. Shortly after his election President al-Sisi launched a campaign to remove street vendors in urban areas, despite the fact that the activity frequently represents the last hope for those who have failed to find other employment, as exemplified by the case of Muhammad Bouazizi in 2010 in Tunisia.

The labour force, in sum, faces increasingly bleak employment prospects and a government intent on preventing further industrial action while being simultaneously intent on finding ways and means to limit spending on government employment, virtually the only segment of the labour market that has prospered since 2011. The temporary respite of reduced numbers of young job seekers will soon give way to a renewed surge in those numbers. Prospects for migration have dimmed as GCC states move to restrict expatriate labour. Other potential foreign labour markets, including Europe and North America, are yet more difficult to access. A growing percentage of Mediterranean boat people and the human traffickers transporting them are Egyptian nationals, as reflected by the country being placed in July 2015 on the US State Department's watch list for global trafficking in persons (*Cairo Post*, 2015). Nothing has been done in recent years to improve the low quality of graduates from secondary and tertiary educational institutions. Such an achievement would, in any case, take years to have an impact on labour markets. In the absence of a dramatic turnaround of the Egyptian economy causing the supply of private sector jobs to surge, the prospects for Egypt's youth, who constitute the lion's share of the unemployed, will continue to deteriorate. The very best that many will be able to envision is a job in Military Inc.; but that segment of the economy, while more robust than others, is unlikely to grow fast enough to make a qualitative difference. In any case the majority of its workers are conscripts, drawn from an overflowing pool in excess of 300,000 men.

4.2 *Key Sectors and Their Maladies*

The two main sectors driving economic growth in Egypt in the first decade of the twenty-first century were tourism and energy/energy-intensive industries. The former's contribution to GDP came to account for about 12 per cent, with a slightly higher contribution to the share of employment resulting from the some 3 million jobs generated by the industry, which rendered Egypt's labour market the world's thirteenth most dependent upon tourism (World Tourism and Travel Council, 2014). The second sector, in the form of gas, steel, cement, ceramics, fertiliser and petrochemicals, came to dominate Egypt's exports of goods and, along with real estate and tourism, the country's ability to attract FDI. The January 25 Revolution has been devastating for both sectors. The prospects for their return to the status quo ante, to say nothing of potential expansion, are not encouraging. Tourism, already down from 2010 totals, fell by two-thirds in 2013 from the preceding year, posting its lowest number of visitors in a decade. The comparative magnitude of this impact is illustrated by the fact that, in 2014, of 184 countries ranked according to the contribution tourism made to gross domestic product (GDP), Egypt was placed 35th, while its ranking with regard to prospects for growth in 2014 was 174th (World Tourism and Travel Council, 2014). Gas exports dried up shortly after the January 25 Revolution as the growth of domestic consumption overtook production. By 2014, accumulated payment arrears to foreign companies that had developed Egypt's gas resources and that are owed shares of its production reached some USD 6 billion before a payment of USD 1.5 billion was made by the government prior to the March 2015 donors' conference in the hopes that new exploration and development contracts would then be signed and so address the growing gas shortage.[17] Cement production fell by 30 per cent in 2013/14 as energy prices escalated. Stopgap measures allowing energy-intensive industries to import their own gas and to construct coal-fired power stations were approved, but the attractiveness of Egypt as a producer necessarily declined as energy costs escalated.

Neither sector will recover quickly. Tourism depends heavily on security and the broader political environment, a fact of which jihadis intent on destabilising the government are well aware. Attacks on tourists in Luxor and the Sinai in 2015, combined with the beheading of a kidnapped Croatian employee of a French energy company that year, reflected this intent. The United Kingdom's declaration in August of that year of most of the Sinai and Western Desert as unsafe for tourism suggested that the prospects for a renewal of the tourist industry had further receded. Egypt's decline on the Global Peace Index in 2014 was the second largest among all countries ranked (Institute for Economics and Peace, 2014). Even if the security and political environments in Egypt were somehow to improve, growing instability in the region, including in neighbouring Libya, would still deter tourists. Egyptian and Western educational, cultural and other institutions based in Cairo or elsewhere in the country, including for example the American University in Cairo, have suffered sharp drops in foreign enrolments, with students, archaeologists and others

17 In 2015 contracts were signed with several international oil companies, which presumably were enticed by dramatic increases in the price offered for the gas that Egypt would buy from them—on average some USD 4.50 per million BTU, more than double the amount under existing contracts. Since this came at a time of declining global gas prices, it suggested Egypt's relative desperation to obtain new supplies.

establishing new institutional relationships elsewhere, such as in Morocco, considered a safer Arab location. Stagnating remittances coupled with tourism's continuing underperformance will dramatically reduce the heretofore vital contribution of services and invisibles to the balances of trade and payments. In the final decade of the Mubarak era annual tourism receipts alone averaged some USD 10 billion, typically offsetting the annual trade deficit in goods. Inadequate reserves of foreign exchange resulting from the decline of remittances and tourism will in turn impact on other productive sectors, most notably that of manufacturing, which depends heavily on the importation of capital goods and raw materials—one of the reasons this sector has declined at a steadily growing pace since 2011, as evidenced by the performance of manufacturing in general and the textile industry in particular.

The energy/energy-intensive processing sector is equally, if not more threatened by the drastic deterioration of the environment in which it operates. Egypt failed to continue development of its hydrocarbon reserves at a rate sufficient to keep pace with expanding local consumption. It then violated production sharing agreements with BG, ENI, BP and other international energy companies by diverting gas intended for exports to domestic consumption. At least two of these companies commenced proceedings against Egypt for contract violations. Given the present availability of hydrocarbon reserves in many other markets now awaiting development, most notably in the Americas, Egypt's attractiveness is substantially lower than it was in the Mubarak era.[18] To restore confidence and attract FDI, Egypt has had to pay some of the arrears and commit to paying the balance, while also offering much more favourable contract terms, virtually overnight more than doubling its energy costs as global prices are declining. In the meantime steadily more energy is required to generate electricity for domestic consumption, a decreasing share of which can be allocated to industry. The future of these energy-intensive industries, which will have to rely ever more heavily on imported energy—whether in the form of natural gas, coal, oil or even electricity, which will be at or near global prices—is bleak, for they were all built on the basis of subsidised energy inputs. None require significant labour forces, so Egypt's potential advantage of cheap labour is minimal. All that remains of comparative advantage is location, especially sitting astride the Suez Canal, so that necessarily will become ever more vital to the country's development strategy. Again, however, that is a long-term prospect, payback from which will require many years to

18 On the impact of the contemporary 'energy revolution' on the Arab world and Egypt, see Springborg (2014).

materialise, thus raising the question of opportunity cost.[19] The key question then is what happens in the intervening years? How is the government going to structure the economy to meet these pressing challenges?

5 Sisinomics: A Model to Meet these Challenges?

This brief review of Egypt's fiscal situation and the state of its labour market and key economic sectors suggests that in all three areas the country is in deep crisis. The magnitude and entrenched nature of the problems in each area are such that they are not susceptible to quick fixes. The new regime, however, desperately needs to augment its questionable legitimacy as soon as possible, lest it face renewed challenges from excluded social and political forces, of which there are several, to say nothing of discontented military and security forces.[20] While it is seeking to substitute ephemeral appeals to nationalism for substantive economic accomplishments, that strategy can buy only limited time. Real personal income—which stagnated even during the boom years of the Mubarak era and which has steadily declined since, with the rate of impoverishment dramatically rising since the January 25 Revolution—requires, for its improvement, both a rapid increase in national income and steps to ensure its more equal distribution.[21] Given the rate of population growth, annual increases in GDP now would have to be well in excess of 7 per cent to have any real impact on average incomes, a rate which was achieved only briefly

19 For estimates of the years required to reap financial benefits from the USD 8.5 billion invested in the canal upgrade in 2014–15, see Springborg (2015).

20 Reports of attempted coups and protests by security personnel have steadily increased since the military seized power. In August 2015, for example, hundreds of police demonstrated in Sharqiya against the Ministry of Interior, which responded by alleging their ranks had been infiltrated by members of the Muslim Brotherhood, an allegation also made in response to previous police strikes in Alexandria and Kafr al Shaykh in February 2014 (*Ahram Online*, 2015a). In May 2015, more than twenty officers suddenly disappeared from their army posts. In August it was reported that they had been tried for, and convicted of, trying to overthrow President al-Sisi, for which they were sentenced to between 10 and 25 years in prison. The group included four colonels (*Middle East Eye*, 2015).

21 It has long been argued that income inequality in Egypt is not particularly pronounced by comparison to other lower-middle and middle-income countries. Recent research, however, calls that proposition into question, presenting evidence to the effect that in the Middle East generally and Egypt specifically income inequality 'is substantially higher than in the US or Europe [and] at least as large as in the most unequal emerging or developing regions (e.g. in Latin America or South Africa)'. (Alvaredo and Piketty, 2014, 2).

during the gas-fired boom years of the Mubarak era. GDP growth in 2014–15 was less than 3 per cent and IMF forecasts for growth in the next few years do not exceed 5 per cent. Since no windfalls are likely, whether in the form of privatisations of state-owned enterprises, confiscation of foreign assets, or a surge of hydrocarbon exports, and since broad economic growth across several sectors would require a thorough overhaul of both state and market, almost any new leadership would find the task of stimulating sustained growth a difficult one.

In the event, Egypt's new leadership is ill-equipped to forge and then implement a successful model for economic growth. Its core of military officers is made up at best of competent managers of companies, at worst of corrupt, rent seeking comrades with a strong sense of entitlement to their privileges. None have substantial experience of broader economic analysis, nor of economic policy formation. The rapid turnover of civilian specialists brought in by the military since 2011 to oversee economic policy suggests that meshing their expertise and recommendations with the preferences and ideas of their officer bosses is not easy. The 'first string' of economists was sidelined, and a second string was then fielded by the al-Sisi government. The present Minister of Finance has a degree in accounting, not economics. Many of these newly recruited experts have neither the professional reputations nor the independent bases of power of their predecessors, suggesting that the officer bosses do not want to hear independent advice, especially from those who might claim to represent constituencies. As for the business sector, the return of cronies indicates that a marriage between them and Military Inc. is being arranged, much to the detriment of other businesses and to the labour force as a whole.

The magnitude and immediacy of the economic challenges faced, combined with the limitations of the al-Sisi government, suggest what the likely strategy and the process of its formulation will not be. Not being an inclusive, representative government, the al-Sisi regime is not going to seek consensus on economic policy. Instead, it will operate more as a military command, with a small group of senior figures who conceive and direct policy. The delivery of goods and services will be conceptualised in a fashion analogous to a military campaign, with top-down orders to field units, many of the key elements of which will be from Military Inc. The notion that the economic forces of civil society can better provide goods and services so long as they operate within conducive governance structures is alien to the military officers in control and even to the cronies at their sides, whose wealth was accumulated through rents, not through market competitiveness. Poverty will be addressed to an extent, but through the delivery of rationed goods and services, many of which are already produced by the military, not through a coherent, unified plan for broad-based, job creating, economic growth. Alongside the 'welfare' component of the economy will be economic activities at which the officers and cronies excel. Most if not all of these depend upon strategic relations with the state, the most important of which include the provision of goods and services to the state, infrastructural development, and other essentially land based activities such as housing construction, as well as agency agreements with international companies seeking access to local markets or relatively small export platforms primarily servicing regional markets. Some of these undertakings will take on the character of national prestige projects, similar to those of President al-Sisi's predecessors, including Nasser's *Mudiriyya Tahrir* (Liberation Province) or Mubarak's Tushka, both ill-fated, large-scale reclamation projects. The example of a much-publicised joint venture between the military and an Emirati real estate company to construct low-cost housing is a case in point in the welfare sector. In the productive economy the main project will be the development of the Suez Canal Zone and surrounding area—the land and maritime access to it being controlled by the military, either directly or indirectly through the Suez Canal Authority and its subsidiary holding companies. The government clearly hopes that this strategic location will provide not just an economic, but a geopolitical inducement for potential investors, presumably including Chinese, Russians and others wanting to sit astride the canal for both political and economic reasons.

Indeed, the mix of economic and political motives is the key to understanding how the al-Sisi government will try to restructure the economy. Just as the geopolitical attractiveness of the Suez Canal may generate rents, so can other of the country's assets, a key example of which is political–military power. Subventions from the GCC states—most of which have gone directly to the military as general budgetary support, for specific projects such as the real estate development just mentioned, or in the form of supplies of oil or gas—are intended by the donors to harness Egypt's hard and soft power for various struggles, whether against Iran, Syria, Turkey, Qatar, Libya or elements of their own populations, key examples of which are the Muslim Brothers and their fellow travellers.[22] This manna from heaven provided to the very core of the Egyptian military-dominated political–economic elite will have the usual distorting effect of rents, as that elite shapes the economy by the very act of pursuing those rents. The Gulf economies are themselves lopsided and rent seeking, struggling to cope with the progressive decline of the rent/population ratio, a decline that accelerated following the collapse of oil and gas prices in the second half of 2014. But even if they were veritable paragons of development virtue, their motive is not Egypt's economic well-being, but rather its political

22 For a review of these subventions provided through the military, see Morsy (2014).

and military support. Keeping Egypt on an economic lifeline that enables the incumbent regime to hold its head above water is, in fact, a better outcome for GCC patrons than an economically independent Egypt. So the rent takers and rent providers will have common interests, but these interests will not prioritise the country's economic development over benefiting those responsible for it. More or less the same can be said of Western support for Egypt, which is increasingly motivated by security concerns rather than by development needs or sheer profit motives. FDI is even more concentrated in the energy sector under the al-Sisi government than it was previously, in part because tourism has lost its investment lure. Integration into global production chains resulting from multinational corporate investment has become an even more distant hope than it was prior to 2011.

Moreover, a fundamental contradiction exists between Egypt's rent seeking and its economic development. The former, reinforced by the regime's need for domestic legitimacy, drives it to accentuate the issues of terrorism, political violence and regional unrest, driven by Islamist fanatics or Shi`a agents of Iran, emphasising Egypt's role as a bulwark against these evils, including—most importantly—domestic ones. The primary message then is that Egypt is at the very epicentre of an existential struggle against terrorism, a message reinforced by the words and deeds of both the Obama Administration and the European Union. This message, however, is not one that reassures potential global or even regional investors in the Egyptian economy. If Egypt is to be integrated into global production chains that would gainfully employ its people, then it needs to be perceived by multinational corporations, even those based in China, as a stable country at peace with itself and its neighbours. This manifestly is not the case, but it should be the government's stated and actual objective if it wants to develop the economy in a meaningful, sustainable way. Instead, however, President al-Sisi is crying wolf out of his need for rents from external patrons and loyalty from his own, fearful citizens, thereby scaring off many potential investors.

The al-Sisi-inspired ideological project of a tough, austere state inspired by the moral virtues of Islam will further accentuate the perception of Egypt as a risky place to invest.[23] One of his first acts upon assuming power—to have the cabinet form a committee to 'fight atheism'—underscored, for observers already concerned about violations of human and civil rights, including those of international journalists, that this is a government hunkering down against many opponents, real and imagined, while emphasising its distinctively

23 For an assessment of the political uses of Islam by the al-Sisi government, see Hearst (2015).

religious character (Saber, 2014). As Noland and Pack have observed, perceptions of this sort are deleterious in numerous ways for a country's development prospects, discouraging—for example—its very own globalised expatriates from committing their skills and capital to their de-globalising homeland (Noland and Pack, 2011, 251–260). An emphasis on struggle, conflict and an austere, religiously inspired morality, with the military and security services playing the key role in combatting evil and doing good, is a message with resonance in Saudi Arabia and possibly Moscow, but not in London, Berlin, Paris, Tokyo, New York or probably even Beijing, or with most Egyptian skilled expatriates. Multinational corporations have already expressed concerns about reputational costs associated with doing business in Egypt with the military and military-owned companies.[24]

6 Conclusion

Al-Sisi's Egypt is doubling down on what preceding regimes in that country and those elsewhere in the world have demonstrated to be a failed strategy for economic development. That strategy is formulated and implemented by a military pursuing mixed and contradictory aims of national economic growth, enrichment and empowerment of itself and its officers, and enhanced coercive powers, both domestic and regionally. Inevitably these regimes emphasise nationalism, conflict and struggle and the central role of those in charge in combatting these threats. Economic development is conceptualised as the task of those in charge, who arrogate to themselves the country's resources in vain attempts to accelerate growth. Civil society and even civilian government are viewed by the officers in charge with suspicion, even contempt, and so are not called upon to, and hence do not, contribute effectively to economic development.

It is, therefore, only a matter of time before yet more profound economic failure, possibly combined with military adventurism, undermines this regime. In the meantime and even thereafter, the Egyptian economy is unlikely to return even to the level of growth achieved under Mubarak, which was inadequate for a smaller population. The key question is thus not how to develop Egypt, but how to save it from becoming a basket case similar to Yemen or Sudan. Sisinomics will not provide the answer.

---

24 The author has been made aware of these concerns through consulting work with various multinational companies presently working in, or interested in working in, Egypt.

References

Abaza, D. (2014a) 'Suez Cement Sees Profits Drop, as Chairman Blames Energy Shortage', *Ahram Online*, 30 October, http://english.ahram.org.eg/News/114349.aspx (accessed 8 May 2016).

Abaza, D. (2014b) 'Egypt Ranks 112th in World Bank's Annual Doing Business Report', *Ahram Online*, 29 October. http://english.ahram.org.eg/News/114251.aspx (accessed 8 May 2016).

Abul-Magd, Z. (2016, forthcoming) *Militarizing the Nation: Army, Business, and Revolution in Egypt* (New York: Columbia University Press).

Ahram Online (2015a) 'Brotherhood behind low ranking policemen strike: Security source' August 22, http://english.ahram.org.eg/News/138537.aspx (accessed 8 May 2016).

Ahram Online (2015b) 'Egypt's Ezz Steel Says Output Hit by Forex Shortage' August 20, http://english.ahram.org.eg/News/138344.aspx (accessed 8 May 2016).

Ali, R. and W. Ahmed (2015) 'Doubts Hover over Egypt's Civil Service Law', *Ahram Online*, August 19, http://english.ahram.org.eg/News/138162.aspx (accessed 8 May 2016).

Alvaredo, F. and T. Piketty (2014) 'Measuring Top Incomes and Inequality in the Middle East: Data Limitations and Illustration with the Case of Egypt', *Working Paper No. 832* (Giza: Economic Research Forum), http://erf.org.eg/wp-content/uploads/2014/07/832.pdf (accessed 9 May 2016).

Assaad, R. and C. Krafft (2013a) 'The Evolution of Labor Supply and Unemployment in the Egyptian Economy: 1988–2012', *Working Paper No. 806* (Giza: Economic Research Forum), http://erf.org.eg/wp-content/uploads/2014/02/806.pdf (accessed 9 May 2016).

Assaad, R. and C. Krafft (2013b) 'The Structure and Evolution of Employment in Egypt: 1998–2012', *Working Paper No. 805* (Giza: Economic Research Forum), http://erf.org.eg/wp-content/uploads/2014/07/805.pdf (accessed 9 May 2016).

Assaad, R., E. Badawy and C. Krafft (2014) 'Differences in Pedagogy, Accountability, and Perceptions of Quality by Type of Higher Education in Egypt and Jordan' *Working Paper No. 828* (Giza: Economic Research Forum), http://erf.org.eg/wp-content/uploads/2014/07/828.pdf (accessed 9 May 2016).

Cairo Post (2015) 'Egypt Downgraded to "Watch List" in Fighting Human Trafficking: U.S. Report' July 28, http://www.thecairopost.com/news/161552/news/egypt-downgraded-to-watch-list-in-fighting-human-trafficking-u-s-report (accessed 8 May 2016).

Charbel, J. (2014) 'Govt Moves to Outlaw Strikes, but is it Promoting Production?' *mada masr*, June 17, http://www.madamasr.com/content/govt-moves-outlaw-strikes-it-promoting-production (accessed 8 May 2016).

Chekir, H. and I. Diwan (2013) 'Distressed Whales on the Nile—Egyptian Capitalists in the Wake of the 2010 Revolution', *Working Paper* 747, (Giza: Economic Research Forum), http://erf.org.eg/wp-content/uploads/2014/03/747.pdf (accessed 9 May 2016).

El-Haddad, A. (2013) 'Political Patronage and Economic Opportunity: The Case of Vertical Integration in the Egyptian Clothing Industry', *Working Paper 756,* (Giza: Economic Research Forum).

Esterman, I. (2014) 'Sisi Meets Egypt's Economic Hurdles' *mada masr,* June 3, http://www.madamasr.com/content/sisi-meets-egypts-economic-hurdles (accessed 8 May 2016).

Esterman, I. (2015) 'Inconsistent Policy Changes are Putting Egypt's Cotton Industry in Crisis' *Mada Masr,* August 19, http://www.madamasr.com/sections/economy/inconsistent-policy-changes-are-putting-egypt%E2%80%99s-cotton-industry-crisis (accessed 8 May 2016).

Hearst, D. (2015) 'The Fatwa of "Ayatollah" al-Sisi' *Middle East Eye,* August 18, http://www.middleeasteye.net/columns/fatwa-ayatollah-al-sisi-1867588370 (accessed 8 May 2016).

Institute for Economics and Peace (2014) *Global Peace Index* (Sydney: IEP), http://reliefweb.int/sites/reliefweb.int/files/resources/2014%20Global%20Peace%20Index%20REPORT.pdf (accessed 8 May 2016).

Krafft, C. and R. Assaad (2014) 'Beware of the Echo: The Impending Return of Demographic Pressures in Egypt' *Policy Perspective,* 12 (Giza: Economic Research Forum).

Mayfield, J.B. (2012) (2012), *Field of Reeds, Social, Economic and Political Change in Rural Egypt: In Search of Civil Society and Good Governance* (Bloomington: AuthorHouse).

Middle East Eye (2015) cited in *Marsad Egypt,* '26 Egyptian Officers Allegedly Jailed for Plotting Coup against Sisi', August 17, http://www.marsad.eg/en/26-egyptian-officers-allegedly-jailed-for-plotting-coup-against-sisi/ (accessed 8 May 2016).

Morsy, A. (2014) 'The Military Crowds out Civilian Business in Egypt', (Washington, DC: Carnegie Endowment), http://carnegieendowment.org/2014/06/24/military-crowds-out-civilian-business-in-egypt/hedq (accessed 8 May 2016).

Noland, M. and H. Pack (2011) *The Arab Economies in a Changing World.* (Washington DC: Peterson Institute for International Economics), 2nd ed., 362 p.

Rivlin, P. (2014) 'Sisi as Sisyphus: Egypt's Economic Emergency', *Middle East Economy* (Tel Aviv University), Vol. 4. No. 6, June 19, http://dayan.org/content/iqtisadi-sisi-sisyphus-egypts-economic-emergency (accessed 8 May 2016).

Saber, A. (2014) 'Govt Announces Campaign to Save Youth from Atheism' *mada masr,* June19,http://www.madamasr.com/content/govt-announces-campaign-save-youth-atheism (accessed 8 May 2016).

Sekkat, K. (2014) 'Is there Anything Special with Intra-Arab Capital Flows', *Working Paper* 812, (Giza: Economic Research Forum).

Shikaki, K. et al. (2011) *The State of Reform in the Arab World: The Arab Democracy Index,* Arab Reform Initiative/Palestinian Center for Policy and Survey Research, http://www.arab-reform.net/sites/default/files/Full%20Report_0.pdf (accessed 8 May 2016).

Springborg, R. (2012) 'Gas and Oil in Egypt's Development' in Robert E. Looney, ed., *Handbook of Oil Politics* (London: Routledge) pp. 295–311.

Springborg, R. (2013) 'Governance in Egypt', in Abbas Kadhim, ed., *Governance in the Middle East and North Africa* (London and New York: Routledge), pp. 399–416.

Springborg, R. (2014) 'The Energy Revolution's Impacts on the Arab World', *Policy Focus Series* (Washington, DC: Middle East Institute), http://www.mei.edu/content/article/energy-revolution%E2%80%99s-impacts-arab-world (accessed 8 May 2016).

Springborg, R. (2015) 'President Sisi's Delegative Authoritarianism', Working Paper 15 (Rome: Istituto Affari Internazionale), http://www.iai.it/en/node/4450 (accessed 8 May 2016).

Springborg, R. (2016, forthcoming) 'Egypt: The Challenge of Squaring the Energy—Environment—Growth Triangle', in Robert E. Looney, ed., *The Routledge Handbook of Transitions to Energy and Climate Security* (London and New York: Routledge).

World Bank (2016) *Gross savings (% of GDP), World Development Indicators*, http://data.worldbank.org/indicator/NY.GNS.ICTR.ZS (accessed on 22 April 2016).

World Tourism and Travel Council (2014) *Travel and Tourism: Economic Impact 2014, Egypt,* (London: WTTC).

Zaazaa Sherif, S. (2014a) 'Tax Talks' *mada masr,* April 22, http://www.madamasr.com/content/economy-week-tax-talks (accessed 8 May 2016).

Zaazaa Sherif, S. (2014b) 'Egypt Reclassified as Frontier Market', *mada masr,* March 10, http://www.madamasr.com/sections/economy/economy-week-egypt-reclassified-frontier-market (accessed 8 May 2016).

Zaazaa Sherif, S. (2014c) 'Egypt Welcomes Back Mubarak-era Cronies' *mada masr,* February 9, http://www.madamasr.com/content/economy-week-egypt-welcomes-back-mubarak-era-cronies (accessed 8 May 2016).

CHAPTER 11

Oil Rent and Regional Economic Development in MENA

Giacomo Luciani

Abstract

Oil rent has created a regional dynamic in the Middle East and North Africa (MENA) whereby major political developments take place at the regional rather than the single-state level. The Arab Spring was a regional phenomenon, and the entire region is today involved in a regional civil war. The regional dimension of democratic transitions has often been postulated and supported in the literature.

In seeking appropriate economic strategies that may support the democratisation process, the regional dimension cannot be forgotten: purely national recipes have little chance of success. Ever since the heyday of pan-Arabism, economic integration within the Arab region has been a recurring theme and objective, but accomplishments remain profoundly disappointing. This chapter reviews findings and the literature concerning the three dimensions of regional integration—merchandise trade, movements of labour and movements of capital—and details the insufficient progress that has been made.

It is difficult to envisage a significant improvement in the development prospects of individual Arab countries unless greater success is achieved in pursuing regional integration. At the same time, the implementation of a new regional economic order also requires a new political order. The main difficulty in this respect is that those countries in the region that have the most economic assets and tools—the major Gulf exporters—are ruled by patrimonial monarchies rather than political forces, and their model of governance cannot be exported.

1 Introduction

The existing state order in the Middle East and North Africa (MENA) has frequently been questioned. Early views, which presented all states in the region as being the artificial creation of colonial powers, have progressively given way to the perception that Arab states—as came to exist at various times during the past century, and in some cases much, much earlier—are here to stay. Thus we tend to analyse political developments in their state-specific dimension.

DOI 10.1163/9789004336452_012

This chapter argues that the oil rent has created a regional dynamic whereby major political developments take place at the regional rather than the single-state level. Essentially all major political movements in the region have a regional, not country-specific, dimension. The Arab Spring was a regional phenomenon, and the entire region is today involved in a regional civil war. The prospects for democratisation will also be decided at the regional level, and will essentially be influenced by the outcome of the civil war underway, which cannot be predicted.

The argument is presented in four sections followed by conclusions. The first section summarises the regional dimension of democratisation processes, and of all politics in the MENA region. The second section discusses the dynamics of oil prices and oil rent and how these have affected regional relations. The third section illustrates how regional economic integration has failed, and how conduits for regional circulation of the oil rent have not been operational or have benefited only very narrow elites. The fourth section argues that that the current regional order is in crisis, and democratic transitions will only be successful if they are accommodated at the regional level and accompanied by closer regional economic cooperation. A short conclusion closes the chapter.

2 Politics in MENA is Regional

The distinguishing feature of the Arab Spring is its regional character. Within weeks of the first manifestations of the movement in Tunisia, many other countries were engulfed in rapid succession: Egypt, Bahrain, Yemen, Syria and Libya. A total of five countries accounting for close to 50 per cent of the total population of MENA were soon fully involved in the phenomenon, while others were more marginally touched—notably Oman and Jordan. In North Africa, only Algeria, which had experienced its own aborted 'Spring' twenty years earlier, and subsequently saw a very bloody civil war, was not involved. In the Levant, Iraq had been experiencing civil war conditions ever since regime change in 2003, and Lebanon has a fragile and very imperfect, yet democratic, order. The major Gulf rentier states (a grouping of which Bahrain is not a member) were almost untouched.

The regional dimension of democratic transitions has often been postulated and tested in the literature (Kuru, 2014; Freund and Jaud, 2013; Elbadawi et al., 2011). It is frequently found that the regional environment has an important bearing on the outcome of individual countries' transitions: democratisation is facilitated in regions where democracy prevails, and more difficult where authoritarian regimes are numerous. There clearly is an imitation effect, and also open support for similar regimes—at least in the case of authoritarian regimes, which tend to fear 'democratic contagion' and support each other more effectively than democracies do. We have seen the same in the Gulf Cooperation Council (GCC—encompassing Bahrain, Kuwait, Oman, Qatar, Saudi Arabia and the United Arab Emirates), a regional body created with the objective of ensuring mutual support among patrimonial monarchies, which quickly intervened to terminate the popular revolt in Bahrain.

Thus, regional influence is not new, but the speed with which the democratisation contagion spread during the Arab Spring was unprecedented, and justifies the quest for regional, rather than purely national causes and interpretations. Looking forward, it is apparent that the battle between democracy and authoritarian rule is also being fought and will be decided at the regional level. In MENA, all domestic politics have a regional impact, and no country's internal equilibria can be independent of regional developments (Luciani and Salamé, 1988). Political permeability inevitably turns the region into an arena for conflict rather than compromise and cooperation. It is the very close interdependence of domestic and regional affairs—close to an extent that has no parallel in any other region of the world—that makes it inevitable that MENA states will be involved in each other's internal affairs.

The region has known 'democratic exceptions' in a context of prevailing authoritarian rule. Israel has been the most prominent case, and in the economic sphere it has been almost completely alienated from its regional environment while pursuing integration with the United States of America (US), Europe and other regions. Lebanon has maintained a democracy, while being constantly on the brink of civil war, in which constitutional dictates are ignored more often than not. Tunisia might possibly also succeed in consolidating a democracy against the regional tide, and pursue a strategy of economic integration with Europe rather than its Arab neighbours. But these are exceptions, and fragile exceptions at that—Israel apart.

At the regional level, the battle is raging: while civil wars are being fought in only four countries (Iraq, Syria, Yemen and Libya) all other countries are in fact implicated. The whole region is engaged in a regional civil war whose active front is primarily in the four countries mentioned, but new fronts may open. And the GCC member states, which have so far succeeded in maintaining substantial control of their territory, are—in any case—active participants, contributing funding, providing weapons or, in the case of Yemen, Syria and Libya, via military involvement on the ground and from the air.

If and when the regional civil war will be resolved, economic policies will also need to be defined at the regional level. The task of providing for the reconstruction of Syria and Yemen will inevitably fall on the shoulders of the major Gulf oil exporters, just as the task of maintaining the Egyptian economy is already theirs. Iraq and Libya are also major producers and might possibly be able to fund their own reconstruction, but they too will need to define a regional economic strategy. The Arab civil war will inevitably define a new regional order, which will be economic as well as political.

In seeking appropriate economic strategies that may support the democratisation process—assuming democratisation will still be on the agenda at the end of the civil war—the regional dimension cannot be forgotten: purely national recipes have little chance of success.

3 The Impact of the Oil Rent on Regional Economic Relations

Oil has exerted a fundamental influence on inter-Arab relations, primarily because of the dialectic between oil-poor and oil-rich states. Interestingly, the oil-rich states are also relatively 'new' in terms of history, having been formed in the first half of the twentieth century, and having gained independence even later; while the oil-poor states have deeper historical roots, in the case of Egypt and Iraq even having existed for millennia (Harik, 1987). Furthermore, the oil-rich states are rentier, meaning that the state is supported by revenues accruing from abroad and independent of domestic taxation; while the oil-poor states became rentier only for a short period, as recipients of unilateral transfers from the oil-rich states in the 1970s and 80s (Luciani, 1987).

The dichotomy between oil-rich and oil-poor states (Kerr and Yassin, 1982) is certainly not the only factor in the extraordinary divisiveness of Arab regional relations, but it has been significant. Although the pan-Arab ideology, which dominated the region at least until 1967, is not directly related to oil—it is rather a reaction to the Balkanisation of the Arab region, which, in turn, is certainly also related to oil—it quickly became entangled with it, hardening the conflict between the historically longer established, progressive, more developed, but oil-poor Arab states and the newly formed, traditional, conservative, oil-rich states of the Gulf and North Africa.

In regional relations the oil-poor states implicitly or explicitly articulated a claim to a share of the oil rent that the oil-rich states never truly accepted as legitimate. Nasser's ideology was not primarily conceived of as a tool with which to destroy the oil monarchies and assert control over their oil riches, but it was soon perceived by these monarchs as aiming precisely at this outcome. Nasser was defeated not only by his inability to deliver progress with respect to the Palestine–Israel issue, but also, and perhaps even more so, by his inability to come to terms with the oil monarchies—or, to be precise, with all oil-exporting countries in the region—even when some (like Iraq in 1958 and Libya in 1969) shed their monarchies and followed the 'revolutionary' path. He lost his battle when he could not prevail in the civil war in Yemen; nor was he able to overcome persistent rivalry with Iraq (even before 1967). The advent of a regime, in Libya, with strong Nasserite and pan-Arab inclinations received little more than an opportunistic and profiteering response from Egypt.

In the 1970s, the increase of the oil rent was so sudden, and its concentration so extreme, that the rentier states felt it was prudent to be generous outside, as well as inside, their borders. They therefore created institutions to redistribute a share of the rent internationally and engaged in granting direct subsidies to neighbouring governments. Jordan, Syria, the Palestine Liberation Organization, and—until it made peace with Israel—Egypt were major beneficiaries of these direct grants. Later, Iraq became a recipient during its protracted war with Iran.

However, the effectiveness of such generosity in purchasing lasting goodwill was dubious, to say the least. Iraq's decision to invade Kuwait, and the attitude that Jordan, Yemen, or the Palestinians adopted on that occasion, proves that generosity sometimes breeds resentment. More recently, the fact that al-Qaeda turned against the Saudi regime is another demonstration of a client turning against its patron.

So, after a short period of time during which the tide of the rent rose so high that it covered the entire region and almost every government became rentier (in the sense of being primarily occupied with capturing oil or strategic rents in the form of direct grants), the region went back to a condition that was common before 1973—that is, being dominated by the dynamics between rentier and non-rentier, or oil-rich and oil-poor, states, and the seeming impossibility of integration between them.

The Arab Gulf States reacted to the Iraqi invasion of Kuwait and the positions taken by several neighbouring countries by radically revising their previously generous attitude, expelling massive numbers of immigrants from the other Arab countries and establishing the GCC as a club of rentier monarchs pursuing an integration project separate and independent from the rest of the region.

The decade of low prices from 1990 to 2000 marked a shift in the attitudes and economic policies of rentier and non-rentier governments alike. The rentiers became more aware of the urgent need for economic diversification, and increased reliance on private sector initiatives, which entailed, among other things, promoting regional trade and investment opportunities. The non-rentiers progressively yielded to international pressure to open up their economies and espouse orthodox fiscal and monetary policies. By the end of the decade, the Greater Arab Free Trade Area (GAFTA) was launched (1997) to pursue an increase in intra-regional trade, which was historically abnormally low. Yet the scar of the mass expulsion of Arab immigrants was only minimally healed: an emphasis on reducing costs increased the attractiveness of importing especially South Asian labour, and limiting the role of Arab immigrants to those occupations where knowledge of the language was necessary or at least a very significant advantage.

But the US-led coalition's intervention in Iraq in 2003 again changed the region's economic environment. There is a close connection between regime change in Iraq and the onset of the oil price cycle that began in 2004 and came to a dramatic end in the latter part of 2014. At the turn of the century oil prices were recovering from the abysmally low levels reached in 1998–99, and the dominant narrative was that of peak oil. Following the terrorist attacks of September 2011 some tension emerged on the markets due to a fear for oil supplies—Saudi Arabia at that time being portrayed as part of the problem rather than part of the solution. However, in the run-up to the allied intervention in Iraq the expectation was that the demise of the Saddam regime would bring an end to the sanctions then in place against the country, lead to the opening of Iraq to investment from international oil companies, and trigger a rapid increase in oil production. As it became apparent that the outcome of the Iraqi adventure was very much different from what had been expected, oil prices started increasing gradually. The upward trend found little immediate resistance: demand for oil showed no sign of decreasing, indeed China's appetite for imported oil exploded; industrial countries were not plunged into recession; and alternative sources of oil were not immediately forthcoming. The market became convinced that prices could rise much higher, and eventually created a bubble. The financial crisis subsequent to the collapse of Lehmann Brothers suddenly drained liquidity from the oil futures market, leading to a collapse in prices in the latter part of 2008—but this proved temporary. Prices recovered quite rapidly and kept climbing until 2011. The outbreak of the Arab Spring contributed to again creating a fear that oil supplies from the Middle East might be seriously disrupted, although this was in fact not the case.

We can therefore identify a clear oil price cycle, which began approximately in 2004 and came to an abrupt end in 2014. This price cycle had momentous consequences in the Middle East region: it further emphasised the distance between the oil exporters of the Gulf and the rest of the region, and created the underlying conditions for the regional upheaval of the Arab Spring.

It is clear that the period of very high prices led to greater regional instability rather than having the opposite effect. It enhanced the distance between the major oil exporters and the rest of the region, and the income concentration within rentier oil exporters non-rentiers alike. In the major oil exporting countries, governments relied again on old and ineffective redistribution policies, which by and large further benefited the haves without offering a significant improvement in the lot of the have-nots. As discussed elsewhere in this volume,[1] low prices for energy products have a regressive impact on income distribution. Infrastructure expenditure benefits local contractors; increased spending leads to higher prices for housing, benefiting real estate investors and damaging the poorer nationals for whom cheap housing is not provided; even the very generous schemes to support nationals studying abroad only benefit a minority, while the majority of adolescents get only mediocre education and are not ready for gainful employment; youth unemployment worsened, as nationals were squeezed out of the market by excessively low wages paid to unqualified expatriates from South Asian countries.

In the non-rentier states, the development model of Dubai and the other Gulf countries became hegemonic: political elites nurtured cronies whose role was to attract investment from the Gulf, offering opportunities to invest in real estate and luxury tourism, and to engage in financial speculation. The economies of the non-rentier countries experienced very satisfactory growth, but the quality of increased investment and value added did not allow for trickle-down to occur.

As I have argued elsewhere (Luciani, 2016) the Arab Spring's eruption and regional dimension cannot be easily explained unless we take into account the dynamics of income distribution at the regional level, not just within each country in the region. National statistics do not show any appreciable worsening of income distribution, but Alvaredo and Piketty (2014) convincingly argue that the data sources that are currently available at the national level in Egypt or other MENA countries are insufficient to derive reliable estimates of top income shares, and that income inequality is extremely large at the level of the Middle East taken as whole. It is the perception of such growing inequality, further fuelled by the growing role of regional media and the constant image of Dubai-style success that they project, that ignited resentment and revolt against the incumbent authoritarian regimes.

Now that the tide of oil prices has turned, will tensions decrease? Reduced financial means may possibly encourage a relatively speedier resolution of the regional civil war, but political stabilisation will require a regional economic order that promises opportunities for all and allows for reducing economic disparities.

1 El-Katiri and Fattouh, this volume; Hertog, this volume.

4 Main Trends and Opportunities in Regional Economic Relations: Labour, Capital and Merchandise Trade

Ever since the heyday of pan-Arabism, economic integration within the Arab region has been a recurring theme and objective, but accomplishments remain profoundly disappointing. It is difficult to envisage a significant improvement in the development prospects of individual Arab countries unless greater success is achieved in pursuing regional integration.

In theory, the Arab region should be expected to provide a model of successful regional economic integration. This is because resources are so unevenly distributed: individual countries within the region face obvious difficulties due to the lack of one or other ingredient in the development recipe, and are thus clearly complementary with each other. Indeed, we have countries with oil resources, but that are mostly thinly populated and largely desert; countries with large populations but limited agricultural potential and little or no mineral resources; and countries with significant agricultural potential, which cannot be fully exploited because of a lack of capital or adequate market access. Greater integration along the axes of movements of capital, labour and merchandise trade is an obvious opportunity.

Yet, little effort has gone into actually pursuing regional economic integration. Endemic political conflict and rivalry, in particular between immediate neighbours, has led to a subordination of economic to political considerations, and systematic reticence towards greater interdependence. The nature of oil as an essentially global commodity trivialises the importance of stable bilateral trade relations, and creates the illusion that a global trade orientation in the absence of regional trade may be sufficient to deliver development. Although Israel has effectively succeeded in developing a modern economy with significant points of excellence while being almost completely isolated from trade with its neighbours, the same experience cannot be replicated elsewhere in the region. The major oil exporters have pursued an industrialisation strategy based on adding value to crude oil and developing refining, petrochemical and other energy-intensive industries that also are structurally global and independent of trade relations with neighbours—but there are evident limits to this model. These same countries also prefer to seek close bilateral trade ties with distant countries—be they in the Americas, in Europe or in the Far East—but are notably reserved about increasing imports from neighbours.

4.1 *Merchandise Trade*

Currently the region is covered by a complex array of trade agreements, many of which have never been implemented and are effectively dead, but continue to exist on paper. The region-wide agreement currently in force and still being implemented—where security and political conditions allow—is the GAFTA, which was established in 1997 and progressively led to some reduction of tariffs on bilateral trade. Among sub-regional agreements, one should of course mention the Gulf Cooperation Council and the Agadir Agreement (encompassing Egypt, Jordan, Morocco and Tunisia). The former group decided, already when it was formed in 1981, to establish a common market, but has not yet succeeded in doing so;[2] the latter is an example of deep integration but as the four countries involved are not contiguous, trade between them is hindered by logistical difficulties.

In addition, there have been attempts to establish trade liberalisation agreements in the context of the Barcelona Process between the EU and the 'Southern Neighbours'[3] (a set that does not include all Arab countries, but only those with a shore on the Mediterranean, plus Jordan; notably excluding member countries of the GCC); and between the US and a select number of Arab countries (Bahrain, Jordan, Morocco and Oman). The latter, dubbed Middle East Free Trade Area (MEFTA), was launched in 2003 by the Bush Administration in the context of other initiatives aimed at reshaping the Middle East (regime change in Iraq being the first and foremost of these), but appears to have been largely abandoned by the Obama Administration. In addition, the EU has officially been pursuing a free trade area with the GCC (separate from the Barcelona Process), but has never succeeded in finding sufficient common ground with the intended partners.

It is, in the literature, well established that trade agreements between the EU and the Southern neighbourhood countries have led to an increase in EU exports towards these partner countries, but not of partner countries' exports to the EU (Parra et al., 2016; Gylfason et al., 2015). Empirical analysis shows that this result might change if trade in agricultural products were liberalised alongside trade in industrial products, but this is not something that the EU has been ready to contemplate.

Notwithstanding its slow implementation, the literature has also found that GAFTA has had a moderately positive impact on South–South trade, at least until the eruption of the Arab Spring and the political disarray that followed. In contrast, the findings on the effect of the Agadir Agreement are not unanimous:

2 A customs union was announced in 2003 and the common market was officially launched in 2007 and should have started the following year, but in practice the member countries have not surrendered sovereignty for all external trade matters to a central authority such as the GCC secretariat.

3 The Barcelona Process or Euro-Mediterranean Partnership was launched in 1995. In 2008 the Union for the Mediterranean (UfM) was created to inject new life into the process, but this objective can hardly be said to have been achieved.

Gylfason et al. (2015) find that the agreement has stimulated horizontal trade, notwithstanding the fact that signatories are not contiguous countries, and conclude that 'deep and comprehensive free trade agreements between contiguous and economically large countries could increase trade flows significantly'. The limited importance of horizontal trade between Arab countries is therefore attributable to conflicts between immediate neighbours, which stifle proximate trade liberalisation. The authors therefore propose to reverse the tide by aiming at a deep and comprehensive trade agreement between Egypt, Israel and Jordan, which they deem politically feasible because these three countries have signed peace treaties with each other—a proposal that is optimistic at best. In contrast, Parra et al. (2016) do not find a beneficial effect of the Agadir Agreement.

Following the Arab Spring and the drift towards a full-scale regional civil war, attention to trade liberalisation is no longer a priority. Yet it is difficult to imagine that a virtuous circle of democratisation can be supported in the absence of a convincing project for trade liberalisation. Is it conceivable that this might be sponsored by outside actors, such as the European Union (EU) or the US? Both attempted to do so in the past, the EU through the Barcelona Process and the US through MEFTA. In each case, the respective projects suffered from their partial nature, being addressed to subsets of the membership of the Arab League and therefore being viewed as having a divisive rather than an integrative impact on the region. Such schemes have justifiably been accused of aiming to impose a hub-and-spoke style trade pattern that would cement the dependence of Arab countries on either the EU or the US, and their isolation from each other. It is possible that a joint EU–US initiative encompassing all Arab countries and aiming at creating serious opportunities for regional integration might, in a context of regional pacification, succeed in finally putting in place adequate agreements, including the necessary supranational institutions and enforcement mechanisms. The conditions for such an initiative do not exist today and have not existed for the past half-century (since at least 1967); they may not be reunited in the future either. Yet, the recurrent temptation to cut corners and launch partial initiatives will, in all likelihood, doom such initiatives to failure.

4.2 *Movements of Labour*

Frustrations with trade liberalisation have in the past led to the conclusion that in the case of the Arab countries economic integration should rather start with movements of factors of production—labour and capital—than with merchandise trade. This view appeared to have empirical support in the 1970s and 1980s, when inter-Arab migrations reached their maximum intensity. At that time, migration was viewed as bringing about a new Arab social order (Ibrahim, 1982) through its impact on family structures and its opening the possibility of capital accumulation for the middle and lower income classes of the sending countries. But this vision was soon aborted: Iraq, a major receiving country, became embroiled in an extended and bloody conflict with Iran, while oil prices collapsed in 1985 precipitating expenditure cuts in all major oil-exporting countries. Then, in 1990, Iraq invaded Kuwait, and some of the major senders of migrant labour—notably Jordan, the Palestinian Territories and Yemen—aligned themselves in support of Saddam Hussein. The reaction was immediate and radical: Saudi Arabia expelled approximately 800,000 Yemeni workers before the end of the year, having cancelled the rule that allowed Yemeni nationals to enter the kingdom without a visa and work without a sponsor (Ayalon, 1990, 725).[4] In addition, 200,000 Jordanians, 150,000 Palestinians, and nearly all Sudanese were effectively expelled from the kingdom (Richards and Waterbury, 2007). In Kuwait, half of the Palestinian population, estimated at 400,000 before the invasion, either fled or was expelled. The rest were also gradually pushed out, and by 2012 the Palestinian population of Kuwait was estimated to be barely 80,000.

In fact, the relative importance of other Arabs in the total expatriate population in the Gulf had been declining systematically even before 1990 as shown in Tables 11.1, 11.2 and 11.3.

TABLE 11.1 *Arab share in foreign populations 1975–2015*

	1975	1985	1996	2002/4	2010/15
Bahrain	22	15	12	15	8.4
Kuwait	80	69	33	30	26.5
Oman	16	16	11	6	2.6
Qatar	33	33	21	19	30.2
Saudi Arabia	91	79	30	33	46
UAE	26	19	10	13	18.4
GCC	72	56	31	32	30

SOURCES: FOR 1975 TO 2004: KAPISZEWSKI, 2006; FOR 2010/15: EUROPEAN UNIVERSITY INSTITUTE, MIGRATION POLICY CENTRE, GULF LABOUR MARKETS AND MIGRATION DATABASE (GLMM DATABASE—HTTP://GULFMIGRATION.EU/GLMM-DATABASE/).

4 In later years Yemenis continued to move to the kingdom in many cases illegally (without a visa) and this led to large-scale expulsions as recently as in 2013 and 2015.

TABLE 11.2 *Estimates of the number of foreign nationals (Arab nationalities), by country of residence in* GCC *member countries (2010–2014)*

Destination	Bahrain	Kuwait	Oman	Qatar	Saudi Arabia	UAE	GCC
Year	2014	end 2012	2010	2013–2014	2013	2013–2014	
Origin							
Algeria	n.a.	845	n.a.	n.d.	n.a.	10,000 [(e)]	10845
Egypt	20,000	482,692	29,877	18,0000 [(b)]	1,370,000 [(d)]	400,000 [(e)]	2,482,569
Iraq	n.a.	15,262	4,159	8,976	20,000	52,000 [(e)]	100,397
Jordan	7,000	55,081	7,403	40,000 [(b)]	250,000	200,000[(e)]	559,484
Lebanon	2,300 [(a)]	42,586	n.a.	25,000 [(b)]	160,000	100,000 [(e)]	329,886
Mauritania	n.a.	142	n.a.	n.d.	n.a.	5,000 [(e)]	5,142
Morocco	800[(a)]	3,495	n.a.	9,000[(b)]	20,000[(a)]	14,000	47,295
Palestine	5,000[(a)]	8,072	n.a.	20,500[(b)]	500,000	150,000[(e)]	683,572
Sudan	14,000[(a)]	4,551	6,867	42,000[(b)]	500,000	75,000[(e)]	642,418
Syria	3,000	135,554	n.a.	60,000[(c)]	1,000,000[(c)]	242,000[(c)]	1,440,554
Tunisia	500[(a)]	2,863	n.a.	15,000[(b)]	12,000[(a)]	4,500	34,863
Yemen	4,700	10,762	n.a.	40,000[(a)]	800,000	90,000[(e)]	945,462
TOTAL	57,300	761,905	48,306	440,476	4,632,000	1,342,500	7,282,487

Figures for migrants in the GCC may be overestimated due to the inclusion of a large share of Gulf-born (second and third generation) non-nationals.
Palestinians are holders of travel documents.
Some of the figures quoted are unverifiable estimates. Therefore, they should be taken as indicative only and should not be used for statistical purposes.
Unless stated otherwise, receiving countries' estimates are from relevant tables in the POP section of the EUI Migration Policy Centre, GLMM database.
(a) United Nations (2013), revision total migrants' stocks by origin and destination countries.
(b) Snoj, J. (2013)'Population of Qatar by nationality' (Doha: BQ Magazine) December, http://www.bqdoha.com/2013/12/population-qatar (accessed on 8 April 2016) and http://gulfmigration.eu/qatar-estimates-of-foreign-nationals-residing-in-qatar-by-country-of-citizenship-selected-countries-2014/ (accessed on 8 April 2016).
(c) Latest figures available as of October 2015, in: De Bel-Air, F. (2015)'A Note on Syrian Refugees in the Gulf: Attempting to Assess Data and Policies', GLMM Explanatory Note, GLMM—EN—No.11/2015. http://gulfmigration.eu/media/pubs/exno/GLMM_EN_2015_11.pdf (accessed on 8 April 2016).
(d) Official estimate: Egyptian workers in Saudi Arabia number 968,000 (end of 2013). https://www.middleeastmonitor.com/news/africa/14187-egyptians-represent-40-per-cent-o--saudi-arabias-total-expatriate-workforce (accessed on 8 April 2016).
Estimates of family dependents: in the absence of any indication of the ratio of worker to family dependents in the UAE, we use data available for Kuwait in 2012: 2.4 workers per family dependent.
Estimates of Egyptians (total): 968,000 + (968,000/2.4) = 1,371,000.
(e) Snoj, J. (2015)'UAE's population by nationality' (Doha: BQ Magazine) April 12.
Table as of December 15, 2015.

TABLE 11.3 *Total population and percentage of nationals and non-nationals in GCC countries (2010–2015)*

Country	Date/period	Total population	Nationals	Non-nationals	% in total population	
					Nationals	Non-nationals
Bahrain(1)	mid-2014	1,314,562	630,744	683,818	48.0	52.0
Kuwait(2)	31 March 2015	4,161,404	1,283,726	2,877,678	30.8	69.2
Oman(3)	25 March 2015	4,149,917	2,324,327	1,825,590	56.0	44.0
Qatar(4)	April 2010	1,699,435	243,019	1,456,416	14.3	85.7
Saudi Arabia(5)	mid-2014	30,770,375	20,702,536	10,067,839	67.3	32.7
United Arab Emirates(6)	mid-2010	8,264,070	947,997	7,316,073	11.5	88.5
Total*		50,359,763	26,132,349	24,227,414	51.9	48.1

* Total provides the sum of population numbers at different dates between April 2010 and March 2015. It is not exactly the total population at any of these dates.

1—Definition

Non-nationals are:

1.1—Persons of the nationality of a foreign state other than the GCC state of residence, or bearing no proof of nationality from any given state (stateless persons and holders of refugee status and travel document in a third country);

1.2—Holders of residence permits residing in the given GCC country at the date of census, as per the definition of residence used in each of the countries. Figures for Bahrain, Saudi Arabia and the UAE are estimates.

2—Sources of data:

Unless stated otherwise, the source is EUI Migration Policy Centre, GLMM database.

(1) Bahrain Central Informatics Organisation (CIO), CIO's website, 'Statistics' and 'Population' sections http://www.data.gov.bh/en/ResourceCenter.

(2) Kuwait Public Authority for Civil Information (PACI), http://www.paci.gov.kw/en/ (accessed on 31 March 2015).

(3) Sultanate of Oman National Centre for Statistical Information (NCSI), http://www.ncsi.gov.om/ (accessed on 5 March 2015).

(4) Qatar Statistics Authority (QSA), Census 2010 http://gulfmigration.eu/population-by-nationality-qatari-non-qatari-census-1970-2010/ (accessed on 8 April 2016).

(5) Saudi Arabia Central Department for Statistics and Information (CDSI), estimates. http://www.cdsi.gov.sa/ (accessed on 8 April 2016).

(6) UAE National Bureau of Statistics (NBS), estimates http://www.uaestatistics.gov.ae/ (accessed on 8 April 2016).

Kapiszewski has pointed to the political activism of early Arab migrants and to the pan-Arab beliefs that they entertained:

> Many young Arabs regarded borders in the Middle East as artificial lines imposed by Western imperialists, and, consequently, expected them to be eliminated. Another popular pan-Arab view, that of a single Arab nation in which labor "circulates" freely, was also rejected by the Gulf governments for security reasons. Yet another problem was related to the regional distribution of the oil-generated wealth. Whereas the oil-producing countries which preferred to retain that wealth began to link the entitlement of oil revenues to state sovereignty, poorer states increasingly stressed their Arab identity as a good reason to demand their share in the revenues: Iraq even used the oil-related arguments as a justification to invade Kuwait in 1990.
>
> KAPISZEWSKI, 2006, 6–7

Such sentiment has not dissipated to this date and is very central to the Arab civil war.

The declining importance of Arab migrants is even more striking when viewed in the context of growing total expatriate numbers. From the point of view of the composition of their populations, cities like Dubai, Abu Dhabi or Doha have effectively become South Asian. The lack of a preference for other Arabs—or even positive discrimination against them—has been a huge lost opportunity for regional economic integration, including from the point of view of trade ties and capital movements (which migration would have facilitated). But the attitude of the Gulf countries has, if anything, shifted in the opposite direction: increasingly some of the Gulf States have tended to deprive even large groups of citizens of their nationality, in order to punish dissidents.

4.3 *Movements of Capital*

With little progress on the trade front and the declining relative importance of inter-Arab migration, the only dimension of regional integration remaining is capital movements. These did intensify progressively as non-oil Arab countries adopted orthodox fiscal and monetary policies, and the major oil exporters were flush with liquidity thanks to rapidly growing oil prices. Inter-Arab investment grew significantly until 2008 (with an exceptional peak in 2005, Figure 11.1), then collapsed in conjunction with the global financial crisis. Investment picked up again beginning in 2010, but then the effects of regional political turmoil began to be felt.

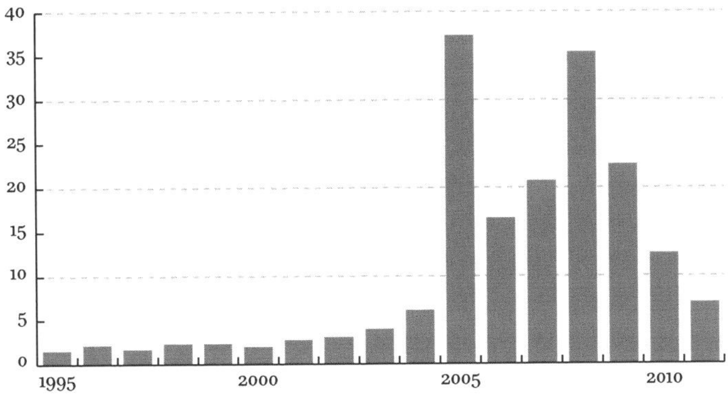

FIGURE 11.1 *Inter-Arab foreign direct investments (FDI) inflows (USD billion, 1995–2011)*
SOURCE: ARAB INVESTMENT AND EXPORT CREDIT GUARANTEE CORPORATION, 2011.

Data on the accumulated stock of inter-Arab investment to the end of 2011 (Table 11.4) point to a prevalence of cross investment within GCC member states, with Saudi Arabia being the main recipient country, due to its larger internal market. Outside the GCC, Sudan, Egypt, Lebanon and Algeria have been major recipients, while Jordan, Syria, Yemen, Tunisia and Morocco have remained at the margins.

Much of this distribution can be explained on the basis of the size of the respective economies, the attractiveness of investment conditions, political/security considerations, or proximity. In this respect the figure for Algeria is a little surprising, because the country has neither a friendly investment environment nor proximity to the Gulf.

With respect to sectors, it is found that inter-Arab investment concentrates heavily in services (tourism, banking, telecommunications…), which absorb close to 70 per cent of the total, while industry absorbs about a quarter.

The 'push factor' of high oil prices generating large surpluses and abundant liquidity is confirmed by data for 2012 (Table 11.5), showing the large investment from Qatar in Algeria, Egypt and Tunisia. The contrast between Qatar and the United Arab Emirates (UAE) is interesting; the latter being evidently more reserved about investing in the region.

It is clear from these figures that inter-Arab investment remains highly concentrated on a few large-scale projects, frequently initiated by state-owned entities. As such, it remains an unstable and occasional source of funding, albeit not an unimportant one. The role of private investors and industrial

TABLE 11.4 *Inward inter-Arab FDI stocks as of end 2011—individual country shares*

Saudi Arabia	27.06
Sudan	13.21
Egypt	11.28
Lebanon	8.38
Algeria	7.81
Bahrain	7.66
UAE	6.38
Morocco	3.66
Jordan	2.61
Tunisia	2.44
Kuwait	2.08
Oman	1.94
Syria	1.85
Yemen	1.68
Libya	0.75
Palestine	0.73
Qatar	0.22
Djibouti	0.19
Iraq	0.07

SOURCE: ARAB INVESTMENT AND EXPORT CREDIT GUARANTEE CORPORATION, 2011.

enterprises is minor, and the employment effects on the receiving countries, effects about which very little is known, are likely to be minor.

In short, so far inter-Arab investment has failed to be the engine of regional growth that many expected and hoped that it might become. In particular, the idea of 'triangulation' (allying finance from the Gulf and other major oil exporters with industrial know-how from Europe, the US or elsewhere and an abundant labour supply in oil-poor Arab countries) has not made any progress at all in practice.

5 Conclusion: The Unresolved Regional Political Order

As we look forward to a potential end to the Arab civil war the need for a new regional political and economic order seems inescapable. In a recent report

TABLE 11.5 *Inter-Arab investment, 2012 (in EUR millions)*

Destination	Origin of FDI flows						
	Bahrain	Kuwait	Oman	Qatar	Saudi Arabia	UAE	Egypt
Algeria				738		91	
Egypt		196		640	160	738	
Jordan		59		18	237	50	
Lebanon				1	11	38	132
Libya	21			129		15	
Morocco		65		15	105	73	
Syria	83	63		36		60	
Tunisia		17		457			

SOURCE: NOUTARY AND TABET, 2013.

proposing three scenarios for the future of the Arab region in 2025, the optimistic scenario is introduced as follows:

> The implementation of a Greater Arab Free Trade Area (GAFTA), coupled with a reduction of 5% in transport costs and the replacement of 20% of foreign labour in the Gulf by Arab workers led to an important U-turn in Arab economies. In Egypt, unemployment rates among skilled workers dropped by 8%; in Morocco, by 7.2%, in Tunisia by 6.9%. GDP rates grew in all Arab countries, but particularly in Egypt (whose GDP grew by 6.2%) and Tunisia (4.2%).
>
> GAUB AND LABAN, 2015, 37

Such emphasis on the regional dimension of economic growth and the importance of integration through trade and migration is fully justified. Individual Arab countries can move towards democracy and implement economic reforms to support such a transition, but in the absence of a convincing and bold regional integration strategy Arab youth will still focus primarily on moving out of the region.

At the same time, the implementation of a new regional economic order also requires a new political order. The main difficulty in this respect is that those countries in the region that have the most economic assets and tools—the major Gulf exporters—are ruled by patrimonial monarchies rather than political forces, and their model of governance cannot be exported. Indeed, patrimonial monarchies find it difficult to engage in regional cooperation that requires any kind of devolution of sovereignty to regional institutions, as demonstrated by the lacklustre progress of the GCC.

In the wake of the Arab Spring, in 2011 Saudi Arabia's King Abdullah called for the transformation of the GCC into a union—a project whose exact implications were never spelled out precisely, although it meant some form of transition from interstate cooperation to at least partial devolution of sovereignty. The call was not met with enthusiasm by fellow GCC member monarchs, and has failed to make any progress. The idea of Gulf integration has significant support in GCC member countries, primarily in business circles—although many would not want to see the Saudi brand of Wahhabism and mores imposed on the rest of the region.

Again in 2011, the GCC invited Jordan and Morocco to become members, much to the surprise of the latter. This too was an attempt at strengthening the GCC and showing that it had regional power of attraction beyond the Arabian peninsula: both Jordan and Morocco are monarchies, of course, but in both countries power is not exclusively centralised in the hands of the monarch and elections are regularly held. Not much progress in this direction has been made.

Finally, Yemen applied for membership of the GCC in 2015, following the launch of the Saudi military intervention in the country.[5] Yemen is obviously seeking free access for its citizens to GCC labour markets, and an opportunity to attract financial support and private direct investment. By the same token, the idea of Yemeni membership constitutes a big problem for the GCC, which has been accused of having many times missed opportunities to integrate their southern neighbour. The political obstacles to the country's membership of the GCC are only too obvious, as Yemen's political reality is totally incongruous with that of the GCC; nevertheless, refusing to offer to its people a reasonable opportunity for development is tantamount to allowing a security time bomb to grow increasingly dangerous, situated at the door of the GCC.

With respect to other countries in the region, the GCC and its members aim to support 'friends' that reproduce authoritarian styles of governance. That such friends are not always well chosen is unfortunately a reality, President al-Sisi being the foremost example. In recent years, Qatar has tended to support its own 'friends', which are not the same as those that the UAE or Saudi Arabia support—a rift that has been superficially but not substantially overcome.

---

5 'Rather than scoffing at the idea of Yemeni membership in the GCC, the Gulf Arab nations should realize that closer integration of the states of the Arabian Peninsula is a historic opportunity—one that they have failed to seize, time after time'. Farea al-Muslimi (2016)'A History of Missed Opportunities: Yemen and the GCC', Carnegie Endowment for International Peace, http://carnegieendowment.org/syriaincrisis/?fa=62405 (accessed on 5 February 2016).

And yet, neither the perspective of a 'fortress GCC' nor that of Arab integration without the GCC has much potential. Kuwait, Qatar or the UAE may aim at isolating themselves from the regional security environment, positioning themselves as political free zones between a troubled region and the global environment; but Bahrain, Oman and Saudi Arabia are inevitably exposed and impacted by regional politics. Conversely, an Arab regional project that does not include the major oil exporters would lack the main growth engine that the financial, labour and consumer markets of the GCC can offer.

It is, then, difficult today to share the vision of the optimistic scenario referenced at the beginning of this section, just as it is difficult to foresee the end of the Arab civil war any time soon. Yet civil wars eventually do end, and the future of the region depends entirely on the political order that will follow.

References

Alvaredo, F. and T. Piketty (2014) *Measuring Top Incomes and Inequality in the Middle East: Data Limitations and Illustration with the Case of Egypt*, Working Paper Series 832 (Cairo: Economic Research Forum), http://piketty.pse.ens.fr/files/AlvaredoPiketty2014ERF.pdf (accessed on 17 March 2016).

Arab Investment and Export Credit Guarantee Corporation (2011). *Investment Climate in Arab Countries, 2011* (Safat: The Arab Investment and Export Credit Guarantee Corporation), http://www.iaigc.net/UserFiles/file/en/archives/annual_reports/Climate-2011-English.pdf (accessed on 8 April 2016).

Ayalon, A. (ed.) (1990) *Middle East Contemporary Survey*, Volume 14, (Boulder: Westview Press).

De Bel-Air, F. (2015) 'A Note on Syrian Refugees in the Gulf: Attempting to Assess Data and Policies', glmm Explanatory Note, glmm—en— No. 11/2015. http://gulfmigration.eu/media/pubs/exno/GLMM_EN_2015_11.pdf (accessed on 8 April 2016).

Elbadawi, I., S. Makdisi and G. Milante (2011) 'Explaining the Arab Democracy Deficit' in I. Elbadawi and S. Makdisi (eds.) *Democracy in the Arab World: Explaining the Deficit*, (Abingdon and New York: Routledge).

Freund, C. and M. Jaud (2013) 'On the Determinants of Democratic Transitions' *Middle East Development Journal* 2013(05) DOI: 10.1142/S1793812013500053.

Gaub, F. and A. Laban (eds.) (2015) *Arab Futures: Three Scenarios for 2025* European Union Institute for Security Studies Report No.22 (Paris: EU Institute for Security Studies) http://www.iss.europa.eu/uploads/media/Report_22_Arab_futures.pdf (accessed on 8 April 2016).

Gylfason, T., I. Martínez-Zarzoso and P.M. Wijkman (2015) 'Can free trade help convert the "Arab Spring" into permanent peace and democracy?', *Defence and Peace Economics*, 26(3), DOI: 10.1080/10242694.2014.886433.

Harik, I. (1987) 'The Origins of the Arab State System' in G. Salamé (ed.) *The Foundations of the Arab State* (London and New York: Croom Helm).

Ibrahim, S.E. (1982) *The New Arab Social Order—A study of the social impact of oil wealth* (Boulder: Westview Press).

Kapiszewski, A. (2006) *Arab versus Asian Migrant Workers in the GCC Countries*, United Nations Expert Group Meeting on International Migration and Development in the Arab Region, Population Division, (Beirut: Department of Economic and Social Affairs, UN Secretariat), UN/POP/EGM/2006/02.

Kerr, M.H. and E. Yassin (1982) *Rich and Poor States in the Middle East* (Boulder: Westview Press).

Kuru, A.T. (2014) 'Authoritarianism and Democracy in Muslim Countries: Rentier States and Regional Diffusion' *Political Science Quarterly*, 129(3), DOI: 10.1002/polq.12215.

Luciani, G. (1987) 'Allocation vs. Production States: A Theoretical Framework' in B. Hazem and G. Luciani (eds.) *The Rentier State* (London and New York: Croom Helm).

Luciani, G. (2016) 'On the Economic Causes of the Arab Spring and its Possible Developments' in K. Selvik and B.O. Utvik (eds) *Oil States in the New Middle East—Uprisings and Stability* (Abingdon and New York: Routledge).

Luciani, G. and G. Salamé (eds.) (1988) *The Politics of Arab Integration* (London and New York: Croom Helm).

Farea al-Muslimi (2016) 'A History of Missed Opportunities: Yemen and the GCC', Carnegie Endowment for International Peace, http://carnegieendowment.org/syriaincrisis/?fa=62405 (accessed on 5 February2016).

Noutary, E. and M. Tabet (2013) *Emerging countries: the new Mediterranean FDI providers? 2012 report on MED Foreign Direct Investment attractiveness*, ANIMA Investment Network, October, http://www.animaweb.org/sites/default/files/ain_fdipartnerships-2012_en_final.pdf (accessed on 8 April 2016).

Parra, M. D, I. Martinez-Zarzoso and C. Suárez-Burguet (2016) 'The impact of FTAs on MENA trade in agricultural and industrial products', *Applied Economics*, 48(25), DOI: 10.1080/00036846.2015.1119792.

Richards, A. and J. Waterbury (2007) *A Political Economy of the Middle East*, Second Edition (Boulder: Westview Press).

Snoj, J. (2013) 'Population of Qatar by nationality' (Doha: BQ Magazine) December, http://www.bqdoha.com/2013/12/population-qatar (accessed on 8 April 2016) and http://gulfmigration.eu/qatar-estimates-of-foreign-nationals-residing-in-qatar-by-country-ofcitizenship-selected-countries-2014/ (accessed on 8 April 2016).

Snoj, J. (2015) 'UAE's population by nationality' (Doha: BQ Magazine) April 12. http://www.bq-magazine.com/economy/socioeconomics/2015/04/uae-population-by-nationality (accessed on 8 April 2016)

United Nations (2013) *International Migration Report 2013* (New York: Population Division of the Department of Economic and Social Affairs), ST/ESA/SER.A/346.

Index